MONEY

Who Has How Much and Why

ANDREW HACKER

SCRIBNER

SCRIBNER
1230 Avenue of the Americas
New York, NY 10020

SCRIBNER and design are registered trademarks of Simon & Schuster Inc.

DESIGNED BY ERICH HOBBING

Text set in Bembo

Manufactured in the United States of America

1   3   5   7   9   10   8   6   4   2

Library of Congress Cataloging-in-Publication Data
Hacker, Andrew.
Money: who has how much and why/Andrew Hacker.
p.   cm.
1. Income—United States. 2. Income distribution—United States.
I. Title.
HC110.I5H27   1997
339.2'2'0973—dc21   97-9038   CIP

ISBN 0-684-19646-8

For Ann and Tim

CONTENTS

PREFACE

YES, THE RICH ARE GETTING RICHER

John F. Kennedy defended the importance of business prosperity by arguing that "a rising tide lifts all boats." It was a deft figure of speech: we imagine tugboats, tankers, and superliners all together on the high water.

However, recent decades have failed to validate Kennedy's thesis. Of course, there can be no denying that the tide of wealth in America has swelled. Between 1975 and 1995, the amount of money in the hands of America's households rose from $2.7 trillion to $4.5 trillion, after the 1975 figure is adjusted to 1995-value dollars. All told, the income of the average household went from $37,365 to $44,938, also in constant dollars, resulting in a twenty-year gain of 20.3 percent.

The table on the next page shows how various segments of the society fared during those two decades. Its figures, which come from annual Census Bureau surveys, simply divide the total number of households into five equal groups, ranging from the poorest to the best-off. So in 1995, each fifth contained 19.9 million homes, consisting of families or of individuals living alone or together. Thus the incomes of those in the middle fifth ranged from $26,915 to $42,002, with an average of $34,106. The Census also specifies the incomes of the richest 5 percent of all households. Lastly, figures are given for the share of all household income received by each segment. Thus in 1995, the middle fifth ended up with 15.2 percent of the total, or $684 billion from the $4.5 trillion.

Clearly, all boats did not rise equally with this tide. Here were the twenty-year percentage increases in the average income for each of the quintiles and also for the top 5 percent:

Richest 5%	+54.1%	Middle 20%	+6.7%
Top 20%	+35.4%	Fourth 20%	+4.4%
Second 20%	+13.0%	Bottom 20%	+1.5%

While all segments of the population enjoyed an increase in income, the top fifth did twenty-four times better than the bottom fifth. And measured by their shares of the aggregate, not just the bottom fifth but the three above it all ended up losing ground. Indeed, the overall share

1975		Household Segments	1995	
Share of all Income	**Segment Average**		**Segment Average**	**Share of all Income**
43.2%	$80,834	Top 20%	$109,411	48.7%
24.8%	$46,417	Second 20%	$52,429	23.3%
17.1%	$31,963	Middle 20%	$34,106	15.2%
10.5%	$19,535	Fourth 20%	$20,397	9.1%
4.4%	$8,227	Bottom 20%	$8,350	3.7%
100.0%	$37,365	All Households	$44,938	100.0%
15.9%	$122,651	Richest 5%	$188,962	21.0%

How Households Divided the Nation's Income: 1975 & 1995 (in 1995-value dollars)

received by those segments, comprising four of every five households, dropped from 56.7 percent to 51.3 percent. At the same time, the average income of the richest 5 percent rose from a comfortable $122,651 to an affluent $188,962.

I will explore the reasons for these shifts in subsequent chapters. For now, let me say that two factors intertwine. On the one hand, more of the 1995 households had two or more incomes coming in. Thus the $109,411 average for the top fifth could represent, say, $65,932 from one spouse and $43,479 from the other. But it is noteworthy that while there were also more dual earnings down in the fourth quintile, their income average rose by only $862 during the two decades.

The second factor is that 1975 to 1995 saw the creation of more high individual incomes at one end of the scale and more low incomes at the other. Thus the proportion of men earning more than $50,000—again, computed in constant dollars—grew from 12.8 percent to 16.5 percent. But overall, the median income for men dropped from $24,007 to $22,562, due to declining wages for those in the bottom tiers. All indications are that these disparities will continue in the decades ahead.

CHANGING STATES

If income disparities are on the rise, they are also being compressed. As the table on the next page shows, in 1960, income in the richest state (Connecticut) was 2.59 times that of the poorest state (Mississippi). By 1995, the gap (Alaska vs. West Virginia) had been reduced to a ratio of 1.93. And if the 1995 comparison stays with the contiguous states (New Jersey vs. West Virginia) the richest-poorest ratio declines to 1.76.

Closing the gap has nurtured a national homogeneity. This is illustrated vividly in the shopping mall, which has emerged as America's most distinctive institution. Set down in malls in New Hampshire or New Mexico, we would be hard pressed to say where in the country we are. All have Gaps and Radio Shacks, multiplexes playing the same movies, and though food markets may have regional names, their merchandise is much the same.

Mobility also plays a role. The 1990 Census reported that over half the residents of New Hampshire, Florida, Wyoming, Nevada, Oregon, Arizona, Colorado, California, and Alaska had been born elsewhere. And by now, Maryland, Idaho, Delaware, Washington, Virginia, and New Mexico are likely to have joined the list. New arrivals adapt quite easily, since each year sees more Americans sharing common attitudes and attributes.

Among the more striking developments has been the economic rise of the South. In 1960, the six poorest states were all from that region, while by 1995 only three were. Indeed, household income doubled in Arkansas, Mississippi, and South Carolina. Among the losers, Ohio dropped to five places behind Virginia, and New York's income fell below the national median.

A Dozen Gainers and Losers					
Gainers' Rank	**1960**	**1995**	**Losers' Rank**	**1960**	**1995**
Wisconsin	14th	5th	Michigan	5th	14th
Colorado	20th	6th	Ohio	7th	21st
Iowa	30th	19th	New York	9th	29th
Virginia	34th	16th	Indiana	16th	28th
Georgia	40th	25th	New Mexico	25th	47th
North Carolina	46th	33rd	West Virginia	37th	50th

Median Household Income for Each State (in 1995-value dollars)

1960	$23,476	USA	1995	$34,076
Connecticut	$29,469	1st	Alaska	$47,954
New Jersey	$29,175	2nd	New Jersey	$43,924
Illinois	$27,386	3rd	Hawaii	$42,851
Nevada	$27,141	4th	Maryland	$41,041
Michigan	$27,117	5th	Wisconsin	$40,955
California	$27,082	6th	Colorado	$40,706
Ohio	$26,666	7th	Connecticut	$40,243
Maryland	$26,543	8th	New Hampshire	$39,171
New York	$26,494	9th	Massachusetts	$38,574
Massachusetts	$26,078	10th	Illinois	$38,071
Delaware	$26,029	11th	Minnesota	$37,933
Utah	$25,804	12th	California	$37,009
Washington	$25,696	13th	Utah	$36,480
Wisconsin	$25,348	14th	Michigan	$36,426
Wyoming	$25,294	15th	Oregon	$36,374
Indiana	$24,914	16th	Virginia	$36,222
Oregon	$24,843	17th	Nevada	$36,084
Pennsylvania	$24,652	18th	Washington	$35,568
Alaska	$23,912	19th	Iowa	$35,519
Colorado	$23,579	20th	Rhode Island	$35,359
New Hampshire	$23,172	21st	Ohio	$34,941
Hawaii	$23,079	22nd	Delaware	$34,928
Arizona	$22,971	23rd	Missouri	$34,825
Minnesota	$22,903	24th	Pennsylvania	$34,524
Rhode Island	$22,736	25th	Georgia	$34,099
New Mexico	$22,726	26th	Maine	$33,858
Idaho	$22,422	27th	Vermont	$33,824
Montana	$22,060	28th	Indiana	$33,385
Kansas	$21,766	29th	New York	$33,028
Iowa	$20,766	30th	Nebraska	$32,929
Missouri	$20,511	31st	Idaho	$32,676
Nebraska	$19,919	32nd	Texas	$32,039
Texas	$19,844	33rd	North Carolina	$31,979
Virginia	$19,811	34th	Wyoming	$31,529
Maine	$19,703	35th	Arizona	$30,863
Vermont	$19,527	36th	Kansas	$30,341
West Virginia	$19,262	37th	Kentucky	$29,810
Florida	$18,694	38th	Florida	$29,745
North Dakota	$18,532	39th	South Dakota	$29,578
Georgia	$17,238	40th	North Dakota	$29,089
Louisiana	$17,214	41st	South Carolina	$29,071
Oklahoma	$16,997	42nd	Tennessee	$29,015
South Dakota	$16,861	43rd	Louisiana	$27,949
Kentucky	$16,415	44th	Montana	$27,757
Alabama	$16,410	45th	Mississippi	$26,538
North Carolina	$16,337	46th	Oklahoma	$26,311
Tennessee	$16,332	47th	Alabama	$25,991
South Carolina	$15,313	48th	New Mexico	$25,991
Arkansas	$12,882	49th	Arkansas	$25,814
Mississippi	$11,388	50th	West Virginia	$24,880

CHILDREN AND WOMEN LAST?

All parents want their children to have a good start in life, and one underpinning is a family budget ample enough to provide a range of opportunities. Yet a rising proportion of children are growing up in homes without the means even for basic necessities.

In 1995, a third of all youngsters lived in homes with incomes of less than $25,000, and one in five were in homes where the income was below $15,000. At issue is what is required for growing up in modern America. More often than not, low incomes bring inferior local schools and inadequate exposure to the manners demanded by the wider world. As a result, millions of American children are deprived of a chance to develop whatever promise they have. Of course, poverty is not the only factor. We all know of youngsters—especially from immigrant families—who move far beyond the world of their parents. Still, two causes of the increased impoverishment of children should be singled out.

Of America's 70.3 million children aged eighteen or under, 31.3 percent are living with only one parent, or with a relative other than a parent, or in a foster home. The 68.7 percent with both of their parents in their home is an all-time low. In 1970, for example, the proportion was 85.2 percent. While it can be questioned whether two parents are necessary for a child's optimal development, the fact remains that single parents earn a lot less money. For two-parent families, the median income is $49,969, almost double the $26,990 for the relatively small group of single fathers and more than three times the $16,235 for single mothers. (The two-parent and one-parent families do not differ much in size. Those with two parents average 1.49 children; and those with single mothers average 1.34.) Nor is childhood poverty due only to marital breakups. Among today's single mothers, an all-time high of 35.6 percent have never been married. In 1970, the proportion was 7.1 percent.

Racial disparities are also reflected in the changing composition of families. As the table on the next page shows, even when black children are raised by two parents, their households are twice as likely as white two-parent homes to have incomes under $15,000. While the $43,946 median income for two-parent black families is fairly close to the $50,594 for whites, the overall black median is only 52.6 percent of the white figure. Moreover, the typical black woman who is raising children on her own must make do with $12,989, compared with $18,099 for the white single mother. These figures suggest that the United States disproportionately denies opportunities to black children. Stated another way, one reason why America's children are not being allowed to show their true talents is that many of them are of African origin.

The Coming Generation			
Incomes of Families Where Children Are Being Raised			
Incomes of White Families	**All White Families**	**Two Parents (76.3%)**	**Mother Only (18.7%)★**
Over $40,000	54.0%	65.0%	15.6%
$15,000–$40,000	32.6%	29.3%	42.6%
Under $15,000	13.4%	5.7%	41.8%
	100.0%	100.0%	100.0%
White Median	$43,091	$50,594	$18,099
Per Black $1,000	$1,901	$1,151	$1,393
Incomes of Black Families	**All Black Families**	**Two Parents (39.7%)**	**Mother Only (54.0%)★**
Over $40,000	28.1%	55.9%	8.5%
$15,000–$40,000	36.6%	35.3%	36.0%
Under $15,000	35.3%	8.8%	55.5%
	100.0%	100.0%	100.0%
Black Median	$22,671	$43,946	$12,989
Per White $1,000	$526	$869	$718

★The remaining 6.3 percent of black children and 5.0 percent of white children are living with their fathers or with other relatives or are in foster care.

THE SALARY SPECTRUM

The table on the following page does not list the incomes of corporate chairmen, medical school professors, or investment firm partners. They and other high earners will be discussed in later chapters. This table records the wages and salaries of full-time workers in forty-two typical occupations.

Despite its reputation as a high-wage economy, the midpoint pay for America's full-time workers in 1995 was a rather modest $24,908, not really enough to give a family a middle-class living standard. The median for the 51.2 million employed men was $27,976, and for the 38.1 million women it was $21,112. (So an average working couple might bring in $49,088, which explains why there are so many dual-earner households.) The table's figures raise several questions and suggest some partial answers.

Women as a group are paid less, but is that because they are clustered in lower-wage occupations? The earnings of bank tellers, hairdressers, and sewing-machine operators suggest that this is the case. Yet the pay for nurses and elementary school teachers—jobs traditionally held by women—have surpassed that of many occupations dominated by men. (Teachers' unions tend to remain strong, while those of construction workers have lost much of their dominant force.) Moreover, each year finds more women in better-paid positions such as pharmacists, financial managers, and college professors.

Indeed, women now account for 33.9 percent of all pharmacists, compared with 12.1 percent in 1970. For insurance adjusters, the respective figures are 74.1 percent and 29.6 percent. And women now make up 48.6 percent of the nation's bartenders, as against 21.1 percent twenty-five years earlier. Yet these shifts do not always bring better earnings. When insurance adjuster was mainly a man's occupation, it paid well for inspecting dented cars and burned-out buildings. Today, most are women who tap claims into computers.

Many of the amenities we desire depend on a supply of low-wage workers. This is clearly the case with those who launder our linen and park our cars. But it is also true of hotel clerks, most of whom are young people who haven't yet chosen a long-term career. Waiters and waitresses also tend to be younger or are older women bringing in a household's second income. Sewing-machine operators, many of

Median Earnings for Full-time Wage and Salary Workers
(with percentage women in each occupation)

All workers, median earnings: $24,908   Percentage women: 42.6%

Above National Median	Earnings	Women	Below National Median	Earnings	Women
Lawyers (salaried)	$58,500	30.1%	Automotive mechanics	$24,232	0.5%
Pharmacists	$51,480	33.9%	Insurance adjusters	$24,128	74.1%
Engineers	$48,100	8.2%	Printing operators	$24,024	16.9%
Computer analysts	$45,344	29.4%	Flight attendants	$23,400	77.2%
College faculty	$43,836	41.2%	Secretaries	$20,592	99.9%
Financial managers	$39,416	51.0%	Telephone operators	$20,228	85.8%
Computer programmers	$38,636	28.6%	Data entry keyers	$18,668	83.6%
Police Officers	$38,376	14.1%	Factory assemblers	$18,408	38.1%
Architects	$37,648	24.2%	Taxicab drivers	$18,304	8.6%
Registered nurses	$36,140	91.3%	Security guards	$17,576	16.4%
High school teachers	$34,996	54.1%	Bakers	$16,640	27.7%
Elementary school teachers	$33,280	83.5%	Bank tellers	$15,600	90.0%
Journalists	$32,084	49.7%	Bartenders	$15,236	48.6%
Designers	$31,096	50.3%	Janitors and cleaners	$15,236	30.3%
Electricians	$30,992	2.0%	Hotel clerks	$15,028	70.5%
Librarians	$30,992	85.1%	Hairdressers	$14,872	90.3%
Realtors	$30,628	53.5%	Garage workers	$14,248	5.0%
Electronic repairers	$30,316	4.7%	Waiters and waitresses	$14,092	71.3%
Motor vehicle sales people	$29,952	7.4%	Laundry workers	$13,468	63.2%
Clergy	$25,896	8.9%	Cooks and chefs	$13,364	38.5%
Brick masons	$25,116	1.6%	Sewing machine operators	$13,052	85.4%

whom are recent immigrants, often labor under third-world conditions. Were they to demand more than their current pay, their employers would probably send their work to an actual third-world country.

ARE WE STILL NUMBER ONE?

For most of the twentieth century, the United States has led the world in industrial production, technological innovation, and personal standards of living. In 1970, for example, America ranked first in per capita output. Our nearest rivals were Sweden, Canada, Denmark, and Switzerland, which like us had escaped being World War II battlegrounds. At that time, even advanced countries such as the Netherlands and Britain were only half as productive as the United States. Yet there were signs that change was under way: a once bomb-scarred Germany had risen to sixth place.

The per capita figures for 1994, the most recent at this writing, show dramatic changes. The United States has fallen to fifth place, a sad descent considering that its primacy once seemed beyond challenge. Two other countries, Germany and Austria, were less than $50 behind America in per capita GDP. (Germany would actually have been ahead had it not absorbed its inefficient eastern sibling.) Most striking is that between 1970 and 1994, Italy, Japan, and Austria all doubled their per capita production. Though Sweden and Australia dropped in the rankings, their output improved while America's was treading water.

Perhaps embarrassed by the GDP measure, which gave the United States fifth place, American economists devised an alternative gauge. This index computes "personal purchasing power" for each country, by noting differing price levels. Example: while hourly wages in Britain and America are quite similar ($9.37 vs. $9.56), the same basket of goods in Britain costs 42.2 percent more. With this new formula, the United States is once again number one, but not because our economy is more innovative or efficient. Prices are lower here due to a combination of choice and circumstance.

Other countries raise much of their public revenue from some variant of a "value-added tax," which is factored into the price of purchases. This charge tends to be "invisible" since it is seldom put on price tags or sales slips. But it clearly raises prices, as can be seen by what a gallon of gasoline typically cost in 1994: Austria, $3.13; Italy, $3.46; Norway, $3.79, Japan, $4.14; United States, $1.24. Other counties tax themselves to provide funds for social services and public amenities. Americans have chosen lower taxes and prices and reduced levels of benefits.

Per Capital Gross Domestic Product & Purchasing Power
(per $1,000 for the United States)

	GDP Per Capita, 1970		GDP Per Capita, 1994		Purchasing Power, 1994	
1.	UNITED STATES	$1,000	Switzerland	$1,438	UNITED STATES	$1,000
2.	Sweden	$857	Japan	$1,339	Switzerland	$943
3.	Canada	$776	Denmark	$1,087	Japan	$826
4.	Denmark	$663	Norway	$1,024	Canada	$824
5.	Switzerland	$662	UNITED STATES	$1,000	Norway	$817
6.	Germany★	$641	Germany	$989	Denmark	$804
7.	Norway	$622	Austria	$965	Belgium	$791
8.	France	$613	Sweden	$914	Austria	$782
9.	Australia	$572	France	$908	Germany	$769
10.	Belgium	$556	Belgium	$886	France	$766
11.	Netherlands	$497	Netherlands	$850	Australia	$735
12.	United Kingdom	$450	Canada	$757	Italy	$720
13.	Austria	$409	Italy	$745	United Kingdom	$703
14.	Japan	$404	United Kingdom	$720	Netherlands	$699
15.	Italy	$365	Australia	$695	Sweden	$690

★West Germany only.

America is the world's largest market, measured by the amount of money available for shopping. With one dominant language, national advertising media, and familiar brand names, economies of scale can be reflected in reduced prices. We have also mastered the delivery of bargains at complexes such as Price Cosco and Wal-Mart, and via mail from Lands' End and L.L. Bean. Other countries are beginning to build supermarkets and shopping centers, but they are still well behind America.

So, yes, the United States has the world's highest living standard—if gauged by the sums we devote to personal purchases. But being the leader in consumption is not necessarily a cause for congratulation. If production is what creates national wealth and the prospect of a prosperous future, America is no longer first and is unlikely to regain its primacy.

MONEY

CHAPTER ONE

SEARCHING FOR SENSE

Two things tantalize us about the people we know and many we don't know. The first concerns their sex lives: What do they actually do and how often do they do it? The second concerns money: How much do other people make or have stashed away? With money as with sex, it is impertinent to inquire. To do so would be a gross invasion of privacy. If you ask even your closest friend, your relationship will never be the same. Of course, our curiosity comes from wanting to know where we stand in relation to other people in those two realms of pleasure and power.

The first purpose of *Money* is to provide objective information on how much Americans make and what they are worth. It will also examine their sources of income, and how individuals and groups compare with one another. Its second aim is to explain why income, earnings, and wealth end up apportioned as they do. Yet in deliberating about money, the details are never neutral; each sum demands an accounting. Simply mention someone's salary, and mental wheels start turning: How did it get that high; why is it so low; can the sum be justified? Here, to start, are a few facts and figures, plus some of the questions that they raise.

- Fifteen years ago, 13,505 American households had annual incomes of $1 million or more, measured in today's dollars. Today, 68,064 families—five times as many—are in that bracket. Where did these new seven-figure incomes come from?

- Immigrants from India have an average income of $44,696 a year, after which come newcomers from the Philippines ($43,780) and China ($36,259). They make more than Americans of English ($34,117),

Swedish ($33,881), and Irish ($31,845) ancestry who have been here for several generations. What does this tell us about the changing contours of our society?

• In 1960, women earned 35 percent of all bachelor's degrees. They now account for over half: 55 percent. As a result, women are receiving more of the earnings pie. But not as much as their skills and training might warrant. How much of the lag is due to bias? Are other factors also at work?

• A radio news director in Vermont is offered a salary of $17,000; in Albuquerque, New Mexico, airline reservationists make $14,000 a year. How do people support themselves on these incomes?

• Orthopedic surgeons have an average income of $304,000 a year, while pediatricians make do with $113,000 a year. Are the former so much more adept, or are they profiting from an esoteric mystique?

• Has there been racial progress? Two decades ago, the typical black family received $605 for every $1,000 made by its white counterpart. Yet, today, the ratio is measurably lower, having dropped to $577 to $1,000. Why are black Americans still so far from parity?

• Is downsizing a recent development? Twenty years ago, America's largest corporations provided 244 of every 1,000 of the economy's jobs. Today, they employ only 169 of every 1,000 workers. Yet the top firms continue to hold the same share of all business assets. Why don't they need as many people?

• The partners in New York City's most prosperous law firm average $1.6 million in annual earnings. For Chicago's top firm, the figure is $685,000, while Boston's highest-paid partners average $490,000. In Seattle and Minneapolis, the amounts are $260,000 and $220,000. These variations reflect more than differences in cost of living. Why do some lawyers make so much more money than others?

• In a recent year, the chief executive of the Disney company received $203 million in salary and other awards. The chairman of Coca-Cola has been given so many options that he now holds $672 million of the firm's stock. How do the directors of these companies justify these payments? Are there explanations other than those given by the directors?

Much of the information in *Money* comes from official sources, including the Bureau of the Census, the Internal Revenue Service, the Social Security Administration, the Securities and Exchange Commission, and the Department of Labor. The United States leads the world in collecting information on income and earnings. But most of it is dispersed in documents few citizens ever see. These reports are public property; indeed, they have been produced for our benefit. It is our right not only to know what they say, but to use their findings to enlarge our understanding. In *Money,* I have recomputed figures from governmental studies and recast categories so that their significance is readily apparent. I have also synthesized findings from several sources to enable us to draw broader conclusions.

Official agencies do not release information on individuals' incomes, which is as it should be. While every American citizen is expected to file annually an accurate statement of income with the Internal Revenue Service, that agency has had an honorable record of guarding our submissions from *public* scrutiny, though it has been known to show our forms to the FBI and to prying eyes in the White House. And, of course, our incomes will become public information if the IRS chooses to prosecute us for not telling the whole truth.

Despite the confidentiality of our tax returns, it is not difficult to find out what a good number of Americans make in the way of wages or salaries. This is certainly the case with the 18 million men and women who have some kind of tax-supported employment, including those in the armed services and public education. In all cases, their pay is public information, starting with the president of the United States ($200,000) and extending to a newly hired deputy sheriff in New York's Chenango County ($16,000). Since I am on the faculty of a municipal college, I have no objection to revealing my last year's salary ($79,277) because you could find it out for yourself if you put in a little effort. And you would have to do that if you wanted to learn how much your mailman made, including his overtime payments and fringe benefits. The Postal Service might try to put you off, leaving you to invoke the Freedom of Information Act. But since your letter carrier is on a public payroll, you are entitled to know and would eventually get the figure. By the way, the average salary of a mail carrier is $33,696.

Still, while the IRS cannot divulge information about individuals' incomes, it can report facts such as that 3,055 of Idaho's taxpayers declared incomes of over $200,000; that, nationwide, 353,859 taxpayers said they received alimony checks, while 629,366 reported signing them; and that among the taxpayers with incomes exceeding $1 million, 225 claimed medical deductions, with those bills averaging $77,700.

The Census Bureau reveals that among the nation's 99.6 million households, 7.1 million now have incomes exceeding $100,000. Its figures also show that the income of a typical black family comes to only 57.7 percent of the white family median. The Census Bureau can also fine-tune its information. Men with bachelor's degrees who are aged thirty to thirty-five and hold full-time jobs average $48,998 a year, while full-time working women of the same age and with the same qualifications earn $35,176 a year, or 71.8 percent of the men's earnings.

The Bureau of Labor Statistics will tell you that for male salaried lawyers the median earnings figure is $60,892, while the typical female salaried lawyer makes $49,816. The Social Security Administration reports that among its 34.6 million beneficiaries, a top tier of 860,000 couples receive pensions reaching $31,824. It also informs us that it sends 366,209 checks abroad every month, ranging from 55,069 to Mexico to 548 to New Zealand.*

Discovering how much people make is also a staple of modern journalism. *Forbes* magazine easily leads the field with its annual lists of the richest Americans, the wealthiest lawyers, as well as the best-paid athletes, authors, and entertainers. In most cases, this calls for intensive investigative reporting. While everyone is obliged to report his or her income each year, there is no requirement to report what is owned. (Upon a person's death, forms must be filed on the estate. But they may show less than the full figure if some of the deceased's wealth has already gone into trusts and bequests.) So *Forbes* dispatches reporters to talk with people who keep their eyes on the wealthy, such as financial

---

*All figures are the most recent that were available at the time of writing, which generally means those for 1995. If other periods had to be used, there may be variations in medians or percentages, since year-by-year baselines are not always comparable. For example, a 1993 Census survey has also been used, since it reports kinds of information that are no longer being released.

advisers and investment analysts. Whatever figures are gleaned are necessarily estimates, but they are the most reliable information we have. Thus for 1996, *Forbes* suggested that Warren Buffett's holdings totaled $15 billion, Steven Spielberg's an even $1 billion, and Oprah Gail Winfrey's $415 million.

Financial World performs the same sort of exercise in the canyons of Wall Street. Leading its 1995 roster of top earners was George Soros, who runs his own offshore hedge funds and took in something like $1.5 billion. In fact, he was so far ahead of the pack that the runner-up, Stanley Druckenmiller, also a member of the Soros firm, came in at $350 million. Closer to the midpoint on the list of Wall Street's highest earners, with $38 million, was Michel David-Weill, the best-paid partner among Lazard Frères's investment bankers. In one-hundredth place was Charles Schwab of the discount brokerage firm that bears his name, who made a mere $9.4 million. But that amount has little meaning, since he is the firm's principal owner, and *Forbes* says he has a personal fortune of $1.1 billion. As owner of the company, it is Schwab's prerogative to decide his own salary. (He gave his second-in-command $5.4 million.)

In the worlds of professional sports and entertainment no one has to state how much he or she makes. But these industries are rife with gossip and cater to a public that's eager to read every paycheck. *People* magazine didn't have to do much digging to report that Sandra Bullock's compensation for the ten or so weeks it takes to film *Speed II* is $12.5 million. And *People* could safely estimate that each of the six members of the twenty-something cast of *Friends* is receiving about $75,000 for every new episode, or at least $1.5 million apiece.

In the sports arenas, *Financial World* tells us, football pays the least: Troy Aikman of the Dallas Cowboys got a mere $6.8 million in 1996. Baseball comes next, with $7.5 million for the Seattle Mariners' Ken Griffey Jr. Mario Lemieux of hockey's Pittsburgh Penguins made $11 million for the season. And Michael Jordan is the George Soros of basketball, with his $25 million from the Chicago Bulls and as much as another $40 million for endorsements.

The Securities and Exchange Commission requires every corporation to reveal the compensation of whichever of its executives sit on the firm's board of directors. *BusinessWeek* is usually the first magazine to collate those figures, which must appear in the proxy statements sent out to stockholders for the annual meeting. In its 1995 rankings,

John Welch, General Electric's chairman, is near the top with $22.1 million. James Preston, the chief executive who has helped to make Avon a very profitable company, was satisfied with $991,000.

The Internal Revenue Service does divulge some individual incomes, but in a roundabout way. Any organization that is exempted from taxes must report what it pays its five top people. The IRS does not release these filings, but it does tell the organizations that they must show the figures to anyone who asks to see them. The *Chronicle of Higher Education* does just that and has published the leading salaries at private colleges and universities. (Public schools aren't included, since their employees' salaries are always available.) At the top of the list of earnings for the 1994–95 academic year was Dr. Wayne Isom of Cornell's medical school, who received $1,729,709. John Silber, the president of Boston University, received $565,018 as the highest single-year compensation for a private college or university president. Further down the list was Michael Krzyzewski, Duke's basketball coach, with a salary of $238,722, although he may have made even more from endorsements and other activities. The best-paid nonmedical professor was Northwestern's Bala Balachandran, who received $294,143 for his courses in accounting informations systems.

Most people, however, prefer that their incomes not be revealed. Gone are the days portrayed by Jane Austen in *Pride and Prejudice* when everyone knew that Fitzwilliam Darcy had an inheritance that brought him "ten thousand pounds clear a year." Why is this privacy so important? In some cases, we may feel that we are not making as much as we should, and we prefer not to let others know of our shortcomings. In other cases, we may fear that people will become envious or angry if they learn the size of our incomes.

People are more defensive about money than any other subject, with the possible exception of the way they raise their children. Well-paid individuals will spin webs of words in the hope of persuading the rest of us that what they get is both earned and deserved. Those with more modest wages seek to show that what they do is worth a lot more than what they are currently receiving. Considering how self-interest warps perceptions, especially when dollars are at stake, it becomes all the more difficult to cull useful explanations of why people make as much or as little as they do.

I once asked a colleague known for his research with laboratory rats what a student of human behavior might learn from his studies of animals. "The marvelous thing about rats," he said, "is that they do not talk. Of course, they communicate via squeaks and a complex body language. However," he went on, "if one rat takes some food from another, he doesn't make a speech explaining why he did it." Turning to me, he said, "The trouble with the social sciences is that they record all the silly and self-serving things that people say." His advice was to observe what people do instead of listening to what they say, as he and his colleagues do with laboratory animals: "Explanations for behavior can be found within and around that behavior, if you look for influential factors and forces."

My colleague's advice is especially valuable in the realm of money because people tend to offer rationalizations rather than reasons for the amounts they make. Yet no principle should be carried to extremes. At times what people say to us can expand our understanding, and listening is a form of observing. For example, in the next chapter we will learn the responses of people who were asked how much they feel they would need to "live in reasonable comfort" and then how much they would want to "fulfill all their dreams." We want to know about those dreams because even fantasies are facts, since they are in people's heads and affect the ways they behave.

So *Money* begins with an invitation to ask skeptical questions, the more unsettling the better. A lot of stereotypes will have to be pierced if we hope to discern how a society such as ours divides up those pieces of paper we call dollars. We should also be ready to look at old issues in new ways. Thus, as the economist Lester Thurow has noted, in the past one reason why people had several children was that they were viewed as "profit centers," since they eventually made a net contribution to their parents' well-being. Today, children have become "cost centers," because indulgent parents lavish so much of the household's income on their offspring. Hence, the tendency for couples to have only one or two children. I am not saying that everything we do has an economic explanation. The point is to identify how our financial situations shape our behaviors as human beings.

As Clemenceau counseled about war and the generals, the subject of money is too important to be left wholly to the economists. My office in the Queens College political science department is down the hall from the offices of my colleagues in economics, and I count many of them as old friends. However, their inclination is to converse with one another rather than to address a general audience. So this is a book for lay readers, without technical terms or abstract equations. Still, tables serve a purpose, since insights may be gained by translating facts into figures. Far from compressing people into chilly columns of numbers, statistics can highlight qualities that make individuals interesting and varied. While it may be too much to claim that a number is worth a thousand words, the tables in *Money* should be regarded as illustrations, specially collated to complement the text.

The recurrent question on these pages will be simple and straightforward: Does the way income is apportioned make any kind of sense? Yet there can be questions within questions, a few of which are noted here. How far does our economic system actually adhere to its own rules? Is competition the best way to uncover talent? Does the public really have the final say by voting with its dollars? Is it rational to pay experienced teachers a fraction of what law firms offer recent graduates? And, assessing the consequences for society and the health of the human spirit, does it make sense when our kind of economy divides the population into winners and losers? Of course, it may be countered that even though much about our system defies logic, not to mention morality, it still makes sense from the perspective of a broader philosophy. The issues the foregoing questions raise are hardly new. Indeed, they were a great concern of this nation's founders. And they are questions that must be recast and posed anew in every era, including our own.

CHAPTER TWO

AMERICA'S WAY
WITH MONEY

Every year, more than $4 trillion changes hands and becomes the personal income of Americans. Just how this money is apportioned will be the subject of this book. Subsequent chapters will also explain why the distribution has its current shape and form. And here it is important to understand that the basic causes go back a long way. It may be agreed that Franklin Roosevelt's New Deal, Lyndon Johnson's Great Society, and Ronald Reagan's supply-side credo all affected who would get how much. But in a wider context, the impact of politics and policies cannot be more than marginal. For the stage was essentially set two centuries ago, in the early days of the republic. Indeed, it is not an overstatement to say that our present distribution is the realized vision of the nation's founders. Even allowing for the passage of time, in broadest outline ours remains the nation that James Madison and Alexander Hamilton intended it to be.

"THE DIVERSITY
IN THE FACULTIES OF MEN"

Every economic system intersects with a view of human nature. As it happens, this nexus was a prime concern of this nation's architects. Most explicit on this score was James Madison, who is rightly called the father of our Constitution, because of the central role that he played at the Philadelphia convention of 1787. In a series of articles now known as *The Federalist,* which urged support for the new government, he also expanded on the kind of economy the emerging nation would have. Terms such as *capitalism* and *private enterprise* never appear in the Constitution; at most, there are some references to "commerce." But unwilling to avoid the matter altogether, Madison, in *Federalist No. 10,* revealed the founders' views of human nature, and how they underpinned the way the economy would work. It would be well, he said, to start by acknowledging "the diversity in the faculties of men."

At face value, this is hardly a controversial proposition. We know human beings vary immensely, especially in having different traits and talents. For our present purposes, we need not consider to what extent these aptitudes are due to distinctive genes or to variations in upbringing. What we can accept is that some people excel at music, others have mechanical skills, while still others can work wonders with a garden.

However, a faculty for playing the flute or raising roses was not what Madison had in mind. He and his fellow founders made clear they were primarily concerned with what they called the "faculties of acquiring property."

Within any population, some people will have a talent for building business enterprises. One such person was Raymond A. Kroc, a salesman who sold milk-shake machines to low-priced eating places. Most were dowdy diners, catering mainly to working men. Kroc sensed that many more people would like a light meal out, especially families who were moving to the suburbs where driving was a way of life. But his vision had a deeper dimension. People also wanted clean surroundings and efficient, friendly service. Now, a half century later, Kroc's McDonald's is still an unmatched success, extending all across the globe. Clearly, it provides something billions of people had wanted, even if they didn't realize it themselves. It is not too much to say that Ray Kroc had a faculty for understanding what his customers desired even if they couldn't put it in words. And this, of course, is how fortunes are made. At the close of his career, Kroc was worth upward of $500 million. And today, McDonald's employs more than two hundred thousand Americans, most of them at or near the minimum wage. The roster of the richest Americans is filled with men and women who had a new idea, and the faith that the buying public would exclaim, "Wow, that's what I've always wanted!"

Indeed, persons possessing this faculty can be found in every kind of society, even those that try to suppress entrepreneurial endeavors. As we now know, many such men and women lived in the former Soviet Union and are presently able to show what they can do. Our nation's founders not only believed that the faculties for building businesses were inherent in some people, but that these capacities also needed to be nourished. For this reason, Madison said, the public must come to understand that "the protection of these faculties is the first object of government."

Accordingly, men and women who show that they have a talent for building enterprises will have first call on the government's attention. Indeed, Madison went on, the need for this protection is why "the rights of property originate." His reasoning, simply, was that the good fortune of the nation depends on the prosperity of its business community. Madison was also candid in saying that the nation would always be divided into "those who hold and those who are without property." And by property, he was not referring to ordinary possessions such as one's home or its furnishings. For him and the other founders, it meant ownership of some magnitude, more like a business of your own or considerable holdings in an enterprise. So they were talking about a fairly small group who had proved their superiority in the economic arena. These few would be America's first citizens, with preferred access to the bodies that make the laws and set the nation's priorities. And why not? After all, they are the ones who bring us the products that make life varied and interesting, who provide most of us with employment, and raise the capital required for developing natural and human resources.

In the Madisonian view, our incomes will reflect the extent to which each of us has "the faculties of acquiring property." While today most of us do not operate enterprises of our own, what we earn is in large part based on how skillfully we sell what we have to offer. In some cases, as the saying goes, if you build a better product, people will find out about it and come knocking at your door. But, as the poet Thomas Gray pointed out, many fine flowers live and die unseen by a human eye. Think of the best-known operatic tenors, who combine superb voices with unabashed marketing skills. Even scientists are expected to sell their findings in television interviews. And if we are tongue-tied or self-effacing, we may employ others to do the selling for us.

THE ISLAND

James Madison believed it a natural truth that disparities in human talents will produce an "unequal distribution of property." This does not mean that the rest of us must accept his belief. Even sages and scholars have devised quite antithetical theories, and since neither science nor philosophy can provide definitive information, we are all entitled to frame our own perceptions and form our own opinions.

No attempt will be made here to persuade the reader of a particular assessment of human character and capacities. A better approach is simply to ask all of us to examine the premises that guide our own reasoning. The following exercise is designed to move us a little further toward that goal. It borrows from the device called a "state of nature," used by such classical thinkers as John Locke and Jean-Jacques Rousseau. To clarify their views of our intrinsic qualities, they created models of precivilized societies where natural attributes held sway.

> For our exercise, next January 1, let us place one hundred American men and women on an uninhabited island, one blessed with an equable climate and plentiful resources. As we land them there, we give each person $10,000 in a form suited for use as currency. We then leave them for a full year.
>
> When we return, on December 31, what might we find in terms of distribution of income, a human hierarchy, and the development of the island?

Well, of course, we'll want more information. So let's set down a few ground rules. It will be a diverse group, consisting of fifty men and fifty women, each over the age of eighteen. As for their prior lives, let's say they had a spectrum of incomes and occupations and that they will not have known one another before they arrived on the island; nor will they bring any wealth they may previously have had.

In your view, what might the island look like on December 31? Some people might say we will probably find it divided into parcels of property, which are now "owned" by various inhabitants. But how many owners would there be, only five or ten, or perhaps considerably more? What about the possibility that after twelve months, some people might be employees, working for others for wages? And that total of $1 million, which arrived equally dispersed: Would a few people be rich, others poor, and some actually in debt? Indeed, twelve months is not too short a time for the creation of additional currency, so could some of the residents already by millionaires? The scenarios are endless. Yet because this is still a fictional island, the scenarios reflect not a reality, but our own ideas about how capacities are distributed among human beings.

Some people might want to raise a quite different speculation. Perhaps that on December 31, we might find that no one "owned" property. The original money would still be equally apportioned, and everyone would be working together to create a congenial common life. To object that such a scenario is utopian does not take us far. If we are concerned with what is humanly possible, we should acknowledge that at times and places—not all of them "primitive"—people have been more inclined to choose cooperation. (Would things be different if all of the islanders were women?) Those who have led more communal lives are not less "human" than persons who thrive on competition. Indeed, it could be argued that the island might encourage the emergence of human traits quite different from those most of us now believe are inherent and inevitable.

The purpose of imagining these island scenarios is to see that our current financial system is not inevitable, though it certainly reflects Madison's augury of the American way.

"THE SPIRIT OF IMITATION, THE FEAR OF FAILURE"

Great Britain produced Adam Smith, the philosopher of a free-market economy. Yet it remained for the United States to take Smith's teachings to heart. Here the pioneer was Alexander Hamilton, the country's first secretary of the treasury. He was convinced that America had a great destiny before it. "It belongs to us to vindicate the honor of the human race," he prophesied in *The Federalist.* And by that he meant that in this new nation, people could realize their full potential, particularly by being part of a vigorous economy. "When all the different kinds of industry obtain in a community," he wrote, "each individual can find his proper element and call into activity the whole vigor of his nature."

Yet Hamilton was also aware of human frailties. "Individuals," he said, "are apt to succumb to the strong influence of habit and imitation, the fear of failure in untried enterprises and new attempts." He believed that people needed to be goaded into using their talents. In a Hamiltonian scheme, none would be able to sit back on their haunches. All of us would have to enter the market, to sell our skills and services in competition with others.

Recall what we learned in Economics 101, which remains largely Adam Smith with a strong touch of Hamilton. The United States has a market economy. There are obvious markets, such as the stock exchanges, where the maneuvering of buyers and sellers determines the price of securities. Anyone who owns a house occasionally wonders what it's worth; hence casual glances at the real estate pages to see what comparable properties are going for. Other markets are more subtle. Yesterday, you walked out of a store without buying a shirt, since you felt the price was too high. If others feel the same way, the garment will gather dust and the merchant will get the message. Hence the next time you see it, the price will have been marked down. The same kind of interplay affects what is paid for human labor.

Some neighborhoods have pickup locations, where landscaping contractors stop to get the laborers they need for the day's work. If they can get the people they need at $6.50 an hour, the next day they may offer $6.25 to see if they can still get the same number and quality of help. (Since the contractors were actually prepared to pay $6.50, a lower rate means they keep more for themselves.) Conversely, if the demand for labor grows, workers may ask for and get $6.75. The same thing happens when carpeted corporations need more computer analysts than they can attract at the wage they have been offering.

Of course, most people's wages do not fluctuate daily. A teacher or an executive may have a contract assuring a settled salary for one or several years. But even during this period, the market is at work. At renewal time, the teacher may find the board not only rejecting bids for raises, but insisting on cuts in benefits. Yet during the same period, the executive may find her talents are much in demand, so her employer will probably give her a hefty hike without waiting to be asked. Hardly ever does this market minuet ask about individuals' needs, their benefit to society, or even—in many cases—how much skill is required for the tasks they perform.

Just about everyone has joined this auction at least once, when we made ourselves available for our first job and took or turned down an employer's offer. The market is a very much a reality for those who leave a position, voluntarily or otherwise, and soon find out what they are worth—or if they have any worth at all—to another employer. But many Americans have not known these interludes of truth. In public service and the academic world, many people remain with the same organization from recruitment to retirement. Until recently, this was also common in the corporate sphere. Among the current chairmen of the one hundred largest firms, forty-four have been on the company's payroll for thirty or more years, and for another twenty-four it has been at least twenty. The chief executives at Ford, Coca-Cola, Caterpillar, and Aetna are forty-year veterans, suggesting they came to the company straight from college.

Still, we are in play in the market even when we don't change jobs. Promotions and bonuses and raises register our current worth, since they calibrate the degree to which our presence is wanted.

Of course, some individuals have been able to avoid having their labor subjected to auction altogether. Most union members—even if fewer today than in the past—are shielded by seniority. The typical airline pilot is now paid significantly more than he would be if he presented himself anew to his current employer or a new one. This is why firms are seeking to install "two-tier" systems, under which newly hired people will enjoy a less generous salary schedule than those who preceded them. Professors are noted for their ironclad tenure, even if this protection is not as freely granted as in the past. Because of having given tenured professors lifelong careers, universities find themselves clogged with senior personnel. At Stanford and Yale, three-quarters of the faculty budgets are absorbed by the salaries of full professors. The higher reaches of business also foster a clublike camaraderie that tends to insulate CEOs from market tests. Indeed, corporate boards generally give chairmen generous raises, seldom wondering whether their top officers might be offered as much elsewhere were they to put their skills on the auction block.

Since most workers see their market value begin to decline when they reach their midfifties, many decide to retire before they turn sixty-five. For many men and women it is a relief to leave the auction. Social Security checks not only arrive regularly, but are raised each year to meet the cost of living. Yet in a sense, retirees are now participants in a political auction. The levels of public pensions are legislated by elected officials, and senior citizens have shown they know how to use their votes effectively.

Are there alternatives to auctions? One proposal, which will be examined later on, is that wages be determined by more rational criteria, such as the difficulty or responsibility adhering to a job, or the training required to perform it or even its social contribution. Another proposal invokes the Marxian precept "to each according to his needs." Yet to implement that rule would require coming to decisions about what is "necessary," whether for each citizen individually or for all people generally. An even more utopian nostrum would be to give everyone the same income, which would have a common floor and ceiling. It seems safe to say that most Americans would deem this proposal not only impractical but grossly immoral. It certainly could not be considered an American way.

Our Hamiltonian legacy posits that the market and its auctions are the best way yet devised to allocate an economy's resources, including the skills sold by human beings. Any other method is seen as authoritarian, if not worse, with decisions reflecting the biases of officials who may begin as democrats but end as despots. Yet it was Adam Smith who noted that businessmen seldom gather "but the conversation ends in a conspiracy against the public," by which he meant prearranging bids before auctions, setting prices to undercut competition, as well as bestowing compensations that bear no palpable relation to services rendered. Even if on paper an auction for human services is a persuasive theory, if given the choice, most of us would rather not be put on the block. At best, the test is seen as suited for individuals other than ourselves, since the scrutiny will build their characters and lower wages will benefit the commonweal. Yet with the diminishing clout of labor unions, weakening job security, and the shrinking of both middle management and the middle class, the future is going to see a lot more Americans realizing that they have become "other" people.

"ACQUISITIONS AND ENJOYMENTS"

Congratulations! You have just heard from a lawyer, a gentleman hitherto unknown to you, who has told you that he represents a law firm in

Melbourne that is charged with distributing an estate. Do you recall your uncle Charlie, the one who moved to Australia some thirty years ago? Apparently even as a toddler, you were a favorite of his. And he has left you $100,000 in his will. Once you sign this document, the check will be in your hands within a week.

That afternoon, you relate your good fortune to a friend, who responds by saying, "That's great! Now you'll have to decide what to do with it." Without a beat, you reply, "No problem on that, I've already spent it."

Well, of course you have. As would any of us. We all have a shopping list in our heads, specifying what we would buy if we came into some money. Of course, the list is always changing, as our priorities shift and items are added or deleted. Some may be material things you can actually feel, such as a car or a coat. But they can as easily be costly experiences, such as a four-star meal or concert tickets or supersonic travel.

Almost all our friends and neighbors will tell us that they lack sufficient money to lead the lives they would like to enjoy. Such plaints may well be valid for the truly poor, most of whom lack sanitary shelter and a balanced and varied diet. Yet one hears similar laments from individuals with six-figure incomes, and even some who have reached the seven-figure bracket. After all, the rich also have their doggies in the window, such as that Picasso at next month's Sotheby auction.

Why do people want more money even when they are comfortable by any objective standard? Perhaps the answers are obvious; but let's not assume that immediately. Of course, one doesn't have to stop at comfort. A Roper-Starch survey, conducted in 1995, shows that Americans use several thresholds when they think about money. As the table on page 40 shows, most agree they could tighten their belts and get by on quite modest incomes. Over two-thirds felt that their families could keep going on less than $35,000 a year, and over half said they could live reasonably comfortably with incomes below $50,000. In fact, the "comfort" median of $41,100 was only $2,300 more than what the midpoint American family made in 1995. But the most revealing responses came when the same people were asked what they would want to "fulfill all your dreams." Less than a fifth yearn to be really rich. Still, they're a considerable group and help to explain the lines at lottery booths. Yet well over half of the people surveyed have shopping lists with a baseline of at least $100,000, an income now enjoyed by only one in twelve

How Much Would You and Your Family Need to . . .	
Just Get By?	
Under $20,000	26%
$20,000–$35,000	45%
$35,000–$50,000	15%
Over $50,000	14%
Get-by median: $25,500	
Live in Reasonable Comfort?	
Under $35,000	37%
$35,000–$50,000	21%
$50,000–$70,000	25%
Over $70,000	17%
Comfort median: $41,100	
Fulfill All Your Dreams?	
Under $50,000	12%
$50,000–$100,000	28%
$100,000–$200,000	28%
$200,000–$1 million	14%
Over $1 million	18%
Dreams median: $102,000	

Americans. Thus their ideal income was derived not from peering at the rich and famous, but simply by seeing what is available at their nearby shopping malls.

Since colonial days, Americans have made clear their desire to keep as much of their money as possible. Taxes, no matter how minimal, were presumed to be illegitimate, with the ideal rate being nil. (Granted, they were imposed by a parliament sitting three thousand miles away. Still, most of these funds remained in the colonies to finance local projects.) This animus remains in place today. Even when legislated locally, taxes are seen as acts of coercion, imposed by alien authorities. By their own choice, citizens of the United States hand over less of their incomes than do those of the nations with which we choose to be compared. But hostility toward government is only part of the equation. Even more elemental is the conviction dear to Americans that they are entitled to keep every penny they earn or otherwise obtain. Stripped of rhetorical flourishes, the reason is very simple: this money is needed because there is so much out there clamoring to be bought, and not just the essentials such as shoes for the children or bread on the table. For Americans, even ephemeral purchases are soon cast as necessities, enjoyments one must have to make life fulfilling and complete.

Alexis de Tocqueville, as a visiting aristocrat, was struck by what he saw as Americans' "inordinate love of material gratification." While this country can take pride in initiating such principles as freedom of speech and public education, it also pioneered the idea of "one-stop shopping," which was born as the general store and is now incarnated as the shopping mall. This country's variant of capitalism was the first to stress popular consumption. Indeed, as Tocqueville observed, the country's commitment to democracy was much more than political. It is not unfair to say that the freedom to shop—to select, from an array of options, whatever appeals to you—is the choice Americans cherish most. We know that in an average election, less than half of all citizens feel moved to use their right to vote. Indeed, for at least a generation the polling booth has been fading as a symbol of democracy. Its replacement, as a site of popular participation, has been the aforementioned shopping mall.

How can America's obsession with shopping be explained? For one thing, America has always had more space than older countries, which meant people built bigger homes on larger plots of land. But capacious homes have to be filled, which imparts to purchasing an aura of necessity. The old fear of emptiness impels us: so long as we lack certain items, our lives will seem less than complete. Hence Alexander Hamilton's remark on the penchant of Americans for "multiplying their acquisitions or their enjoyments." Compounding the pressure is the desire of an aging republic to see itself as a young nation. Hence the stress on keeping up with the most recent and the latest: not only in material possessions but also in ideas and fashions and trends. Hence, too, the impulse to discard even recent acquisitions, for fear one might be seen as out of touch or out of date. It is not surprising that Americans lead the world in per capita accretion of garbage, exacerbated by the fact that—even with garage sales—there is little demand for used or secondhand items.

Alexander Hamilton, more than any other individual, can claim the title of the founder of this nation's economic system. In his *Report on the Subject of Manufactures,* written two centuries ago, he showed how supply and demand interplay in a market economy. When Hamilton wrote, America was primarily an agrarian society: nine of every ten persons made their living on the land. Both the farms of New England and the plantations of the South relied on human sweat and muscle to provide the necessities of life. In Hamilton's mind, to continue this reliance on agriculture would consign the United States to what we would now term a Third World status. His mission was to persuade the American people that national greatness required an industrial base.

Hamilton believed that the advent of industry would spur individuals to use their intellects and imaginations, since "manufactures opens a wider field to exertions of ingenuity than agriculture." In the Hamiltonian vision—a forecast that became self-fulfilling—America would honor the scientist, the inventor, the engineer. As so we have, from Thomas Edison and Henry Ford to Walt Disney and Bill Gates. America's first treasury secretary was certain of what would happen once technology became the prime mover for a free economy. "The multiplication of factories," he asserted, "creates a demand for articles such as were either unknown or produced in inconsiderable quantities." Here, a single phrase—"creates a demand"—identified the way capitalism works. The system extends a challenge to enterprising individuals, inviting them to put on the market products that are designed to arouse a response from the purchasing public, such as have the Big Mac, the Barbie doll, Arnold Schwarzenegger movies, and the novels of Danielle Steel.

So it is suppliers who create demand. Of course, consumers choose what they want, and they demand an ample array of options. (Recall the malaise of Soviet socialism: the lack of variety sapped the human spirit.) Yet if we take a closer look at those wish lists—things people would buy if they came into some money—they consist of things already on the shelves. In other words, the "acquisitions and enjoyments" we want have been put there by entrepreneurs who think they have a fair idea about what will turn us on. In this sphere, as in others, most people are not very inventive. We would be hard-pressed to imagine items not already available that we might like to see at our local malls. Thus a demand was created for Swatch watches and Power Rangers, for sushi and coffee bars, plus utility vehicles and movies about dinosaurs and extraterrestrials.

But for Americans, purchasing is not simply a pursuit of pleasure. The "material gratification" of which Tocqueville spoke serves another purpose. All those possessions, carefully selected, become dimensions of our identities. This is certainly true of our wardrobes, where each item expresses or accentuates some part of our personalities. Most of us have collections of musical recordings that, taken together, reflect who we are or would like to be. The same may be said of the places where we choose to travel, even the kinds of foods we buy. Americans, Tocqueville observed, are quick to abandon their antecedents and are constantly reinventing themselves. "Every citizen," he wrote, "is lost in the crowd." So by our purchases and possessions, we make an attempt to persuade the world and ourselves that we are original, unique, indeed that we truly exist.

Part of being an American is to feel that you deserve more than you have. (How many of the people you know do *not* feel that they are underpaid?) Thus Tocqueville noted how the average citizen "conceives a more lofty opinion of his rights, of his future, of himself; he is filled with new ambitions and new desires, he is harassed by new wants." To be sure, not all these wants are economic. People also want love, respect, and recognition; some may seek sensual pleasure, others peace of mind. But in the end, Americans of every class feel the want— indeed the need—of incomes discernibly higher than the ones they currently have.

No law of nature decrees that human beings must feel this way, or that they need so expansive an array of acquisitions. Rather, the history of our time has created for Americans a culture based on status and style, seduction and temptation, and symbols of success used to mask the anxieties of uncertain identities.

CAPITALISM AND CATHEDRALS

Some of the finest tributes to capitalism were bestowed by a gentleman named Karl Marx. "The bourgeoisie," he said, referring to the presiding class of the system, "has accomplished wonders far surpassing Egyptian pyramids, Roman aqueducts, and Gothic cathedrals." Even as Marx wrote those words, a century and a half ago, capitalism was changing the shape of the world by its

> applications of chemistry to industry and agriculture, steam-navigation, railways, electric telegraphs, clearing of whole continents for cultivation, canalization of rivers, whole populations conjured out of the ground.

His theories of socialism and communism aside—witness the demise of regimes bearing his name—Marx's insights into market economies still inform our thinking. As the preceding passage shows, he stressed that the pursuit of profits depends on new technologies. Thus the leading players in the capitalist drama are entrepreneurs and engineers. It is their interplay that shapes the configuration of classes, determining the distribution of income and the contours of careers.

This system, Marx went on, "cannot exist without constantly revolutionizing the instruments of production, and with them the whole relations of society." Far from being conservative, owners and managers are constantly searching for new technologies whose effect will be to recast the way human beings experience life. That has certainly been the impact of familiar inventions, all ushered in by capitalism: the automobile and air-conditioning, television and commercial aviation, the computer and the birth-control pill. The last, an artifact of biochemical technology, had a crucial role in starting the sexual revolution, which has in turn shaped much of the society we know today. While not every woman used the pill when it became available, to all women it signaled the freedom to choose careers other than motherhood.

New machines and processes also create forms of employment—some well paid, many not—just as they eliminate others. Such displacements are especially evident in the American variant of capitalism, which has never made the creation of jobs a primary goal. Help Wanted signs go up only if people are needed; they come down when they are not. This logic is not easily refuted. Why, it must be asked, keep people on a payroll if their services are not needed? The implications of this premise will recur throughout this book.

For several generations, the craft of tool and die making was an esteemed occupation. It required an arduous apprenticeship, which led to a well-paid artisan career. Limited entry also ensured that workers would be in short supply, with employers bidding for their services even in depressed times. Simply stated, tool and die makers built the machines that made other machines, from the presses that shape automobile bodies to molds for perfume bottles. Their work called for dexterity of hand and eye, plus a mind for applied mathematics. These blue-collar aristocrats could often be seen counseling college-trained engineers.

In 1970, there were approximately 200,000 tool and die makers in a workforce of approximately 80 million. By 1995, there were only 143,000 of them within a workforce of 125 million, which is the equivalent of less than half their earlier number. Why the decline in demand for a service that had once been so crucial? It is not as if they were akin to blacksmiths, whose skills were no longer needed in an automotive age. Yet to an extent, something similar was happening. For one thing, many of the products once made in the United States are now manufactured abroad. In some cases, the decision to do so was made by American companies, since outlying labor costs are lower. In other cases, foreign firms were making things Americans chose to buy. In either event, skills that were once the province of Cleveland and Detroit are now reliably piled in Seoul and São Paulo.

Impending advances of capitalism, Marx said, would devastate those in the more vulnerable reaches of the middle class:

> The lower strata of the middle class . . . sink gradually into the proletariat, partly because their diminutive capital does not suffice for the scale on which modern industry is carried on . . . and partly because their specialized skill is rendered worthless by new methods of production.

It is not simply that tasks are now being performed in other countries. An even more radical change has been that skills that were once unique to individuals are now contained in software programs. Where tool and die makers once gauged minute tolerances with micrometers, computers now do the scanning and make immediate adjustments. This sort of transference became apparent in the early 1990s, when crafts workers at Caterpillar went out on strike. The company's managers found that lower-paid replacement workers could turn out tractors of equal quality, once the company installed technologies to ensure the fine-tuning.

Marx's statement also referred to smaller entrepreneurs, who find they lack the capital to compete with nationwide chains. He could be speaking of the many Main Street merchants who have been forced to close their doors soon after a Wal-Mart or a Home Depot opens on the outskirts of town. Or, to cite another example, the typical pharmacist was once not only a college graduate, but someone who owned his own store and ran it as if he were a professional. Indeed, he was welcomed at the local Rotary Club, where he ranked with dentists and accountants and the high school principal.

However, "the scale on which modern industry is carried on" is now manifested in the huge drug chains, which are driving local pharmacies out of business. Now pharmacy graduates have to settle for weekly wages from Rite Aid or Walgreen's or do what is essentially assembly-line work for mail-order services or health maintenance organizations.

Indeed, our current economy may be going Marx one better by declaring even executives obsolete. Entire echelons of managers who once had corner offices are being told that what they do is no longer needed. Papers pass through fewer hands for opinions and approval; more stringent tests are now applied to see who actually contributes to the bottom line. Downsizing and flattening have been most pronounced in our largest corporations, and these processes have been under way for the better part of a generation. The table on page 47 shows that in 1973, the nation's 800 largest firms presented paychecks to 229 of every 1,000 employed Americans. By 1993, the top 800 provided jobs for only 169 of every 1,000. The dip was even more graphic among the 500 largest in the industrial sector, whose payrolls dropped from 184 per 1,000 workers to 97 per 1,000. Relative to overall employment, the largest insurance companies and utilities also made do with fewer workers. The main gains have been in banking and retailing, which are more prone to use temporary and part-time workers. So while total employment rose by 41 percent between 1973 and 1993, the largest firms were cutting their payrolls by 34 percent.

QUINTILES AND BELL CURVES:
NATURE'S LAWS OR HUMAN DESIGN?

According to classical economists, the spreads of incomes and earnings will follow "natural" distributions if free markets are allowed to oper-

How Many Jobs Are the Top Companies Providing?

Corporate Fields	1973	1993	Change*
500 Manufacturers	15,531,683	11,546,647	-47.4%
50 Banks	427,412	934,429	+54.7%
50 Insurance	410,918	473,948	-18.4%
50 Financial	355,062	790,813	+57.6%
50 Retail	2,683,337	4,023,949	+6.1%
50 Transportation	924,314	1,372,045	+5.0%
50 Utilities	1,275,943	1,042,527	-42.2%
800 Largest Firms	21,608,669	20,184,358	-33.9%

And How Much of the Economy Do They Own?

	1973	1993
Assets of largest 800	$1.6 billion	$9.4 billion
All U.S. corporations	$3.3 billion	$20.0 billion
Largest 800 share	49.6%	47.1%

*Between 1973 and 1993, overall employment in the U.S. rose from 84 million to 119 million. So the *Change* column has been computed to reflect shifts in the top 800's employment relative to the larger 1993 workforce. Example: While in absolute numbers, jobs in insurance rose by 15.3 percent, in light of the growth in the total workforce, they in fact fell by 18.4 percent.

ate. But nature at best is laconic, challenging us to pick up clues and cues that give glimpses of her laws. To get better acquainted with her design, the human species created sciences and mathematics. So far as we can ascertain, nature wants us to use numbers in this endeavor. Calculus began as a blackboard exercise, a method for measuring the area under a curve. But it was then found that the very same equation could compute the speed of falling bodies, which plummet toward the ground at accelerating rates. So calculus was much more than an academic model; it turned out to be an instrument for revealing how nature rules the physical world.

Every so often, nature allows the human population to produce some extraordinary minds, people with powers of perception that have been denied to the rest of us. It was such uncommon intellects who discovered that deoxyribonucleic acid formed the basis of heredity, and that the energy of the velocity of matter is equal to its mass times the square of the velocity of light. Thus far economists have yet to match the elegance of DNA's double helix or the simplicity of $E = mc^2$. But not for want of trying. Hence their deployment of devices such as Lorenz curves, Pareto coefficients, and Gini indices to explain the allocation of wealth and income and earnings among households and individuals.

America's founders, as we know, accepted that there would be disparities in material success, reflecting natural variations in the capacities of human beings. Thus Alexander Hamilton argued that "society naturally divides itself into the very few and the many." James Madison saw it in nature's design to create "unequal faculties of acquiring property." By allowing these capacities free rein, America would become a competitive arena, in which citizens would vie for slices of what we have come to think of as the national pie. And we accept that there will be winners and losers. But it is not enough to proclaim that such an outcome is ordained by nature. It must then be ascertained whether nature has created distinctive profiles for these distributions.

One of the most common ways to depict economic distribution is to divide the population into fifths, then see what proportion of all income goes to each of the quintiles. In 1995, for example, $4.5 trillion was the aggregate amount received by the nation's 99.6 million households, from earnings and other sources. As the table on page 49 shows, the 19.9 million households whose incomes put them in the best-off fifth came away with 48.7 percent of the national aggregate, while those in the poorest 19.9 million ended with 3.7 percent of that total. The table makes clear that since 1935, there have been changes in the configurations, and they will be analyzed in later chapters. But it can be as easily argued that a basic pattern has persisted for almost two-thirds of a century. To be sure, over the years, each quintile has lost or gained some part of its share. Yet it is equally striking that the second-highest quintile has never had higher than a 24.8 percent share, and the middle quintile has never surpassed 17.4 percent; that the next-to-lowest peaked at 10.5 percent, and that even the poorest fifth's best year gave it only 4.4 percent.

It would seem unlikely that natural laws or forces decree these exact numbers. But the numbers themselves suggest that the structure and the culture of the nation's economy causes these disparities to remain steady. They also suggest that the system has surprising endurance, considering the successive impacts of the Depression, the New Deal, and World War II, as well as the administrations of Franklin Roosevelt, Dwight Eisenhower, Richard Nixon, and Ronald Reagan. So what we take as historic turning points for ourselves and our society may have only marginal effects on the distribution of income.

Whether as anthills or pharaohs' tombs, something about the pyramidal shape strikes us as natural. Certainly, many societies have their majorities clustered at the bottom, tapering to a small class at the top. As the figures on pages 50 and 51 show, it is possible to array American incomes and earnings that way. But to apply a pyramid to incomes, every family that makes less than $45,000 would have to be placed in the bottom tier. At this point, few people would say that such an amount spells poverty or even ranks as a low income. Even so, a pyramid shows that most Americans live in households of modest means, especially as their incomes often require two or more earners.

A pyramid makes more sense when used to depict the paychecks of individuals, since a sizable majority does make less than $25,000. At the same time, it should be noted that the pyramid includes the wages

Share of Aggregate Household Income Received by Each Fifth the Richest 5% of Households				
	1935	1955	1975	1995
Best-off fifth	51.7%	44.3%	43.2%	48.7%
Second fifth	20.9%	24.5%	24.8%	23.3%
Middle fifth	14.1%	17.4%	17.1%	15.2%
Fourth fifth	9.2%	10.5%	10.5%	9.1%
Poorest fifth	4.1%	3.3%	4.4%	3.7%
Top 5 %	26.5%	18.0%	15.9%	21.0%

Distribution of Income Among America's Families

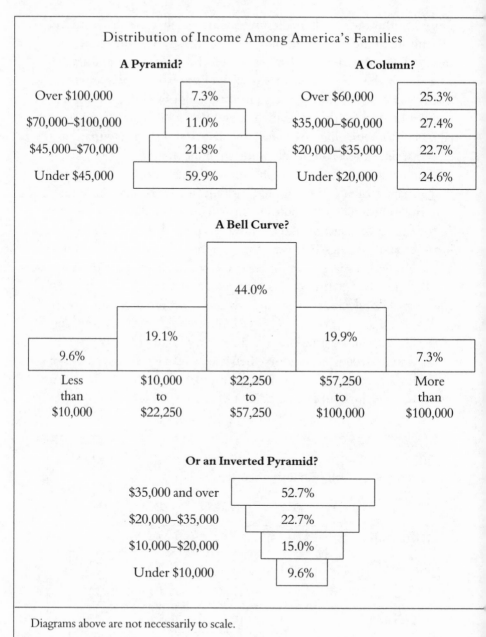

A Pyramid?

Over $100,000	7.3%
$70,000–$100,000	11.0%
$45,000–$70,000	21.8%
Under $45,000	59.9%

A Column?

Over $60,000	25.3%
$35,000–$60,000	27.4%
$20,000–$35,000	22.7%
Under $20,000	24.6%

A Bell Curve?

9.6%	19.1%	44.0%	19.9%	7.3%
Less than $10,000	$10,000 to $22,250	$22,250 to $57,250	$57,250 to $100,000	More than $100,000

Or an Inverted Pyramid?

$35,000 and over	52.7%
$20,000–$35,000	22.7%
$10,000–$20,000	15.0%
Under $10,000	9.6%

Diagrams above are not necessarily to scale.

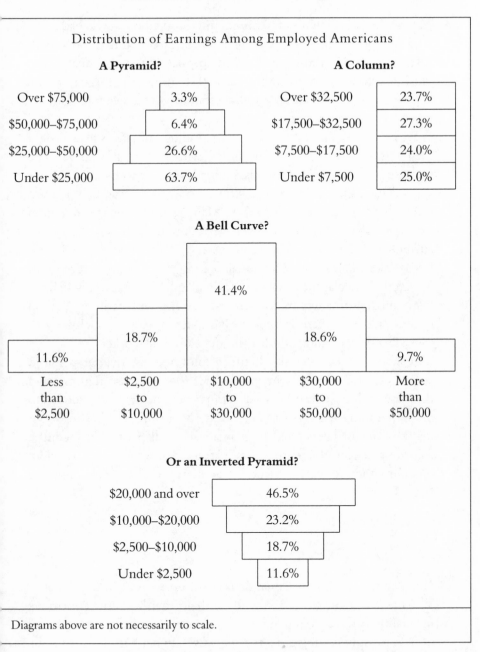

Distribution of Earnings Among Employed Americans

A Pyramid?

Over $75,000	3.3%
$50,000–$75,000	6.4%
$25,000–$50,000	26.6%
Under $25,000	63.7%

A Column?

Over $32,500	23.7%
$17,500–$32,500	27.3%
$7,500–$17,500	24.0%
Under $7,500	25.0%

A Bell Curve?

Less than $2,500	$2,500 to $10,000	$10,000 to $30,000	$30,000 to $50,000	More than $50,000
11.6%	18.7%	41.4%	18.6%	9.7%

Or an Inverted Pyramid?

$20,000 and over	46.5%
$10,000–$20,000	23.2%
$2,500–$10,000	18.7%
Under $2,500	11.6%

Diagrams above are not necessarily to scale.

and salaries of the almost 140 million men and women who had some kind of paid employment during 1994. So it contains persons with part-time jobs and those who worked only part of the year, many if not most of whom fall in the under-$25,000 stratum. Still, this part of the labor force is very much a part of the economy and in fact represents its fastest-growing segment.

We can all recall teachers who, after reading our class's tests, would then regrade them so they accorded with a "normal" curve. The premise is that if over half the class initially got As and Bs, then the test was too easy, since a "natural" distribution would locate the midpoint somewhere nearer to a B- or a C+. Many psychologists are drawn to the "bell" shape, which they believe represents a natural spread of attributes and talents. The same exercise can be performed with households incomes and individuals' earnings. For income, it requires having the range at the center run from $22,250 to $57,250, which is a fair enough estimate of middle-class status. But with earnings, the top of the middle segment is a relatively modest $30,000, which is again caused by the mingling of full-time and part-time workers.

It is not necessary to ask whether a column or an inverted pyramid comes closer to nature's intentions. All four of these figures—and there are undoubtedly others—are simply graphic devices, intended to draw attention to facets of a single reality. More will be said later about distributions of talents and their relations to disparities in incomes. And we will also address the ways that forces at work within a nation, including the interplay of structure and culture, shape the geometric figures we find.

A CEILING TO CLOSE THE GAP?

"I am conscious that an equal division of property is impracticable," Thomas Jefferson conceded. Still, he held that because "enormous inequality produces so much misery, legislators cannot invent too many devices for subdividing property." However, in neither his time or our own have lawmakers heeded Jefferson's advice. Among the world's modernized countries, the United States has the most glaring income gaps.

In 1995, for example, a Wall Street money manager named George

Soros made $1.5 billion, while in 1993 another American named Mike Tyson received a total of $237 for the jobs he undertook in an Indiana correctional institution. A single year also saw Michael Eisner, the chairman of the Walt Disney company, being paid $203 million, whereas the state of Texas allowed a $2,130 welfare stipend for a mother with two children. True, Eisner's award was considerably above the norm for CEOs. Yet in 1995, the paychecks of corporate chairmen averaged 190 times that of a typical worker, up from a ratio of 40 times twenty years earlier. Within the population as a whole, the average income in the best-off 20 percent of all households ($109,411) was thirteen times higher than that going to the poorest 20 percent ($8,350). In South Korea, well on its way to becoming a modern country, the top fifth is content making six times what its bottom fifth receives.

One widely used measure of inequality computes how far the richest and poorest households in a country are from the national midpoint. As the table on page 54 shows, comparing their respective shares provides an "index of inequality." Finland turns out to be the most egalitarian nation, followed by Sweden and Belgium. The United States has the greatest income disparity, partly because its rich receive more than their counterparts in other countries, but mostly because those who are poor get so much less.

Of course, this country redistributes income in a variety of ways. Whenever we buy a movie ticket, we contribute to the salaries of the stars. These offerings are voluntary—no one is forcing us to see the show—so we don't hear many complaints. (When you bought some Heinz ketchup, would it disturb you to learn that you were providing a part of its chairman's $24-million salary?) Of course, transfers via public agencies are much more visible and are not always perceived as being voluntary. Undoubtedly, the most begrudged outlays are those commonly called "welfare," wherein taxpayers have provided money payments and other grants to families made up mainly of single women raising children. In fact, poor Americans receive a relatively thin slice of the redistribution pie. Social Security pensions subsidize the middle class and, in fact, the very rich. Even workers with minimum-wage earnings are made to support senior citizens with benefits well above the amortized worth of the recipients' own contributions. A middle-class family that sends its children to its state university, vacations in national

		Share of National Income: Rich-Poor Ratio	
Best-Off Tenth	**Poorest Tenth**	**Country**	**Inequality Index**
153%	59%	Finland	2.6
152%	56%	Sweden	2.7
163%	59%	Belgium	2.8
175%	62%	Netherlands	2.9
162%	55%	Norway	2.9
185%	54%	Switzerland	3.4
187%	54%	New Zealand	3.5
193%	55%	France	3.5
194%	51%	United Kingdom	3.8
187%	47%	Australia	4.0
184%	46%	Canada	4.0
198%	49%	Italy	4.1
209%	50%	Ireland	4.2
206%	35%	United States	5.9

Percentages show the proportion of each nation's median income received by the midpoint household within its poorest 10% and also for its best-off 10%. The index of inequality is the ratio of the two percentages for each country.

parks, and commutes on interstate highways gets more value from these public amenities than it paid in taxes. Not to mention corporate farms, which receive generous government payments, making possible lavish profit margins.

While Jefferson's heirs continue to cite the most visible disparities, this country has been disinclined to use legislation to compress the income gap. True, tax rates rise as incomes grow, but well-off Americans are allowed to keep enough to live very comfortably. And measures to maintain some kind of floor (or "safety net") offer little more than subsistence stipends, the minimum needed so that visible signs of malnutrition are not seen on the streets. Indeed, many Americans feel redress has gone too far. Hence the recent moves to end programs that are seen as supporting individuals who are regarded as making no productive contribution to society. Yet neither side has calculated how the economy might look if steps were actually taken to compress the income gap. The exercises that follow are intended to provide some answers.

Studies for 1994 by the Census Bureau and the Internal Revenue Service found that some 1.1 million households had pretax incomes in excess of $200,000. This would seem a likely group to be called upon to contribute toward a redistribution of wealth. The average income for its members was approximately $475,000, and together their incomes added up to about $520 billion. However, all that money can't be used in the exercise. Households in higher brackets already pay higher-than-average taxes. That money would still be needed by the government for the other functions that it currently performs, including current income transfers, and would not be available for additional redistribution. Therefore, the exercise can only use what remains after taxes: about $375 billion, which works out to an average of $340,000 among the 1.1 million households.

Suppose that the highest allowable income was $200,000, the current salary of the president of the United States. If the current incomes of the 1.1 million households were all reduced to $200,000, this would leave them an aggregate of $220 billion. Thus the amount left for transfers comes to $155 billion, which just about equals the current Medicare budget.

We now know who would be doing the paying; so it is time to decide on the recipients. For present purposes, the target group can be the poorest 20 percent of all households, whose current income averages about $7,760. Were the entire $155 billion to be made over to them, every household in the group could have an income of at least $15,530. Given such a national minimum, the ratio between households now at the $200,000 ceiling and those at the $15,530 floor would work out to about thirteen to one.

But, we can hear some observers arguing, why allow some people to keep as much as $200,000? To them, that doesn't look like an egalitarian outcome. After all, no one really "needs" that much money. So let's see what happens if the ceiling is brought down to $100,000, a little less than today's base pay of a four-star general. This would in fact add another 3.4 million households to the group that would have to give up something, in some cases a great deal. After subtracting taxes already paid and leaving enough for the $100,000 incomes, the

---

Redistributing Dollars Via a Maximum Income
(with transfers to poorest 20 percent of households)

Households That Would Benefit by Income Transfers

Number to benefit	19,798,000
Average income now	$7,764

Households That Would Lose by Income Transfers

Possible maximums	$200,000	$100,000
Number to lose	1,096,000	4,499,000
New minimum income	$15,527	$22,219
New high-low ratio	12.9:1	4.5:1

---

amount on hand for transfer would come to $285 billion, almost double the amount yielded by the $200,000 ceiling.

Once transferred, the money from the $100,000 ceiling could create a national floor of $22,220, if it were distributed among the bottom 20 percent. The ensuing ratio would give the best-off group about four and a half times the income of those at the minimum. Indeed, with a floor of $22,219, it could be argued that there would be no poor at all. And with a $100,000 ceiling, there wouldn't be any rich either.

While this is only a paper exercise, we might want to remind ourselves that the great majority of households make less than $100,000 and thus would lose nothing by the transfers. On the other hand, quite a few Americans have dreams of getting up there with the really rich. One has only to look at the number of people who line up to buy lottery tickets in hopes of hitting a $1-million pot. Or who fantasize of making it big in some other way. So even if now they are well below it, would they support the idea of a $100,000 ceiling?

56

THREE NATIONS

GETTING BY, BARELY

In New York's Chenango County, deputy sheriffs start at $16,000. A radio news director in Vermont is offered $17,000, while in Albuquerque, New Mexico, airline reservationists make $14,000. The average salary for lay teachers in Chicago's parochial schools is $21,000. In fact, according to a recent Census survey, a third of all full-time jobs pay below $20,000. Many who hold these jobs are women supplementing the family budget; but for the first time, men account for almost half the workers in this bottom tier. These are working Americans, not individuals who are unemployed or receiving public assistance. The paychecks just mentioned might suggest that a significant segment of the workforce is falling perilously close to the poverty line.

But the $17,000 news director and the $16,000 deputy sheriff will be quick to tell you that they do not view themselves as poor. They may agree that they are just getting by and sometimes feel the pinch. Yet they are aware of the term *poverty* and in no way do they wish to be associated with it. That they can and do feel this way conveys a lot about how the economy operates.

Just as America remains two nations racially, so it contains equally real economic divisions. Whether or not to call these components "classes" is a matter of ideological taste, and we should be wary of outdated dualities. To draw the divide between "rich" and "poor" fails to mirror current reality, if only because the rich are so small a stratum that the "poor" would have to include the entire middle class. Karl Marx's ideology, which split society into owners and workers, also pushed salaried and professional people into his proletariat. James

Madison, the principal author of our Constitution, would have had no major quarrel with Marx. He saw the break, very simply, separating "those who hold and those who are without property." Still, what must be answered is whether that "property" represents impressive holdings, or if it can refer to a more modest stake. If it must mean a business or other assets capable of yielding a comfortable income, then not many Americans can be called persons of property. It was left to Alexis de Tocqueville to illuminate the American way of thinking on this issue. This was the gist of his analysis:

> Among a great democratic people there will always be some members of the community in great poverty and others in great opulence. Between these two extremes stands an innumerable multitude almost alike, without being exactly rich or poor. But the poor, instead of forming the immense majority, are comparatively few in number.

Some commentators have chosen to describe this "multitude" as a large middle class. There is no harm in doing this, so long as we are clear on what kind of income or occupation is needed for inclusion in this stratum. If $30,000 is set as a minimum middle-class income, less than a third of all employed persons will make the cut. Even at $20,000, only about half get included. But things look a bit better for a sizable middle class if we focus on family incomes instead of individuals' earnings. Some 60 percent of all households have incomes of $25,000 or over, and slightly more than half are above $30,000. So even as we aver that a majority of Americans are not poor, many of them are still at a distance from what is usually seen as a middle-class income.

This country still has a considerable working class, which generally means factory jobs or related occupations in transportation and construction. Workers in General Motors plants in Ohio can still draw close to $70,000 a year, although that calls for considerable overtime. But each year, fewer Americans enjoy the safeguards that were common in the days of union protection. When it can, General Motors shifts jobs to North Carolina, where the going rate is nearer to $20,000. Still, even if modestly paid and lacking job security, this group of workers sees itself—and is encouraged to see itself—as distinct and separate from the poor.

America was the first society to essay what was and continues to be an unusual fusion: a politics that expounds the principle of human equality and an economy that produces visible disparities in income and wealth. Such a system will only work if it can induce most of its citizens to believe that they are faring well under its auspices. Thus the way the economy works must have majority support. Of course, citizens can and will be critical, on occasion sharply so. But in the final reckoning, they must feel that all in all they have been treated fairly. The heart of this strategy, as Tocqueville told us, is to ensure that the "multitude" does not see itself as poor.

In a word, the majority must be able to live sufficiently well so that they see themselves as "haves." It is not charity or compassion, but a sense of self-preservation, that led the system to ensure that income is so dispersed that most people feel they are getting by. The 1995 Roper-Starch survey cited earlier found that seven in ten people felt they could manage decently on less than $35,000 a year and would need only $15,000 more for "reasonable comfort." Indeed, during a stroll through their local shopping mall, the majority of Americans will find that much of what they see is within their means.

Symbols also play a role. Perhaps the most fervid is found in the word *welfare,* which will also be discussed later on. As an object of opprobrium, public assistance serves several functions. For one thing, it allows a distinct group of Americans to be isolated and identified as poor. They are also deemed to be legitimate targets for censure or worse by anyone who pays taxes. And since public funds are involved, taxpayers feel even more entitled to criticize recipients' values and behavior. But perhaps the greatest role of welfare is to heighten the self-image of those not on its rolls. Thus the rest of the population is allowed to congratulate itself by declaring that they work or are otherwise self-supporting. The $14,000 airline reservationist can say that she makes do on even less than welfare recipients, given all of the extra benefits attached to public aid.

How do people get by on $14,000, $16,000, $17,000, or $21,000 a year? The short answer is to double up, if you have not done so already. Among the country's 35 million married couples aged twenty-five to fifty-four, in 73 percent of the households both spouses work. Often, the wife only works part-time or has a less demanding job. In marriages where the husband earns between $20,000 and $30,000, the wife averages $15,954. (However, when he gets to the $50,000 to $75,000 range, her earnings decline to $13,786). To make do on modest paychecks, young people share quarters with one or more roommates, while those from affluent homes sometimes get subsidies from their parents. A surprisingly large number continue to live at home, since they cannot yet afford a place of their own. The last two Censuses testify to a visible change in the kinds of roofs Americans have over their heads. As the table on this page shows, fewer Americans can afford to own the traditional dream home. In 1970, such a newly built house cost about twice a young couple's annual income. By 1994, the price tag on a typical new home was almost four times their income.

Where Americans Live		
1970		1990
66.3%	Detached single-unit homes	59.0%
3.1%	Trailers or mobile homes	7.2%
30.6%	Apartments & other housing	33.8%

Perhaps the chief accommodation Americans have made to this new economic fact of life has been to postpone marriage and having children. This can be seen by looking at women aged thirty to thirty-four, first in 1970 and again in the mid-1990s. In 1970, only 6 percent had not yet been married, and only 8 percent had not yet had a child. By the mid-1990s, almost 20 percent had not been married and over a quarter had yet to become mothers, and it seems likely that some will never take those steps. But this does not mean that young people are abjuring sex. More nonmarried couples are living together today than ever before, and in varied pairings of genders and orientations. While affection is what usually binds these households, the fact that both have modest incomes can reinforce the decision to share bed and board.

The number of conceptions is probably as high today as it was in the past, but thanks to *Roe v. Wade,* fewer now eventuate in births. However, the fact that abortions are available is not itself the cause of declining reproduction. Rather, it is that for growing numbers of adults, not only in the United States but in most advanced countries, parenthood is a lower priority. If the number of children being born is declining, the chief reason is that raising them is seen as too expensive. Prior to 1970, a typical couple had already had two children before reaching the age of thirty, and they did not stop to ask if their income was sufficient for that responsibility. In those early postwar days, most fathers made what was then called a "family wage," which was enough to support a full household.

How did a single income do it in 1970? The short answer is that what was seen as an optimal life required fewer amenities. In 1970, for example, only 28 percent of families owned two cars; today, 54 percent do so. In 1970, also, 2.9 million of us traveled to Europe. Last year, 7.1 million did, which signals that jet-setting is no longer confined to an elite. Therefore, the Consumer Price Index, which is based on a typical market basket of purchases, is not a wholly reliable mirror. If wages seemed to go further in 1970, one reason is that shopping lists were simpler. Those were the days of Keds and typewriters and turntables. Today, the Index includes Nikes, laser printers, and multiple-CD changers, which cost more because they do more. Even bread has been upgraded: croissants and exotic grains have replaced blander white loaves; Starbucks costs more than Maxwell House. Since cars have so much high-tech gear, a new one costs about half of a young couple's income, visibly up from 38 percent in 1970. And it is hardly necessary to add that Americans eat out and take out food much more often than was done a generation ago. It may not be gourmet cuisine—Burger King or Taco Bell will do—but even fast-food drive-ins cost more than meals prepared at home.

Much has been made of the disappearance of blue-collar jobs, especially those that paid well even if they entailed enervating work. In fact, though, not much more than the color of the collars has changed. Tens of millions of new jobs are essentially on assembly lines, albeit without the clanking of heavy machinery. An apt example are the polite and well-spoken ordertakers at mail-order merchants such as Lands' End and L.L. Bean, who sit at computer screens and tap in shirt sizes. It has been claimed that entering such data makes them a part of an "information industry." Perhaps. Certainly, the first requirement for work of this type is to have your fingers trained for QWERTY. So despite all the fretting about subliteracy, it is worth observing how many $14,000 workers can make a keyboard do their bidding and know more than their elders about high-tech appliances. From this arises a feeling that these new occupations belong in the middle class, even if they are poorly paid. America has always tried to wish away the thought that it might have a proletariat. The customer calling L.L. Bean wants to converse with someone who sounds like her favorite niece. Of equal if not more importance is where the person tapping in the order feels she fits in the social scheme.

The important divide, then, is between the poor and those who are not, even if the latter group is not receiving much more than the minimum wage. If the gap is seen as between the have-nots and the haves, what the haves have are manners and skills that give them a decent chance of finding a place in the employment market. Not the least of these attributes has been a readiness to roll with the tide, to understand that they must make the best of the cards being dealt to them. Thus far they seem fairly sure that there will be limits to their descent. The system probably has enough sense not to betray that promise.

THE POOR: ALWAYS WITH US?

Since 1959, the Bureau of the Census has been computing an annual "poverty threshold." This is the level above which you must rise if you wish to escape being defined as poor. In 1995, the threshold for one person living alone was $7,763, or about $150 a week. For a single parent with two children, it came to $12,278, about $236 a week for this family of three. In fact, this poverty income is so low that survival seems problematic without added assistance. At best, one might be more likely to get by in a rural area, where costs tend to be lower and being poor is less evident, since not as much is available for purchase.

On the whole, though, the official poverty figures understate the number of Americans living at a subsistence level. Still, they offer insights into who the poorest Americans are and where they can be found. The highest poverty ratios are for city dwellers (21 percent); women living on their own (25 percent); and families headed by single mothers (53 percent). As hardly needs remarking, the figures for black and Hispanic individuals and families are over twice those recorded for whites.

Many of the programs of Lyndon Johnson's administration were designated as a "war on poverty." As can be seen in the table on page 63, the 1960s did bring a visible decline in the ratio of Americans below the poverty line. How much this was due to government initiatives and how much to broader factors cannot be stated with precision. This was a prosperous period, with opportunities for people who might otherwise have been unemployed. Parents were also having fewer

Which Americans Are Poor?

Number and Percentage in Each Group Who Are Poor

In Total Population	36.1 Million	13.8%
Children under 18	14.7 million	20.8%
Men 18–64	7.5 million	9.5%
Women 18–64	10.9 million	13.3%
Men 65 and over	0.8 million	6.2%
Women 65 and over	2.5 million	13.6%
White	16.3 million	8.5%
Black	9.9 million	29.3%
Hispanic	8.6 million	30.3%
Asian	1.4 million	14.6%

Below the Poverty Line, 1960–95

	All Families	Persons Over 65	Children Under 18
1960	18.1%	35.2%	26.9%
1970	10.1%	24.6%	15.1%
1980	10.3%	15.7%	18.3%
1990	10.7%	12.2%	20.6%
1995	10.8%	10.5%	20.8%

children: two instead of four can make a modest income go a lot further. Relevant, too, was the continuing migration from the Southern states, with workers exchanging rural wages for better-paid factory jobs. Unions were still strong, and immigration was at nominal levels. If the 1960s was a decade of political protest and civil unrest, they also saw more Americans living better than they ever had before.

The bad news, however, was that the downward trend in poverty would be short in duration. The 1970s saw increases in the poverty rates for families and children, a trend that has continued through the 1990s and shows no sign of abating. The only exception has been persons over sixty-five. For them, the role of government has been crucial. Between 1960 and 1994, in dollars adjusted for inflation, the average Social Security payment to a retired worker came close to doubling, rising from $4,347 to $8,089. The average payment for a retired couple now exceeds $15,000. Each year also sees more marriages where both spouses have worked, so checks arrive in each of their names. As of 1996, if both had top earnings records, together they would receive $31,824. A growing number of Social Security recipients also have private pensions, plus savings and investments of their own. Among retired couples, median outside income is slightly over $10,000, and almost a third have $20,000 or more.

Among the aged poor, women outnumber men by a three-to-one margin, putting their poverty rate above the national average. Their numbers consist largely of widows living alone who never had sustained work records and must make do on reduced pensions with their husbands dead. Their median Social Security stipend is $7,693, and their outside income averages $2,000. Many bolster their budgets with food stamps, of which the weekly value for a single person comes to about $15. They are also eligible for Supplemental Security Income, which typically yields $2,923. In addition, the federally funded Nutrition Program for the Elderly serves 3.3 million senior citizens some 250 million meals each year.

The Supplemental Security Income program also gives stipends averaging $4,597 to 4.5 million children and adults who have been classified as physically or mentally disabled. They are then eligible for treatment under the respectable aegis of Medicare, receiving an average of $5,426 in treatment, rather than having to line up at a crowded Medicaid clinic. Another seven hundred thousand or so persons on the SSI rolls are listed as "alien recipients." As is well known, our immigration laws give high priority to "family unification." In many cases, this means young adults come first and then send for older family members. Thus a growing group within the alien recipients consists of grandparents who came here too late to build up pension rights. Until recently, they have been able to receive Supplemental Security Income instead of Social Security. In this way the government relieved their children, most of whom are now citizens and many of whom had comfortable incomes, of having to support the parents they brought here. In 1996, Congress revoked this allowance, on the ground that people who decide to live in the United States should not become a burden on the taxpayers.

The most disheartening trend has been the rise in childhood poverty, from 15 percent of all youngsters in 1970 to 21 percent in 1995. The chief reason is that many more are being raised only by their mothers, which generally means on only her income. Since 1970, their percentage has more than doubled, from 11 to 24. This change has also been the largest single influence on the overall poverty rate: families headed by women now make up 27 percent of all households.

The rise in the number of female-headed households does not mean that disappearing and defaulting fathers are enjoying great bachelor lives. In fact, the poverty rate for single men is also at a new high, although it is not captured in most official statistics. Yet one official figure begins to paint the picture: the nation currently has about 1.5 million of its men incarcerated. At last count, the United States was vying with Russia for leadership in inmate population. Given our current spate of prison construction—this is one bill taxpayers seem willing to foot—we may already be in first place.

America has a growing group of men who have never had steady employment, at least of the legal kind. Many lack a high school level of literacy and the social deportment most employers expect. On the streets of the nation's cities can be seen worn-out men in their forties, begging or searching for soda cans. More than a few are graduates of the prison system, which is hardly a recommendation when seeking a job.

Most of the inmate population will eventually be released. The larger society does not even want to think about what these men will do when they come out. There is, of course, the hope that most will "go straight": rejecting crime for a law-abiding life. But to do so requires employment, and thus far no one has drawn up a list of honest occupations former felons might seek. Indeed, the opposite is often the case. In New York City, an uproar arose when it was discovered that some of its school janitors had served terms in prison. In other cities, people with prison records are barred from becoming taxicab drivers and security guards, even though they are positions suitable for those seeking a fresh start.

At this point, it seems logical to ask whether America would have a much lower incidence of poverty if its economy were able to provide full employment. For example, it has been argued that a key reason why many men do not stay to raise the children they sire is that they lack steady jobs that would make them reliable providers. This idea has an inherent plausibility; the only hitch is that millions of middle-class fathers are also leaving home, but not for economic reasons. In other words, it should not be assumed that steadily employed blue-collar men would be more dutiful spouses than their white-collar counterparts. Still, jobs for all is a salutary goal, even if it can't mend broken marriages, which are a major cause of childhood poverty.

Except during the depths of the 1930s depression, this country has always had more job openings than people available to fill them. This was most graphic during the last century, when employers sent recruiters to Europe to announce that they were hiring. Even today, there are millions of unfilled positions. Hotels in many parts of the country are desperate for chambermaids and kitchen help and offer bonuses to employees who bring in friends or relatives. This is why the country has absorbed so many immigrants. It is almost as if the circulars have been sent out again, but now to Asia and Latin America and the Middle East. There is work waiting to be done, ranging from harvesting crops to designing silicon chips to medical residencies in inner-city clinics. Or services Americans did not realize they wanted until they became available, such as the Korean-owned manicure salons that cater to busy professional women.

The reason why unemployment persists even when jobs are available is quite obvious. The economy has always wanted things done, but is only willing to pay a certain price. And, immigrants, for their part, have been willing to work for wages that citizens of longer lineage would never deign to consider. Nor does it help to tell the long-term unemployed that they should apply for the jobs that immigrants are eager to take. For better or for worse, even poor Americans feel that any work they do must pay what they—like the rest of us—deem to be an American wage.

THE $100,000 LIFE

The real income explosion has been in the topmost brackets. Not only are the rich getting richer, more Americans are becoming affluent or are moving close to that category. For present purposes, an income of $100,000 will be considered sufficient for membership in the comfort class. Of course this is far from being rich; given today's expectations, that takes $1 million or more a year. Nor does comfort connote wealth; that requires having enough in assets to enjoy your prosperity without having to work.

Six-digit incomes were once considered a rarity, indeed an eminence ordinary people could never hope to attain. No longer. The most recent details on Americans in the $100,000 bracket are for 1995. In that year, 6.3 million of the nation's families, 9 percent of the total, were at this level. In 1980, using constant dollars, only 4 percent of families had that kind of purchasing power; while in 1970, less than 3 percent did.

But there's a crucial caveat. Eighty percent of these incomes come from having two or more earners in the family. Indeed, such multiple employment is at all-time high. Dad may make $52,498, Mom brings in $33,501—this is a typical division—while Sis contributes the $17,221 she earns at the mall. Only one in six of the $100,000 households attains it with a single earner, usually a well-paid husband. Still, this tells us that when wives don't have to work, quite a few choose not to. Almost a tenth of the $100,000 families have one or more members over the age of sixty-five, pointing to a growing class of affluent retirees.

We often hear that families now need two or more paychecks just to keep up with the bills. This rings true for households where one member makes, say, $28,000. But when multiple earnings boost domestic incomes above $100,000, one wants to ask what are all those "necessities" households feel they must have.

Both spouses work in almost 60 percent of the nation's marriages, so two-income homes are now found at all economic levels. Even if the husbands make $100,000, generally enough to support a household, the wives also work in 60 percent of those marriages, which in fact is a point or so above the national norm. The Census found 120,000 couples where both make at least $75,000, and 45,000 have both passed the $100,000 mark. In this category are Bruce Willis and Demi Moore, who together can command $20 million for a pair of movies. Or Marion and Herbert Sandler, the joint CEOs of Golden Western Financial, who in tandem have been making about $5 million a year.

Washington has always had well-paid couples. During the 1996 presidential campaign, the contenders declared their incomes for the previous year. The Clintons' total was $316,074, which included Bill's $200,000 salary and payments due to Hillary for past professional work. The Doles declared $533,415, to which Bob contributed $148,000 as Senate majority leader and $17,700 for his army disability, while most of the rest came from Elizabeth's $200,675 salary for heading the American Red Cross. (Ross Perot's income was whatever he decided to take as walking-around money from his $3.3-billion fortune.) In some instances, both incomes come courtesy of the taxpayers, as was the case with Anne Bingaman, an assistant attorney general who received $131,400 in 1996, and Sen. Jeffrey Bingaman of New Mexico, whose pay was $133,600.

But there's another $100,000 explosion. Last year's Census study found 2.7 million working Americans—2.4 million men and 300,000 women—who had six or more digits on their paychecks. So if the rich are getting richer, there are also more of them: the group making $100,000 or more now matches the adult population of Los Angeles. For instance, Princeton now pays a star psychology professor $233,546. Pilots at Federal Express average $128,000, earning them the tag of "flying vice presidents." The minimum in major league baseball is $109,000, even for players just out of high school.

Pressure for six-figure salaries extends across a growing array of professions. For example, we were once told the people entered the civil service for security, light work, even to promote the public good. Still, at last count, the federal payroll had 15,266 "senior grade" officials who averaged $102,338. Of course, academics are in it for the love of learning and the joys of stirring young minds. Even so, 5,858 of the nation's 79,323 full professors—7.4 percent—also make over $100,000. Close to half of these prospering scholars are at five schools: Harvard, Stanford, Yale, Princeton, and Cal Tech. MIT pays an ace professor of electrical engineering $321,967, while Wellesley shows that women's colleges also reward their stars, giving $141,023 to an eminent classicist.

Medicine has long been the one field that all but assures a six-figure income. According to the most recent American Medical Association survey, the nation's 407,044 physicians who have their own practices take home a median of $176,000. Fewer than a quarter make less than $100,000, and most of them are just starting out. The AMA also estimates that salaried physicians average about $130,000, with government employment at the low end and some hospitals paying their pathologists and radiologists considerably higher.

It isn't so easy to generalize about what lawyers are getting, since we

now have 894,000 attorneys, surpassing the combined adult populations of Atlanta, Pittsburgh, and St. Louis. At the top are liability
experts, who take a slice of every multimillion-dollar award and fly to
trials in their own Learjets. Chicago starts its public defenders at
$32,772, and law clerks for federal judges get $36,426. The Census cal-
culates the lawyers' median at $72,144, with close to 250,000 making
over $100,000. According to the *American Lawyer*'s most recent survey,
the 13,131 partners in the country's hundred largest firms average
$446,000. In New York City, first-year associates can start at $85,000,
while in lower-living-costs New Orleans, offers are more like $53,000.
Associates in Los Angeles can expect $100,000 by their fifth year.

Corporations prefer not to state what they give upper-middle executives. (Top-tier pay must be shown in stockholders' proxy notices and
gets wide publicity.) The Census computes that about 800,000 "managers, executives, and administrators" earn more than $100,000, but
that total includes small-business owners who can take what they
choose from the till. Texaco has reported that 875 of its people make
more than $100,000, while IBM has 1,350 at over $150,000. Leading
financial firms now start newly minted MBAs at $100,000. But there's
a catch. They are expected to put in twelve hours per day, six days a
week. Figured on an hourly basis, the checks look considerably
smaller. (Manhattan rents are another shrinkage factor.) But an arduous apprenticeship can pay off. Last year, some 1,500 Wall Streeters
made more than $1 million.

Why are so many people paid so much? The most heard answer is
that talent is in short supply, so there is fierce competition for the top
performers. Derek Bok, who for twenty-two years was president of
Harvard, argues that every society contains only "a limited supply of
highly talented people." Hence the bidding wars that drive compensations up. In some areas, this hypothesis seems sound. When the major
league baseball players went on strike, it was evident that replacement
teams from the minors couldn't, well, replace them. Networks ascribe
the sad state of prime time to a shortage of good comedy writers.
"There's just not enough talent to go around," lamented a CBS executive. Perhaps, although the continued success of soap operas suggest
that ways can be found to expand the pool. High-paying law firms say
they must compete for a finite fund of brains. At this point, someone
might shout, "Whoa!" Each June sees the graduation of forty thousand

new J.D.s. True, not all are from Harvard. But could it be that the big firms find it beneath them to scout for prospects at the University of Iowa? After all, Economics 101 taught us that one way to solve talent shortages is by opening doors to new people.

Another claim is that modern work calls for more sophisticated knowledge. Think of investment analysts and their mathematical models. Or lawyers who must become expert in silicon and DNA. But every era says this of its well-paid professions. Tool and die making became a princely craft because it depended on having a head for applied mathematics. (Software does much of the job today.) Novelists of Jane Austen's era may have used quill pens, but it would be hard to argue that they were not as brainy as word-processing writers. True, more of us spend more years in classrooms, ostensibly because our age has more to learn. An alternative reason is that we store people in school since the labor force has little need for workers prior to their twenties.

If Economics 101 said that increased demand should give rise to new sources of supply, it also told us that the equation can work in reverse. Perhaps the strongest force behind all those $100,000 salaries is the increasing supply of things clamoring to be bought. Whether goods or services or entertainments, in recent years the possibilities for purchasing have become more elaborate and intriguing. As always, much is material merchandise, ranging from kitchenware and clothing to cellular phones and powerboats. The economy also highlights new experiences, ranging from sitting at a sushi bar to backpacking in Nepal. Here is a sampling of items advertised during the 1996 Christmas season: a stainless-steel home stove for $13,900; a digitalized putting green costing $1,195; a high-tech desk lamp at $6,800; for him, a polyurethane car coat at $2,145; for her, an alligator briefcase at $7,780; for both, an embroidered cashmere blanket at $3,585; plus a $2,700 reproduction Queen Anne dollhouse for the children. These are just things to have around the house and do not include tough-terrain cars and furnishings for a second home.

These add up to the "new necessities," things to be owned or known in order to lead a full life. In the past, unions sought a "living wage" for their workers. Today, the process is less overt. The economy and employers tacitly agree that a sizable stratum of Americans should be able to enjoy high-end shopping.

One such expense is college tuition, especially for parents who feel that their offspring must attend a college that has a national reputation. An upscale degree is not wanted simply to open doors to desirable careers. That elite circle of colleges imparts added stature to its graduates, an association that cannot be erased. But simply to attend classes at Amherst costs $22,007 during the current academic year. Harvard is slightly cheaper at $21,900, and Stanford looks like a bargain at $20,500. Even a lower-tier school such as Vanderbilt charges $20,200, while a small college such as Carleton is asking $21,100. But tuition is just the beginning, after which comes bed and board, plus textbooks and travel, not to mention all the gear students must now have during those formative years. To be sure, a car and ski equipment are not absolutely necessary for higher education. Still, such extras help a student make the most of that unique experience. Modestly, having one child at college can exact $35,000 a year. As a result, even families with $100,000 incomes have been known to ask for—and receive—scholarship aid.

In theory, employers do not raise wages because they like playing the role of benefactor, nor even feel obliged to elevate their workers' living standards. But economies are not only guided by economic considerations. During the 1980s, abetted by the Reagan ethos, the expectation emerged of the "the $100,000 life." This was not a pie-in-the-sky dream, depending on a legal settlement or a lottery ticket. Rather, the figure was regarded as a realistic aspiration, approximating how much one had to be paid to enjoy an optimal life.

This is not to argue that employers began to raise salaries to create a new class or to satisfy expensive tastes. Decisions are seldom made in so deliberate a way. Yet it is not totally off base to conclude that law firms and corporations and colleges, even the civil service, all felt that their stature would be enhanced by expanding their echelon of $100,000 people. In return, they would have representing them men and women who could embody a standard of life that was becoming a new national norm. And surely visitors will be impressed by all those BMWs in the corporate parking lot. And aren't investors more likely to trust advice emanating from a $2,000 suit? No wonder clients keep coming to those law firms whose partners average $446,000. That they are paid so much, we tend to reason, even if against our better judgment, must be evidence that they are the best people in the field.

CHAPTER FOUR

$1 Million a Year

For present purposes, America's rich will be defined as all individuals and households that, in a given year, have incomes of at least $1 million. In 1994, the most recent year for which figures are available at this writing, a total of 68,064 forms were received by the Internal Revenue Service declaring incomes in that bracket. It seems likely that everyone at the $1 million level sends in a 1040 return. Whether they reveal all of their income is, of course, another matter. But they have no compelling need to cheat, since at their level, there are many perfectly legal strategies for sheltering their income from taxes.

These 68,064 returns comprise about one-twentieth of 1 percent of the 116,147,596 forms received in 1994. The average income in this bracket came to $2,483,081, and the federal tax bill averaged $787,994, or 31.7 percent of the income declared. Since these are people who had at least $1 million passing through their bank or brokerage accounts in a year, they can appropriately be called rich. This is not to say that in some communities and states, an income of $500,000 would not warrant that designation. But in large cities and lavish suburbs, where there is so much to buy and to do, $1 million makes more sense as a bottom line.

Understandably, the Internal Revenue Service only provides aggregate information for the filers in this bracket. So we are told that 87 percent of them said they had earnings from wages or salaries, and 19 percent reported professional income or proceeds from a self-owned business. Even so, money from employment accounted for only 33 percent of the overall income at the top tier. Thus we have no way of knowing, for example, how many among the 68,064 derived most of their $1 million from working. In fact, a large number do and many of their names are household words.

In 1995, 246 football players, 241 baseball players, and 159 hockey players made $1 million or more. The National Basketball Association prefers not to release the individual salaries of its 346 players, although the contracts of the top stars invariably make the headlines. But since the average for all players was $1.6 million, it seems valid to estimate that close to half of them made a minimum of $1 million.

During 1996, according to *Entertainment Weekly,* 133 Hollywood stars were paid or could expect to receive at least $1 million per picture. For the most part, this would be most of their annual income, since nowadays not many actors appear in more than one film a year. The magazine listed 96 men and 37 women, itself a revealing ratio. The best-paid men were Jim Carrey, John Travolta, Mel Gibson, Tom Hanks, and Arnold Schwarzenegger, all of whom were getting about $20 million for one picture. Among the women, the best paid were Demi Moore and Julia Roberts, who received $12 million, followed by Sandra Bullock and Michelle Pfeiffer, both of whom could ask for and probably get $10 million. Over recent years, stars such as Gibson, Hanks, and Schwarzenegger have obviously built up personal fortunes. Even so, most of their income still comes from wearing makeup and submitting to retakes before a camera.

No precise information is available on how many physicians and attorneys earn $1 million or more a year. In fact, very few doctors make the list, since there tend to be limits on what they can charge for a procedure, and how many they can perform in a working year. (It's only in the movies that a sultan or head of state offers a cardiologist $1 million for an exotic bypass.) The doctors who do best tend to have medical school affiliations, which they use to justify premium fees for treating their most affluent patients. (Not the least benefit of having money is to be able to boast that your personal physician is on the faculty of a leading institution.) Still, while many doctors make in the high hundreds of thousands, few break the $1-million mark. A recent survey of medical school salaries found only ten professors in the entire country—five at Cornell, three at Columbia, and one each at Stanford and the University of Pennsylvania—at that level. However, healers have other ways to get rich, and these will be discussed in a later chapter.

Nor is the law as easy a road to riches as many think. An investigation by *Forbes* magazine in 1995 found only two dozen corporate attorneys whose incomes had surpassed $2 million. It is unlikely that more than a thousand make $1 million. This is a relatively small number, given that, in 1995, the Bureau of Labor Statistics counted 894,000 men and women employed as lawyers. Of this number, 13,121 were partners in the hundred largest firms. However, in only five of these hundred firms, which had a total of 405 partners, did compensation average $1 million per partner. But that does not mean that all 405 received that much. Averages being what they are, we should surmise that no more than 200 of them, and probably a lot less, ended up with $1 million. Of the compensations in 1995 for the twenty-seven corporate counsels sampled by the *National Law Journal,* only the four at Philip Morris, Time Warner, TRW, and Viacom received over $1 million. The truly huge awards go to trial lawyers. Four in Texas alone have matched Tom Hanks's and Mel Gibson's yearly earnings of $20 million. But those who hit it big in liability suits are also a relatively small group. According to an official of the National Association of Trial Lawyers, not many more than one hundred steadily net $1 million.

Wall Street may be the single largest contributor to the $1-million earnings list, since compensations are based on the amount of money involved in a deal, rather than set fees or hourly rates. When AT&T spun off some of its divisions in 1996 to create the new Lucent corporation, securities firms were paid close to $120 million for chaperoning the new offering. As with law and medicine, we have a fair idea of what the very top people get. Each year, *Financial World* lists Wall Street's one hundred top earners. Not surprisingly, what it takes to make the annual list reflects the ups and downs of the market. Thus in 1992, it took $6 million to be on the list; in 1993, one needed $10 million. The next year, 1994, required only $5 million, while the bottom of the 1995 roster repeated the 1993 high of $10 million. In 1993's boom year, the 161 partners at a single firm—Goldman Sachs—all made more than $5 million. Toward the end of 1996, an exceptionally good year, predictions were being made that as many as 1,500 men and women would finish with at least $1 million.

Stratospheric paychecks are by no means the rule in the corporate world. Only the top five hundred or so companies give their chief executives packages that total $1 million or more, even when bonuses and stock options and other benefits are added to the base salary. And together those companies may have perhaps two thousand more people who also cross the $1 million threshold. However, the great majority of executives—including many who come to head a company—never rise above six figures. Despite some noteworthy exceptions, committing one's life to a corporate career offers modest prospects of becoming rich. Information on who gets how much—and why—will be provided in a later chapter.

Americans still draw a firm line between public-service and private-sector success. In the federal government, no salary can exceed the $200,000 a year given to the occupant of the White House. While no one in government is allowed near the $1 million mark, exceptions have been allowed for quasipublic bodies like the Federal National Mortgage Association (Fannie Mae), whose head receives close to $4 million a year, supposedly because the job is beyond the skills of a garden-variety bureaucrat. Nonprofit organizations are beginning to emulate their business counterparts, on the grounds that they, too, must compete for good people. Thus Kurt Masur of the New York Philharmonic Orchestra and the administrator of that city's Mount Sinai Medical Center both receive $1.1 million. So far only a single union, the one representing professional football players, pays at this level, giving its president $1.2 million.

But just a few moments with a calculator will show that the individuals and occupations mentioned so far do not add up to the 68,064 persons or households on the Internal Revenue Service's $1-million list. The short answer, which will be expanded upon later, is that most of the rich are largely unknown to the public. Many are owners of small enterprises, which sometimes employ fewer than a hundred people. In more than a few cases, these small-business owners live in towns and smaller cities, where they hold leading positions in the local economy. Typical of them were the one-quarter of the delegates to the 1996 Republican National Convention who reported that their incomes were in the $1-million category. Among the 746 millionaires who live in Alabama may be a food wholesaler and the owner of an insurance agency. The 189 in Idaho could include livestock breeders and potato processors. And that Texas has 4,245 millionaires suggests that oil still underwrites high incomes.

Another anonymous group consists of heirs of fortunes that were amassed in earlier eras, or even in recent decades. Many of them have no interest in joining the firms that their grandfathers may have founded, preferring to live comfortably on dividends and capital gains.

To have an annual income of $1 million coming from conservative investments would require an inheritance approaching $15 million. To net $2.5 million—the average income in the top tier—would require inheriting close to $40 million. From time to time, some of these heirs and heiresses gain public attention, due to a flamboyant divorce or other escapades wherein they are identified by whatever product it was that gave them their money. On the whole, though, most stick to golf or visiting friends who, like themselves, have time to spare. But the composition of this cohort is constantly changing. Each year, some fortunes of recent vintage are bequeathed to newly enriched heirs. Concurrently, some in today's $1-million circle pass on, dividing—and thus dispersing—their holdings among their own children.

Information submitted to the IRS offers additional insights into the nation's millionaires.

- The 68,064 households have a total of 184,889 family members, approximately the population of Grand Rapids, Michigan, which is America's eighty-third-largest city. Together, they could fill all the seats at Denver's Mile High Stadium, Chicago's Soldier Field, and Boston's Fenway Park.

- It would appear that the rich have strong family values: 88 percent of their households include married couples, compared with only a 55 percent rate for the country as a whole. At the same time, the 68,064 families together claim only 30,135 children as dependents, which tells us that most of their offspring are now on their own and that the parents are largely middle-aged. (At the same time, 961 list their own aged parents as dependents.)

- Taxpayers do not have to state their ages. But we do know that 10,509 of the people who have incomes of $1 million or more, about one in seven of the rich, are over seventy. That is the number who reported cashing checks sent by the Social Security Administration. Upon reaching seventy, everyone—even the wealthiest billionaire—is entitled to collect a pension, regardless of how much they receive from other sources. Might some not bother to apply for such modest stipends? On the contrary, we are reminded that one gets and stays rich by minding the pennies. Indeed, it turns out that $1-million households averaged $17,569 from Social Security, which is not only more than pennies, but substantially ahead of the $11,203 averaged by other retired taxpayers.

• But not all is marital bliss. No fewer than 3,454 of the rich send alimony to a previous spouse. Still, the payout seems quite modest for persons of their affluence, since the average was only $61,339 a year, less than 3 percent of a typical top-bracket income. In fact, many of the wealthy prefer to wrap it up with a single settlement. When Amy Irving and Steven Spielberg parted ways, she agreed to $100 million. Anne Bass, after twenty-three years with Sid Bass, made it $200 million. And Patricia and John Kluge's nine years together ended with her receiving a round $1 billion. The income from such sums elevated these women, and doubtless others, to the $1-million echelon

Only sixty rich Americans reported receiving alimony, and those who did averaged $100,317, which is a relatively modest figure. It means that the alimony recipients in the $1-million group had to have substantial income from other sources. Perhaps they decided to make their ex-spouses pay, not because they needed the money, but for the pleasure of putting them through an emotional wringer. Didn't several Preston Sturges movies have plots with that kind of twist?

• Before examining how and where the rich get their money, let's look at a few more facts that highlight their way of life. As all of us know, one cannot deduct all medical expenses: only those that exceed 7.5 percent of one's total income. So a household at the top tier average of $2,483,081 would have to pay the first $186,233 from their pockets and could then deduct the rest. As it happens, only 225 claimed medical deductions, which averaged $77,702 and would mean that a typical household in this group had a grand total of $263,935 in medical expenses. Hard to believe? Not necessarily. For example, instead of sending an ailing relative to a nursing home, someone who is rich can afford to arrange for around-the-clock attention at home. This could entail four nurses for a 168-hour week and might easily come to $200,000 in salaries and fringe benefits. To which may be added hospital-quality equipment to enhance the care. For less serious ailments, one may spend several weeks or months at the kinds of resorts that specialize in afflictions of the rich. Not to mention first-class travel, which your physician obligingly prescribes. And since the rich insist on "the best," the bills they receive will be at a level that brings their own physicians close to the millionaire level.

• Again, attending to the pennies, 1,396 millionaires claimed child-care credits, averaging $590. But this benefit applies only for children under the age of thirteen, and in cases where both parents have jobs or can show they were looking for work. This offers an estimate of how many of the rich are young couples who combine careers with children. Jane Pauley and Garry Trudeau are one such couple, who doubtless put an extra $590 to good use.

• But it would appear that not all $1-million earners can depend on year-round paychecks. Perhaps as many as 251 of them did not in 1994. That is the number who declared that at least one member of their household received unemployment compensation, averaging $3,275, during the year. It might be for a still dependent son, who can't seem to hold a job. Or it could be for a television star who was paid $2 million for twenty-three weeks of a series, which means she was entitled to benefits for the remaining twenty-nine weeks of the year. We can also visualize heads turning at the unemployment office as she waits in line like everyone else.

• An employee or a self-employed individual may deduct moving expenses if his job requires a change of locale and he must pay the bills himself. Here, 255 among the rich took advantage of that provision, with an average tab of $15,387. Among the rest of the nation's 1040 filers, 787,441 claimed moving expenses, but their bills averaged only $1,891. Obviously, the rich have larger houses and more possessions to transport. Still, it may be worth recalling that the rest of the taxpaying public subsidizes their multiple-van moves.

• One would think that the rich have enough money to pay cash for their residences or would at least have have paid off their mortgages by now. Not so. No fewer than 41,362—six of each ten—still have mortgages on their home or homes, for which they claimed interest deductions averaging $32,814. That sum suggests fairly elaborate dwellings, which means that other taxpayers are underwriting a lot of tree-lined driveways and tennis courts.

- The rich are generally perceived as the group who will make fullest use of deductions for charitable contributions. The tax laws allow gifts of up to 30 percent of adjusted gross income to offset other taxes, giving the $1-million households a chance to combine generosity with reducing their own tax bill. Yet most take only limited advantage of this allowance. Annual donations among the rich averaged $61,269, less than 4 percent of their tiers' total income. Indeed, this is less than the proportion given by many Americans of lesser means. Moreover, the $1-million group had 6,795 filers who either used the standard deduction or failed to specify any donations at all.

- Regarding sources of income, 87 percent of the $1 million households—a total of 58,964—contained one or more persons who reported receiving wages or a salary during the year, with these paychecks averaging $875,802. This would suggest that only 13 percent did no work at all, a group that was once called "the idle rich." But at least some of them may be entitled to a little leisure. Recall we found that 15 percent of the $1-million cohort are over the age of seventy and are collecting Social Security.

- For many of the rich, the "wages and salaries" income is not for full-time executive service. Rather the income may be payments for occasional contributions to firms in which they have an ownership stake, perhaps for showing up at board meetings, or for providing financial advice. Most of the rich do work. But what they do may be diffused among a variety of enterprises, and their "salaries" are quite different from those of most ordinary earners. Much the same conclusion would seem to hold for reports from the rich that they average $322,057 in "business and professional" income.

- Not surprisingly, the major sources of income for the rich are investments of various kinds. As can be seen in the table on page 82, almost all of them profit from dividends and interest-bearing securities or accounts. And about two-thirds augment their incomes by selling assets. The latter source makes clear that unlike the rest of us, the rich can decide how much they will need each year for walking-around money. To buy a gentleman friend a pair of Cartier cuff links, one could cash a few dozen shares of Boeing stock. Or if it's time to build that ski lodge in Montana, your broker may advise selling your interest in an Indianapolis office complex. Thus your income may be $1.8 million one year and $3.2 million the next. It's basically your decision.

• Other investments have a more limited ambit. Only about 7 percent have income from estates or trusts, the traditional source for heirs who are allowed limited access—or none at all—to the capital sum. This suggests that most of the rich are still actively making money, and that the passive wealth identified with Palm Springs and Palm Beach accounts for only a small share of their overall meanings. Two other income sources have ambiguous meanings. One is "rent and royalty" income, where the average amount is $130,977. But only a small fraction of the "royalty" income goes to authors such as Tom Clancy and Toni Morrison. For the rich, the word is more apt to apply to returns from oil wells or sulphur mines. And only a minute part of "partnership" income refers to earnings that accountants and attorneys divide up at the end of the year. Partnerships are now a favored form of investment among the rich, involving a stake in undertakings ranging from a racehorse to mortgages and theme parks.

The $1-million stratum is largely a world of wealth and capital, whose members receive and spend money derived from investments. As has been noted, employment earnings—wages and salaries, or one's own business or a profession—amount to only a third of their aggregate income. At the same time, a case can be made that this bracket is becoming more meritocratic and democratic. Comparing IRS reports for 1979 and 1994 reveals how dramatically it has changed in only a decade and a half.

The most striking development has been the rise of $1-million returns from 13,505 to 68,064. (In fact, the 1979 figure is for filers who had incomes of $500,000 or more that year, which was the equivalent of $1 million in 1994.) Allowing for the overall increase in taxpayers, the proportion of returns in the top tier rose from .015 percent to .059 percent, effectively a fourfold increment. Moreover, the average

Tax Returns with Incomes of $1 Million or More: 1979 and 1994				
1979* 13,505 Returns				**1994** 68,064 Returns
$2,175,092		Average Income		$2,483,081
Percent with Source	**Share of Income****	**Sources of Income**	**Percent with Source**	**Share of Income**
77.8%	21.4%	Wages and salaries	86.6%	30.6%
76.2%	35.6%	Sale of assets	65.0%	27.2%
31.5%	2.2%	Partnerships	61.3%	26.4%
98.5%	7.2%	Interest	99.6%	8.6%
92.7%	23.0%	Dividends	92.3%	5.5%
28.1%	5.0%	Business and profession	18.7%	2.4%
27.0%	2.5%	Rents and royalties	34.9%	1.8%
11.9%	0.2%	Pensions and annuities	23.0%	1.3%
19.6%	2.1%	Estates and trusts	6.7%	0.8%

*Incomes for 1979 are the equivalent of $1 million in 1994.
**Shares do not total 100% since some are pre-loss amounts.

income in the tier went from $2,175,092 to $2,483,081 in 1994 dollars. Where did all these new high incomes come from?

Part of the answer is that the economy has been creating many more $1-million salaries. In 1979, for example, fewer than one in ten of the top eight hundred corporate chairmen was being compensated at that level. In 1994, almost three-quarters received at least that amount, in constant-value dollars. As was seen in the table on page 82, the share of income stemming from work of some sort rose from 21.4 percent of the total to 30.6 percent. At the same time, the average sum from that source increased from $598,153 to $875,802, a surge of 46.4 percent. In 1979, a fairly sizable 22.2 percent of the rich declared they had not performed any activity warranting a wage or a salary. By 1994, that group had shrunk to 13.4 percent.

Slightly offsetting this shift was the decline in reports of professional income. One reason is that many professionals, both individuals or in partnerships, have incorporated their practices. (That "P.C." after your doctor's "M.D." does not signify a medical specialty, but stands for "professional corporation.") Under this arrangement, she pays herself a salary from the practice's income, a maneuver that brings considerable tax benefits. On the other side of the spectrum has been a sharp drop in individuals with money from estates and trusts. While inherited wealth shows no sign of disappearing, it now has a less prominent place in the high-income pantheon.

The last fifteen years have also seen a substantial decrease in tax rates for the rich. In 1979, those with $1 million or more paid an average of 47 percent of income in federal taxes. Not long thereafter Ronald Reagan took office and persuaded Americans that the economy would thrive if people could keep more of their money and spend it as they pleased. So in 1994, the rich had to give only 32 percent of their income to the federal coffers, which means they have more cash not only for luxurious living but also to build up their holdings.* In addition, those with wealth can employ accountants and advisers who show how money can be sheltered or otherwise protected from IRS exactions. In the firmament of this financial cosmos are "umbrella partnership real estate trusts," "zero-cost collars," "safe harbors," "deferred equity compensation," "supplemental executive retirement plans," "accelerated charitable remainder trusts," and even a concoction called "shorts against the box." With some of these contrivances, taxes must eventually be paid, but they often leave the option of picking a propitious year. In theory, this extra money at the top should go into investments that create more employment and enhance the general prosperity. However, ours is an age when money is as apt to be used for creating financial pyramids as to build productive capacity.

The stratum we have identified as the rich are a mixed group. As was noted at the opening of this chapter, the $1-million bracket includes athletes and corporate chairmen, movie stars and litigation lawyers, plus golfers in Palm Springs and party goers in Palm Beach.

---

*For comparison, an average household in the $1–million–plus tier had an income of $2.5 million and paid 32 percent of that in taxes. An average filer in the $100,000-to-$200,000 bracket made $131,000 and sent 19 percent to the IRS. Therefore, while average income in the top tier was almost twenty times that in the $100,000 to $200,000 group, the share of its income paid in taxes was only 1.7 times the rate imposed on those who earned between $100,000 and $200,000.

But the key finding has been that the dominant share of the group's income comes via their brokerage accounts. Of their average incomes of $2,483,081, a very hefty $1,663,664 flows from sources other than employment, reflecting their ownership of much of America's wealth. Certainly, receiving large salaries enables many people to live very comfortably in any given year. But only by amassing sufficient capital will they be able to retain that comfortable lifestyle after the paychecks stop coming in. And that, after all, is the point of being rich.

Most Americans live from paycheck to paycheck. Or on checks that provide pensions, disability payments, or public assistance. Even in the $100,000 to $200,000 bracket, almost 80 percent of all income is derived from employment. This is why *Money* has thus far focused mainly on income and earnings, and little has been said about wealth. There is a simple enough reason. The bare truth is that most Americans have only modest financial assets, and many have none at all. The group of citizens that deserves to be called wealthy is very small indeed. So one aim of this chapter is to identify this group and estimate its size.

Sweat of Our Brows?

Share of Income from Employment

Over $1 million	33.0%
$500,000–$1 million	55.4%
$200,000–$500,000	68.2%
$100,000–$200,000	79.3%
$75,000–$100,000	86.1%
$50,000–$75,000	87.7%
Under $50,000	84.9%

Proportion of aggregate income in each bracket derived from wages, salaries, professions, and personal businesses.

True, many of us have some savings, which might keep us fed for a few additional months. However, in recent years, households have been saving only about 4 percent of their disposable personal incomes, a sharp drop from the 8 percent of the 1970s. It is also true that about two-thirds of the nation's families own their own homes or have paid off part of a mortgage and thus have that equity. But it is also the roof over their heads and not really a functional asset.

The most frequently cited estimate is that the best-off 1 percent of the population owns between 40 and 50 percent of the nation's wealth. In 1995, 1 percent added up to 970,000 households having 2.6 million members, which is a fairly large group, almost the population of Chicago. As reported in their tax returns, the incomes of the top 1 percent start at $200,000, by no means a modest figure, and more than six times the national median. While that order of income can underwrite a comfortable life, it is still some distance from being rich, let alone wealthy. In fact, almost 70 percent of what they take in depends on earnings from employment or a self-owned business or profession. So most members of this 1 percent get up to an alarm clock like the rest of us. While they usually have investments, what comes in from that source may make a nice supplement, but is not the major factor in their budgets.

The last comprehensive study of wealth was conducted by the Census Bureau in 1991, and its findings are essentially applicable today. The median net worth of the 94.7 million households they surveyed turned out to be a not exactly opulent $36,623. And after subtracting paid-off equities in homes, the remaining holdings totaled an extremely modest $10,263. But this should not be surprising. For the great majority of Americans, having property has never meant much more than owning a house and a car, perhaps a second vehicle, or maybe a motorboat. (In the past, things were hardly different, since most farms were held under liens by the local bank.) The creation of a national middle class has been based on salaries and status, not portfolios of assets. Even rights to a pension are not really property but a claim on funds that others hold. (And, as many Americans discover each year, the funding is less solid than they were led to believe.)

Since the great majority of households lack sizable assets, the next step is to find when and where substantial wealth begins. The 1991 study concentrated on two groups. The first was the top 20 percent of all households as measured by annual income. To gain entry to that bracket, one needed $56,760, an amount that could be called a reasonable bottom line for an upper-middle-class family. Indeed, within this top fifth, the average income was a quite comfortable $88,130. The median net worth for this best-off one-fifth of all households came to $123,166 when home equity is included, but dropped to very modest $48,893 when it is not. The most common assets were money market accounts and certificates of deposit, plus IRA and Keogh plans. Only about one in five families in the top fifth had invested in money market funds or government securities or had equity in a business or a profession. About 45 percent had purchased stocks or mutual funds, and almost as many owned real estate apart from their family's home. Still, the bottom line is that while those in America's top fifth have fairly decent salaries, their nonhome holdings add up to less than most of them earn in a year.

Of course, the accumulation of assets always takes place over time. So a more realistic measure of this group's net worth would focus on what people have at the end of their careers. And as the table on this page shows, by the age of sixty-five, those in the top quintile had a net worth just under $300,000, which represents their assets over and above an average $125,000 equity in their homes. The $300,000, invested prudently, can certainly provide extra comforts in one's retirement years. But it is still too small a portfolio to qualify as wealth.

Financial Assets of America's Households			
Income Ranking	**Total Worth**	**Minus Home**	**Over 65s★**
Richest 20 percent	$123,166	$48,893	$299,679
Second 20 percent	$49,204	$16,352	$121,154
Middle 20 percent	$28,859	$8,661	$68,372
Fourth 20 percent	$19,191	$5,588	$29,152
Poorest 20 percent	$5,224	$1,143	$3,577

★For over 65s, net worth in excess of value of home.

For a different perspective, the Census decided to examine the wealthiest 3.6 percent of all households measured by property holdings, a smaller group that is considerably higher on the economic scale. However, even their assets remained in the six-figure realm. Their median net worth added up to about $480,000, of which their home equity averaged $95,000, leaving some $385,000 in other assets. As might be expected, they had a more varied array of investments. Even so, over a third did not own stocks or shares in mutual funds, and half had not bought money market funds or government securities. While $385,000 is by no means a paltry sum, we are looking at the top 3.6 percent: that is, people who are better off than over 96 percent of their fellow citizens. Some in this group, too, are relatively young, and more of their savings and investments will come in the years ahead. Unfortunately, the Census did not provide net worth figures for members of the top 3.6 percent who are ready for retirement. Still, assuming their homes are finally paid off and they have continued investing, they may reasonably be expected to have a net worth of about $900,000 by the age of sixty-five.

With prudent investments, this top 3.6 percent should have another $55,000 to $65,000 to supplement their Social Security benefits and whatever other pensions they have. With this cushion, some could be receiving more than $100,000 a year, which while certainly a comfortable income, is still not enough to rank them as "wealthy" or "rich." So even members of this stratum, who are better off than 96 percent of their fellow citizens, close their careers within the middle class.

CHAPTER FIVE

AT THE VERY TOP

In 1996, *Forbes* magazine's annual—and indispensable—inquiry into wealth identified 137 Americans who had personal fortunes exceeding $1 billion. The 6 men who headed the list were each worth over $5 billion, a figure surpassing the tax collections of either Oregon or Colorado. Another 52 individuals had between $2 billion and $5 billion, which gave each one more than the fiscal revenues of Kansas or Alabama. Each of the 79 men and women with $1 billion to $2 billion still had holdings exceeding tax receipts taken in by Baltimore or Houston.

While many countries have people of great wealth, the United States has always led the world in encouraging the creation of huge fortunes. Indeed, as will be seen, one outcome of this ambience is that the roster of the hugely rich is constantly changing. There are also several ways to enter this echelon.

Pride of place should be given to individuals currently among us who, within their own lifetimes, have amassed their money on their own. The compilers of the *Forbes* list estimate that at least half of its four hundred fortunes can validly be called self-made. At the top of this group are Bill Gates and Paul Allen, who started Microsoft; Warren Buffett, the itinerant investor; John Kluge, who assembled Metromedia; and Philip Knight, the founder and chief executive of Nike. In the past, the greatest fortunes were made from oil and steel and railroads. It is instructive that in our times, a similar order of wealth can be built on athletic shoes.

A second group includes sons—thus far no daughters—who preside over enterprises started by earlier generations. Thus one can find a Johnson heading the wax company, a Wrigley turning out chewing gum, while two Mars brothers still take care of the candy. These heirs show up at the office every day and the companies continue to thrive. (There are usually other offspring who are not interested in the business and elect to do something else with their lives.) Clearly, none of these heirs can be called self-made, since they stepped in at the top. Yet there are also sons who have enlarged their inherited stakes into even greater undertakings. This is true of Rupert Murdoch, who transformed his father's Australian newspapers into a worldwide media empire, and Walter Annenberg, who also had a wealthy father, but went on to create such magazines as *TV Guide* and *Seventeen*.

A third group might be called second-generation heirs, the sons and daughters and widows of self-made men who died fairly recently. With this group we encounter a recurring issue concerning wealth. If someone amasses a huge amount of money by hard work or ingenuity or a run of good luck, the American presumption is that they are entitled to whatever comes their way. Assuming that no criminality has been involved, and others are not unduly exploited, ascending to the top bracket is not seen as immoral. (At most, there will be arguments over how much such individuals should be made to pay on April 15.) However, less sympathetic judgments may be made of holders of inherited wealth. Especially if such scions are seen as leading indolent lives and maintaining no links with the enterprises and communities from which their good fortune came.

Rather than trying to exonerate the playboy or dilettante, defenders of inherited wealth may argue that economies need even idly rich people, since they can afford to underwrite investments that cannot find support elsewhere. Another justification is that people who make a lot of money should be able to dispose of it as they wish. True, there are inheritance taxes; but with prudent estate planning, not much need go to the government. The theory is that if the original Henry Ford knew that his fortune would be dissolved at his death, he wouldn't have applied his energies to pioneering a legendary car. In fact, most successful entrepreneurs leave most of their money to their wives and children. So we should not be surprised if among the wealthiest Americans are quite a few heirs who can live as lavishly as they like and do little or no work. Thus three Bass brothers in Texas have at least $2 billion each, from the oil fortunes created by their father and uncle. The widow and children of Wal-Mart's Sam Walton together now have title to some $23 billion. And Ray Kroc's widow, Beverly, still gets a penny or two from each hamburger that McDonald's sells.

Warranting separate consideration are older family fortunes, whose heirs comprise a fourth group of very rich Americans. As it happens, most of these fortunes are not as huge as we might think. Over time, the nation has seen the rise—and fall—of wealthy dynasties. Even if names such as Astor and Vanderbilt and Morgan have historical resonance, they are no longer found on contemporary lists of the wealthiest Americans. In fact, only one name with a truly venerable lineage—du Pont—remains on current rosters. Compared with the du Pont fortune, which originated with the opening of a Delaware gunpowder factory in 1802, the Rockefeller wealth is relatively recent. So are the fortunes of the Mellons, the Hearsts, and the Dorrances, the last a legacy to the charms of Campbell's soups. On the whole, though, few family fortunes remain in the top tier for more than two generations, for reasons that will be cited later in this chapter.

The rise of personal wealth has always intersected with the corporate world. Companies such as the New York Central Railroad, Standard Oil of New Jersey, and Sears Roebuck created fortunes for the Vanderbilts, the Rockefellers, and the Rosenwalds. The same thing is happening today. America is still the best place in the world for launching a new product or testing a hunch that you can offer something that people will want to buy. Here are the names of ten extremely rich Americans that remain unrecognized in most households: Arthur Blank, Gary Corner, Thomas Monaghan, Frederick Smith, Russell Solomon, Ted Arison, Harry Wayne Huizenga, Daniel Abraham, Lawrence Ellison, Edward Johnson. Yet most Americans are familiar with the enterprises that made them millionaires: Home Depot, Lands' End, Domino's Pizza, Federal Express, Tower Records, Carnival Cruises, Blockbuster, Slim-Fast, Oracle, and Fidelity Investments.

Also instructive is how rapidly these fortunes have been made. Of the ten individuals just mentioned, only two—Arison of Carnival Cruises and Smith of Federal Express—had accumulated enough wealth to be on the first Forbes 400 list, published in 1982. Other entrepreneurs with newly minted fortunes are Bill Gates of Microsoft, Leonard Abramson of U.S. Healthcare, and Michael Dell and Charles Schwab of the computer and brokerage firms bearing their names. In rising, they displaced people from the list whose wealth was not keeping pace, including the three Hunt brothers, who lost almost all of their inheritance when they tried to rig the market for silver.

The sources of wealth convey a lot about the texture of the country. The first reliable roster of the richest Americans was also published by *Forbes* magazine, in 1918, and was limited to thirty names. But they were titanic figures, most of them still recalled in popular folklore. At the summit, and well apart from the rest, was John D. Rockefeller. He was followed by such men as Henry Frick, Andrew Carnegie, Edward Harkness, J. Ogden Armour, Henry Ford, William Vanderbilt, Vincent Astor, J. P. Morgan, Cyrus McCormick, James Duke, George Eastman, Daniel Guggenheim, and Pierre du Pont. In most cases, their fortunes came from turning raw materials into manufactured goods: oil and chemicals, copper and steel, railroad lines and farm equipment, cameras and motorcars, cigarettes and sausages. Of course, a few, such as Morgan, were financiers. But the majority superintended the production of things one could actually touch and see. John D. Rockefeller was estimated to have $1.2 billion, equal to about $12 billion now, not terribly far from Bill Gates's and Warren Buffett's present holdings. But below the summit, the world of wealth has been expanding. To make it into 1918's top thirty, one needed to have $50 million in that year's dollars. With today's equivalent at $500 million, some 340 Americans are now worth that much, which works out to four times as many, after taking account of the population's growth.

The last dozen or so years have seen a continuation of these changes. In 1982, when *Forbes* resumed its roster of the richest Americans, it lengthened the list to four hundred individuals and also included families whose members taken together had very large holdings. To get on the 1982 list, a person needed about $90 million, equal to $150 million in 1996. But by 1996, the amount needed to get into the top 400 had risen to $415 million, in real dollars nearing three times the 1982 figure. This means that many who were on the first list wouldn't have made the most recent one. Stated another way, you now must be a lot richer to be among the very rich. And with more people competing to get into the highest bracket, even more billions are needed to reach the summit. The leader of the 400 in 1982 was the now deceased Daniel Ludwig, a shipping magnate pegged at $2 billion, which comes to about $3.3 billion in 1996 dollars. That sum would have given him only twenty-second place on the 1996 list, well behind front-runner Bill Gates's $18.5 billion.

The *Forbes* compilation of the four hundred wealthiest Americans is a prodigious undertaking and provides an invaluable service. No bureau of the government asks or requires individuals to report their assets. How much Americans have in their bank accounts, the worth of stocks or bonds they may own, the possible sale value of an art collection or a piece of real estate—all this is private information, and no federal or state law requires that it be revealed.

At least, it needn't be revealed as long as we stay alive. Once we expire, tax officials will want to know the value of our estates. And in a divorce or other actions where claims are filed against us, a court may order a disclosure of our holdings. Also, when anything is sold—whether a family business or a stamp collection—what we get must be listed as taxable income. But those amounts, too, are supposed to be kept confidential, between you and the IRS (unless they take you to court for misrepresenting the proceeds).

So how does a magazine uncover the worth of someone who owns her own business or of a Wall Street investor or a third-generation heir? Some of the figures are public. People who sit on a board of directors must list how much of that company's stock they own. And local records show the assessed valuations of business and residential real estate. But after that, the search begins. For example, *Forbes* reporters chat informally with people whose jobs involve watching the wealthy: securities analysts, financial journalists, accountants familiar with what privately held firms may be worth. Thus far no one has charged *Forbes* with egregious errors, nor have any of its four hundred gone public in an effort to show that the magazine's estimates have been too high or too low.

Of the more than one thousand Americans who have been on the successive lists, five have been women who founded enterprises of their own. The most recent is Oprah Winfrey, a sophisticated syndicator as well as a talented performer. An early entrant was Mary Hudson of Mission Hills, Kansas, who built a chain of 250 gasoline stations in thirty-five states. And an original member of the Forbes 400 list is Estée Lauder, herself a household word. More recent arrivals have been Janice Davidson and Pamela Lopker, both the founders of California software fortunes.

Five on the list have been black: Berry Gordy of Motown Records; John Harold Johnson of *Ebony* and *Jet;* Reginald Lewis of Beatrice Foods; plus Bill Cosby and Oprah Winfrey. Twenty-three of those on the 1996 list were immigrants, including Rupert Murdoch from Australia and Edgar Bronfman Jr. from Canada, who felt they could better oversee their businesses if they became American citizens. When the list started in 1982, New York led with eighty-two of its residents on the list and California came in second with forty-six. But by 1996, only fourteen years later, there had been a complete reversal: California boasted eighty-nine of the richest Americans, while New York was down to fifty-six. The youngest person to make it on his own was Michael Dell, who came on at the age of twenty-six. So far only two salaried CEOs, Disney's Michael Eisner and Coca-Cola's Roberto Goizueta, have made the list.

The *Forbes* list also shows that great wealth is concentrated in families whose members are recent or distant offspring of those who founded the original fortunes. The twenty most affluent families, shown on the table on page 95, together have holdings worth some $145 billion, a sum that exceeds Denmark's gross domestic product. In fact, they are a varied group. Members of the du Pont clan have been near the top almost since the nation was founded. However, the Waltons joined the group only recently, in 1992, when Sam Walton's death turned his widow and children into the principal owners of the Wal-Mart stores. The Rockefeller fortune began soon after 1870, the inaugural year of John D.'s oil business. Dorrance money became family money when the founder of Campbell's soups died in 1930. The Haases wealth comes from from Levi Strauss jeans, while all that Mars money is based on M&M's and Milky Ways.

Following the top twenty wealthiest families are ninety other families, each with holdings of $430 million or more. Their combined assets total about $100 billion, or slightly more than Finland's gross domestic product. So the assets of the twenty wealthiest families are almost half again as great as those of the next ninety. The *Forbes* lists of families are also scenes of arrivals and departures. Of the forty-one families that had places in 1982, seventeen no longer had the assets required for the 1996 roster. Among those dropping out were the historic Cabots of Boston, the McCormicks and Pattersons of Chicago, and the Pews of Pennsylvania. Also gone were some familiar house-

The 20 Largest Family Fortunes

Family	Fortune Founded	1996 Worth (in billions)
Walton (retailing)	1962	$24.8
Du Pont (chemicals)	1802	$13.9
Mars (candy)	1911	$12.0
Rockefeller (oil)	1870	$9.9
Newhouse (publishing)	1922	$9.0
Haas (jeans)	1873	$8.6
Bass (oil)	1930s	$8.1
Cox (newspapers)	1898	$8.0
Cargill (grain)	1865	$7.9
Dorrance (soup)	1876	$7.7
Pritzker (finance)	1902	$6.0
Mellon (banking)	1869	$5.8
Lauder (cosmetics)	1946	$4.1
Scripps (newspapers)	1870s	$3.6
Upjohn (pharmaceuticals)	1885	$3.2
Ziff (publishing)	1927	$3.0
Smith (machinery)	1889	$2.8
Davis (groceries)	1925	$2.3
Chandler (newspapers)	1894	$2.1
Gund (food, banking)	1919	$2.1

hold names: the Entenmanns of Brooklyn's bakeries, the Mayers of sausage celebrity, as well as the once and still political Kennedys. In 1996, almost three times as many families had enough money for inclusion, and two-thirds of them had not been on the 1982 list.

Why do we have so many more millionaires today, as well as a higher bottom line for getting to the top? The chief reason is that the shape of the economy is altering in fundamental ways. A generation ago, wealth was more likely to be based on assets such as steel mills and railroad tracks, or manufacturing plants that turned out cars or cameras or industrial chemicals. While market twists and turns might run up the value of these enterprises, they could not deviate too far from what it cost to make a Chevrolet or what customers are willing to pay for a Kodak. In contrast, most of today's fortunes are based in large part on what Robert Reich has called "paper entrepreneurialism." Thus much of the new wealth comes from soaring stock valuations, notably in computer-connected companies. The table on this page lists the twenty richest Americans who either founded their own fortunes or have made significant additions to holdings they inherited.

Because contemporary technologies are so novel and continually taking new forms, there are no solid criteria for assessing their

---

The 20 Wealthiest Americans
Who Are Self-Made or Largely So

Personal Worth in 1996

★William Gates (Microsoft)	$18.5 billion
Warren Buffett (investing)	$15.0 billion
★Paul Allen (Microsoft)	$7.5 billion
John Kluge (Metromedia)	$7.2 billion
★Lawrence Ellison (Oracle)	$6.0 billion
Philip Knight (Nike)	$5.3 billion
★Ronald Perelman (buyouts)	$4.0 billion
★Steven Ballmer (Microsoft)	$3.7 billion
Gordon Moore (Intel)	$3.7 billion
Kirk Kerkorian (investing)	$3.4 billion
Sumner Redstone (Viacom)	$3.4 billion
Ross Perot (EDS)	$3.3 billion
Richard DeVos (Amway)	$3.2 billion
★Rupert Murdoch (media)	$3.2 billion
Jay Van Andel (Amway)	$3.2 billion
William Hewlett (H-P)	$2.9 billion
★Jon Huntsman (chemicals)	$2.5 billion
★George Soros (fund manager)	$2.5 billion
Marvin Davis (oil)	$2.2 billion
Ted Turner (media)	$2.1 billion

★Not on the first *Forbes* list in 1982.

"worth." An engineered chromosome, a new hip-hop recording, a software system, even an investment fund, can give rise to sudden riches by catering to a market for products reputed to be "in" or "hot" or "cool." Here is how some of the richest Americans got to the top.

- Bill Gates, Paul Allen, and Steven Ballmer all owe their fortunes to being the founders of Microsoft. Together, the three young men are worth some $30 billion, reflecting their holdings in the company's stock. Microsoft, the world's largest software company, has products such as Windows 95 and a cybermagazine named *Slate*. Still, much of the firm's revenues comes from owning the patent for MS-DOS, which yields it a royalty whenever computers using that system are sold. In fact, Microsoft's income in 1995 was a quite modest $5.9 billion, which gave it 219th place on that year's *Fortune* listing of the 1,000 largest corporations ranked by revenues. After all, how much can they charge for a floppy disk or access to the Internet? It isn't easy to say what the company will be doing or making, say, a decade from now. So what has made Gates and Allen and Ballmer wealthy is that Microsoft remains a Wall Street favorite; its stock was valued at $60.8 billion in March of 1996. In contrast, as the table on page 98 shows, while General Motors had revenues more than twenty-eight times those of Microsoft, its stock had only two-thirds the value.★

- A company called Berkshire Hathaway had revenues of $4.8 billion in 1995, which placed it 292nd on the *Fortune* ranking. Yet its shares were worth 30 percent more than those of the Ford Motor Company, which had 1995 revenues of $137 billion. And it is Warren Buffett's ownership of 43 percent of this firm that has made him the second-richest person in America. Berkshire Hathaway is, for all practical purposes, Buffett's personal portfolio for buying and selling properties he believes will turn a profit. Thus far, investors have been willing to pay tens of billions to ride along with Buffett. Which is another way of saying that his wealth depends on their continued confidence.

★Of course, Wall Street prefers price-earnings ratios in advising on investments, stressing current profits and forecasts for future growth. The "wealth-worth" ratios employed here are intended to illustrate the shift from physical assets to valuations based on brainpower and speculative skills.

Wealth from Worth
The Old Guard

	Revenues	Worth	Ratio
General Motors	$168.8	$39.8	$0.24
Ford	$137.1	$34.9	$0.25
Kmart	$34.7	$4.7	$0.14

The New Wealth

	Revenues	Worth	Ratio
Microsoft	$5.9	$60.8	$10.31
Berkshire Hathaway	$4.5	$43.9	$9.76
Oracle	$3.0	$21.3	$7.10

Revenues: Company's revenues in billions for 1995. *Worth:* Value of all company shares in billions on March 15, 1996. *Ratio:* Value of shares per each $1 in revenues.

- George Soros has easily set the record for stratospheric earnings. According to *Financial World*'s rankings of Wall Street earnings, both in 1993 and 1995, he made $1.5 billion. (His intervening year was disappointing: a mere $70 million.) Soros runs "hedge funds" for very rich investors, who expect spectacular results. These mixed portfolios can contain all manner of traded items, ranging from avocado futures to foreign currencies. Soros, who has a sixth sense for impending shifts in financial markets, takes about 20 percent of the money he makes for others.

- Another road to wealth is illustrated by Ronald Perelman and Kirk Kerkorian, who buy all or parts of companies, usually with borrowed money, and then wait for their market value to rise so they can sell at a profit. Perelman's "leveraged" ventures have involved Revlon, Consolidated Cigar, and Marvel Comics, as well as failed savings and loan associations, which the government sold him at distress prices. Kerkorian has been in and out of Chrysler and MGM. Leveraged buyouts can also bring outsize gains from a single deal. In 1992, Thomas Lee, a

Boston financier who runs his own fund, bought Snapple beverages for forty-four cents a share. Two years later, he sold the company to Quaker Oats for thirty times that price, netting him $150 million. Henry Kravis and George Roberts each made $75 million in 1995, augmenting their fortunes, which are now nearing $1 billion, by buying companies such as Borden and selling Duracell.

• The media have placed John Kluge, Sumner Redstone, Rupert Murdoch, and Ted Turner among the top twenty wealthiest. All four have committed themselves to running enterprises with material assets: motion picture studios, television stations, video stores, newspaper offices, publishing houses. Yet it is instructive that the major assets of these enterprises are not the physical books or cameras or cassettes. Rather, the billions these men have made are dependent on a steady stream of ideas, images, and illusions.

In time, all fortunes will dissipate. Of the thirty wealthiest Americans in 1918, only three—John D. Rockefeller, Henry Ford, Pierre du Pont—have descendants on the current list. Doubtless there are Astors and Harrimans and Vanderbilts with comfortable inheritances; but none rate membership in the top four hundred. And since 1982, the number of individual du Ponts ranking among the very rich has declined from twenty-nine to nine, and most of those nine are now well into their eighties. Only three Rockefellers were wealthy enough to make it onto the 1996 list.

With each new generation, a limited supply of silver spoons must be divided among a greater number of heirs. The Chandler family of the *Los Angeles Times* may as a group be worth about $2 billion, but there are now more than one hundred adults and children to dig into the estate. Over two hundred Richardsons have claims on the Vicks pot, and close to three hundred Weyerhausers are related to the timber fortune. While much money can be made from beer, the Coors family have now reached their fourth generation, and the Buschs are into their fifth. And at last count, there were over seventeen hundred du Ponts, which must make each one's fraction of the family wealth relatively modest. (With the notable exception of the nine senior members, who together still have $4 billion in their own right.)

It will be instructive to see what the Waltons, the Cargills, and the

Mars brothers will do with their money. Earlier founders of great fortunes were often called robber barons and condemned for supposedly lying and cheating and stealing their way to the top. Yet they are also known for their legacies. Consider those on *Forbes*'s 1918 list. Graduates of Harvard, Yale, and Columbia all recall Joseph Widener's library, Edward Harkness's residence halls, and George Baker's football field. James Duke turned a bucolic college into the university bearing his name, while George Eastman gave a music conservatory to the University of Rochester. Andrew Carnegie and John D. Rockefeller endowed foundations that remain preeminent today, as did Henry Ford's heirs. Carnegie became well known, and deservedly so, for donating 1,679 libraries to 1,412 communities in every region of the country. J. P. Morgan, Henry Frick, and Daniel Guggenheim put together impressive art collections and then made them widely available by building museums. In another object lesson, the current generations of Morgans, Fricks, and Guggenheims are either unwilling or unable to provide sufficient funds to pay the galleries' bills. So members of the public are now solicited to make up the shortfalls.

Certainly some of today's rich are carrying on in this vein. Among notable donations have been William Hewlett's and David Packard's $197 million to Stanford University, Jon Huntsman's $100 million to the University of Utah, John Kluge's $60 million to Columbia, and Michael Bloomberg's $55 million to Johns Hopkins, as well as Bill Cosby's $20 million to Spelman College and the $340 million that Walter Annenberg has distributed among many universities as well as to the United Negro College Fund. Yet it is interesting to note that all these contributions have been to existing institutions, which have spent the money in quite conventional ways.★

It has been many years since the Du Pont Company was headed by a du Pont. And David Rockefeller was the last of his name to head one of the family's enterprises, in his case the Chase Bank. Some heirs

---

★As the story goes, Leland Stanford, the California railroad magnate, lost a son to illness late in the last century. He and his wife decided to create a memorial and thereupon paid a visit to Charles Eliot, who then headed Harvard. "President Eliot, we have an odd question," Mr. Stanford began. "How much would it cost today to build the Harvard you have now?" Eliot mused for a few moments, then said he felt it might be done for a then $50 million. Stanford turned to his wife, patted her hand, and said, "My dear, I think we can manage it."

choose other professions, including electoral office. West Virginia, Arkansas, and New York have all chosen governors named Rockefeller, and a du Pont has held that post in Delaware. (In the spirit of the times, he asked voters to call him Pete, rather than Pierre, the name passed down through four generations.) The West Virginia Rockefeller has also served in the Senate, as has a Heinz of the ketchup clan and a Danforth descended from Ralston Purina. But a larger number prefer a leisurely life, which as always is a rightful option for inheritors of wealth. This is not to say that they do absolutely nothing. Perfecting a golf swing and deciding what to wear at a benefit require more time and dedication than the rest of us might think.

It is highly unlikely that any of today's family fortunes will keep their primacy as long as that of the du Ponts, who have taken pains to ensure that some of their members retain exceptional wealth. As has been seen, the more usual pattern is for holdings to diminish as children and grandchildren divide up the original stake. And even now, there are schoolchildren recently arrived from Bolivia, Bombay, and Barbados preparing to supplant the heirs of the Waltons, the Gateses, and the Buffetts.

DO AMERICANS RESENT THE RICH?

In the first decade of this century, Theodore Roosevelt mounted a rostrum to excoriate "the malefactors of great wealth." Such sentiments are seldom heard today. Indeed, there is little evidence that Americans of modest means spend much time or energy feeling resentful toward the rich. If anything, it appears that taxpayers vent more anger toward families receiving public assistance than they do worrying about the perquisites and privileges of those with wealth.

At the same time, there may be residual resentments. Rather then let them fester, it is best that they be given an outlet. Thus at periodic intervals, the public is allowed to pass judgment on the misbehavior of the rich. A recent example was the prosecution of Leona Helmsley for diverting corporate funds and failing to pay her full taxes. While Americans do not regard the rich as unusually dishonest, they get pleasure from watching the travails of someone once protected by wealth. This appetite was fed by the indictment of Claus von Bulow for attempting to murder his heiress wife; and it accounts in part for the public's fascination with the O. J. Simpson trials. And each year sees the indictment of some corporate officers and financiers, for felonies such as price fixing and insider training, which show that the rich are also within the reach of the law.

Clearly, Americans feel relatively little resentment toward those who are seen as having earned their money. But this does not tell us much, since *earned* literally means merited, and to merit something implies it is deserved. But the word *earn* might apply in a more neutral way, as simply receiving payments for work done or services rendered. While only one television program is actually titled *Lifestyles of the Rich and Famous,* the subject matter is a multistage production on which the curtain never falls. Stated simply, the allure of the rich never abates, and some of their number must be available to play leading parts. It helps when there are photogenic heiresses. An earlier era cast Barbara Hutton and Doris Duke as poor little rich girls searching for love but never finding it. A more recent drama starred a kidnapped Patricia Hearst, who later aided her captors in robbing a bank. On occasion, a self-made tycoon or an indolent heir gains public favor by his flamboyant demeanor. A divorce or custody suit featuring affluent adversaries, especially if spiced with sex, can lend legitimacy to wealth, at least by virtue of its entertainment value. Were the rich removed from our midst, we would find ourselves bereft of a pleasing diversion. It would also be a sore loss for fiction. Engaging millionaires have long been a literary staple, and novelists from Anthony Trollope to Judith Krantz have based their characters on real-life models.

Others members of the top income tier do their bit by amusing their fellow citizens with their offbeat personalities. Ross Perot and Malcolm (Steve) Forbes fill that bill, by presuming that they could purchase the presidency. Sam Walton delighted us by choosing to remain in Bentonville and drive a pickup truck. Bill Gates became an icon for looking like an undergraduate while amassing record-breaking wealth. That his Microsoft offers a window into the coming century commingles business fact with science fiction. There is even something beguiling about Michael Eisner, photographed alongside Mickey Mouse, as if daring anyone to say that he did not deserve the $203 million that Disney gave him in a recent year.

Athletes and others who divert the public are seldom begrudged their salaries, whether it was Babe Ruth's $80,000 in 1930 (equal to about $700,000 today) or Michael Jordan's $25 million in 1996. Indeed, that money can be construed as a sign of public consent. After all, it flows from purchases that are willingly made, be they tickets or recordings or products emblazoned with endorsements. Dollars take the form of ballots, and the winners are the people and the products that receive the most of these votes.

To be sure, there will always be commentators ready to remark that something is sadly askew when an athlete gets $25 million for a season's play and movie stars receive $20 million for even less time on a set. They are exclaiming, as a business magazine once did of high executive pay, "It doesn't make sense!" Well, of course it doesn't. Or at least not in *moral* terms. As matters now stand, or until the pie gets bigger, giving $20 million to a superstar will mean that a lot of people down the line will be paid less than they were getting before. Nor does it make much sense to pile more money on individuals who do not need it and who, until recently, never dreamed that so much cash could come their way. The only "sense" arises from a rationale that avers that under the way our system works, we are all entitled to accept with a clear conscience whatever someone else freely offers us. Not many Americans would reject that reasoning. (After all, look at how many buy lottery tickets featuring $20-million jackpots, every cent of which they would certainly want to keep.) For these reasons, moral or otherwise, the very rich have a supportive constituency, if not an avid cheering section. How many begrudge Oprah Winfrey and Estée Lauder the millions they have received for giving pleasure to so many millions of their fellow citizens?

CHAPTER SIX

HAIL TO THE CHIEF!

CEO.

Most Americans know what these initials signify. And it is well that they do. Just as dukedoms and baronies dominated the feudal era, so corporations today shape the nation's economy and social texture. Yet chief executives are notably anonymous. People who follow the news can perhaps identify a dozen governors and senators, but most would find it hard to name half that number of our top corporate officers. This should not be surprising, since we elect politicians, who themselves seek credit for their acts and thrive in the public eye. While corporation chairmen are not averse to respectful recognition, they prefer that the public not see them as possessing significant power.

At last count, the nation had some 3.9 million corporations, or at least that was how many submitted tax returns. This is an accurate enough count, since if you choose to form a corporation, it isn't easy to do so without informing the IRS.

Some corporations are nonprofit bodies, such as the Harvard Corporation, which governs the university bearing that name. Others having a corporate form are bodies such as the American Red Cross, the Educational Testing Service, and the Carnegie Corporation, one of the country's foremost foundations. These organizations differ from business concerns in that they do not have shareholders, since they do not sell or issue stock. While legally they are overseen by boards of directors, those trustees tend to be self-selecting, which means that corporations of this kind are essentially owned by themselves. As a result, they have considerable freedom when deciding what to pay their chief executives and even themselves.

Some of our major enterprises are unincorporated, since they are still owned by the founding families. This is the case with the Mars company, which supplies the world with Milky Ways and M&M's. Another is the Newhouse conglomerate, which owns the book-publishers Knopf and Random House, as well as the magazines *The New Yorker* and *Vanity Fair.* Some of the largest insurance firms are also outside the corporate ambit. Companies such as Prudential and Nationwide are owned not by stockholders, but by the individuals and organizations who hold their policies. If you are such an owner, you are entitled to vote for their board of directors, although the companies do not encourage widespread participation. So State Farm, which has almost $40 billion in revenues, ranking it between Chrysler and Du Pont, for all intents and purposes has no outside owners. A downside is that having no shares means that their executives cannot be awarded stock or options and thus have to live on their salaries and bonuses. (This lack of a bountiful perquisite is a major reason why many mutual insurance firms have shifted to the corporate form.)

Moreover, many of the 3.9 million corporations are only paper entities, designed to hide sources of control. A single motion picture may be incorporated in its own right, sometimes to minimize taxes or to attract investors. Even a solitary taxicab may be given a corporate identity, the better to limit its liability. (If sued for damages, the cab's owner can declare the "corporation" bankrupt and declare as its assets a single dented vehicle.)

But when we speak of CEOs, we have in mind the men—and in our time, all but a handful are men—who head the nation's most prominent firms. But as has been noted, even the individuals heading the top dozen corporations are not widely known. Only a few, such as Ted Turner and Lee Iacocca, combine distinctive personalities with a penchant for publicity. Some become newsworthy due to an arrogance that eventually sends them falling, although it is equally noteworthy how soon they are forgotten. Others, such as Sam Walton and Bill Gates, become public figures because they create new kinds of enterprises. However, the typical chief executive has spent his whole career as, essentially, a corporate civil servant.

A corporation, as we know, is an association of assets, which can range from Exxon's refineries to that dented taxicab. And as our textbooks taught us, they are often called "public" companies, since they are often owned by outside parties: that is, shareholders, who purchase stock, usually in hopes of enjoying an appreciation in value or a share of the profits.

For this reason, textbooks emphasize that a corporation is the property of its shareholders. So even highly paid executives are employees, who must satisfy the owners if they want to keep their jobs. Each year sees well-publicized cases in which boards of directors dismiss CEOs who had hitherto been receiving high-flying compensation. There are even instances where the individual who founded the company is told he has to go, which happened at Apple Computer and TWA. And this can be achieved after a firm has gone "public" and outsiders come to own most of the shares.

Starting early in the 1990s, the new heights in compensation for chief executives became a running story. Citing several staggering sums, *BusinessWeek* felt obliged to ask, "Is Anybody Worth This Much?" It has been average paychecks like those in the first part of the table on page 108 that have roused such questions and expostulations. Clearly, Disney's awards to Michael Eisner averaging $46.5 million were not typical. Yet even lower figures in the $10-million range are new as well as high, when compared both with what chief executive received in the past and to earnings elsewhere in the economy. In the 1960s, corporate chairmen tended to receive thirty times the wage of an average worker. By the mid-1990s, CEOs' compensations had soared to a two-hundred multiple.

To be sure, single-year payments, such as the $203 million that Disney's Eisner received in 1993, can be unusual, since they may be regarded as rewards for services performed over many years. So the table includes what these chief executives *averaged* over the five-year period from 1991 through 1995. What emerges is that well-known corporations are either approaching eight-figure compensations or are already there.

Along with *BusinessWeek,* we may ask, "Is anyone worth this much?" Here again in the answers to this question, we encounter webs of words, woven by those who are disposed—or paid—to justify the higher realms of remuneration. As often as not, the reasons for a CEO's astronomical compensation are released by a board of directors, usually after the prose has been polished by a growing cadre of communications consultants.

The most common rationale is that the chairman's leadership has brought the company to new financial heights. Thus in 1992, General

For Services Rendered: CEOs' Compensation

Company	1991–95 Total CEO Compensation	Annual Average
Lavish		
Disney	$232,700,000	$46,500,000
Travelers	$199,700,000	$39,900,000
Heinz	$119,100,000	$23,800,000
Generous		
Colgate-Palmolive	$ 54,500,000	$10,900,000
Mirage Resorts	$ 49,539,000	$9,900,000
General Electric	$ 45,400,000	$9,100,000
Merrill Lynch	$ 39,500,000	$7,900,000
Modest		
Caterpillar	$ 7,300,000	$1,500,000
Kimberly-Clark	$ 7,200,000	$1,400,000
Kroger	$ 5,700,000	$1,100,000
Delta Airlines	$ 3,900,000	$800,000

How Much Incentive Does a CEO Need?

CEO and Company	Years as CEO	Stock Awards as of 1995
A Lot		
Roberto Goizueta (Coca-Cola)	15	$672,400,000
Sanford Weill (Travelers)	10	$251,400,000
Anthony O'Reilly (H. J. Heinz)	17	$198,100,000
Michael Eisner (Walt Disney)	12	$184,100,000
A Lot Less		
Joseph Dionne (McGraw-Hill)	13	$9,300,000
John Clendenin (BellSouth)	12	$6,900,000
John Roach (Radio Shack)	15	$6,600,000
John Hall (Ashland Oil)	15	$2,900,000

Electric's profits came to $4.6 billion, close to double the previous year's earnings of $2.6 billion. For that, it was argued, the chief executive deserved more than his customary salary. Disney's directors recalled that during Michael Eisner's tenure, the company's stock had risen in value by $5 billion. They argued that $203 million—an honorarium of 4 percent—was not out of line for putting so much money in the owners' pockets.

Still, even if one agrees that a chief executive's paycheck should be related to performance and that it is rational to reward a winner, or to express gratitude to someone whose achievements have exceeded expectations, one can still wonder how the size of the gratuity is determined. Why not $200,000 or $2 million? And here, no conception of rationality can tell us which figure makes the greatest sense. Even were it asserted that one doesn't insult high-flying chairmen with $200,000, that hardly provides an analytic explanation; it merely reflects the current corporate culture.

Other considerations intrude on the foregoing explanation. Any appreciation of a company's stock may have little or nothing to do with its CEO's actions. In some cases, the strategies that proved successful were put in place by his predecessor. As with any group endeavor, the issue of who deserves credit for what is not easy to resolve. Also, much of a rise in a company's shares may result from a nationwide mood of optimism, from which all firms benefit. Then, too, a favorable position of the dollar relative to other currencies can bring unanticipated profits or capital gains.

Some insights into chief executives' compensation may be gained by examining what happens when a corporation's directors feel a new hand is needed at the helm, and they undertake to bring in a chairman from outside the company. Needless to say, they will want someone with a proven record, which usually means that he is happily situated at another enterprise. It also means that he knows his value and will play for high stakes. Thus when IBM decided they wanted Louis Gerstner who was then the CEO at RJR Nabisco, they had to make a strong offer. In addition to the usual stock options, they agreed to a salary and bonuses that came to $7.7 million in his first year, and $12.4 million during his second. As it happened, to succeed Gerstner, RJR Nabisco also sought an outsider and met his terms, which resulted in a $16-million pay package over his first two years.

However such outsize contracts result from a curious logic. Let us assume that the directors have set out to hire someone they feel is the best person for the job. Could that person be presented as "the best" if he consented to come for an unassuming sum? Unusually high compensation is often an attempt to convince the world: "This man must really be good, look how much we had to pay to get him!" Suppose for a moment that the best candidate said he would take the job for a nominal sum; he had enough money to live quite comfortably and saw the job as a challenge. There is little doubt he would be told that while such an outlook is admirable, to act on it could only harm the company.

An important fact, though, is that it is not customary to seek a CEO from outside the company. Among the country's one hundred largest firms, only thirteen currently have chief executives who were brought in from outside. Among the other eighty-seven, seven were the original founders of the firms, and the remaining eighty were executives already on the premises. In the most typical cases, they held the rank of vice chairman or president and were being groomed as heir apparent for the top spot. And when the promotion comes, there is usually a leap in pay. Thus when Arthur Martinez was anointed head of Sears Roebuck, the directors quickly changed his compensation from $2.1 million to $6.6 million. Was a raise of that magnitude necessary? We can probably presume that Mr. Martinez was anxious for the job, which would cap his career with the company. In private, he might even confess that he would have been happy to take the top job without a raise in pay. The rationale for luring outsiders does not apply to inside candidates, who may be had for much more modest compensation packages. When they are given more than they might ask for, which frequently happens, it is for another set of reasons, which will be considered in due course.

Corporate officers are highly paid, we often hear, in order to match outside offers or to keep them from being lured away. In fact, only rarely is the chief executive of a company sought by other firms. To be sure, there is considerable raiding and head-hunting in corporate America; but it generally takes place at lower levels. Prime candidates are often persons who get passed over in a CEO sweepstakes and who do not want to stay on as subordinates to the winner. As for the CEOs themselves, it is worth recalling that at any given time, half of their number are midway toward retirement. Among the one hundred largest corporations, the typical CEO is fifty-seven years old and will hold the job for about five more years. Approximately a third are in their sixties and nearing the end of their careers. It could even be argued that a CEO's compensation ought to be reduced as his trajectory begins to ebb. Indeed, for most employed Americans, earnings actually decline after the age of fifty-five.

There are instances, certainly, where high pay is given to keep a valued employee from leaving. In some cases, an outside offer has been made, and its terms are matched or exceeded, although even a star performer probably cannot use this ploy more than once or twice. More often, firms try to keep their key people content by paying them above the going rate. Indeed, some employees have never had to ask for a raise, since their superiors are aware of their worth and make sure that such requests are unnecessary.

But even in an age of downsizing, there are executives whose market value has not been measured, or at least not recently. As has been noted, were we to put classical theory into practice, all of us would have to ascertain our true economic worth, perhaps annually, along with a medical checkup. Not so long ago, one company's board of directors approved generous stock options for an entire echelon of high executives. When asked whether all of them merited that, the response was "not really." Some were close to retirement, and others did not have track records that would have caused them to be lured away. Why then, it was inquired, did they not confine the options to executives of proven value to the company? "No, if we did that," came the reply, "it would hurt the others' feelings."

The president of the United States actually has his own song, "Hail to the Chief!" (Second line: "Who in triumph advances!") And it is played on state occasions when the nation's chief executive enters the room. While corporate chieftains do not expect such heralding, to a great extent they are monarchs in realms of their own, which do not lack for regal trappings. The business world gives its highest officeholders a singular personal power unknown in other institutions. (This helps to explain why executives rarely perform well in government.)

Not all CEOs subscribe to the single-leader theory. Robert Eaton, who was hired from General Motors in 1992 to superintend Chrysler, expressed his sentiments succinctly: "I'm a very strong believer that individuals can't and don't accomplish much." Although the company's sales, profits, and stock prices rose after his arrival, he insisted, "I don't take credit for any of it, I make hardly any decisions." Of course, this may be verbal byplay; any CEO who comes in from outside must be ultradiplomatic. After all, he faces a preexisting organization, not to mention subordinates who either wanted his job or are loyal to those who did. Even so, Mr. Eaton put his money where his words were. He urged the board to give his second-in-command, who had been a competing candidate for the top spot, compensation equal to his own.

In recent years, boards of directors have had second thoughts about the individuals they have chosen as chief executives. During the 1990s, CEOs at such firms as General Motors, American Express, Time Warner, Philip Morris, IBM, Apple, and Kodak were all shown the door well before they were ready for an honorable retirement. Yet even in these instances, directors tend to be quite generous with golden parachutes, giving considerably more than legal agreements would require. Borden's board even gave the CEO it had just ousted an extra one hundred thousand stock options. W. R. Grace provided their fifty-five-year-old mistake with a $849,000 annual pension for the rest of his life. In part, this largesse may be a tacit payoff, to ensure that the departing chairman stays quiet. And he probably will, since most parachutes are predicated on year-by-year payments. Moreover, the corporate community looks after its own. Even after Roger Smith was removed at General Motors, the boards at Citicorp, Johnson & Johnson, International Paper, and Pepsico all kept him on as a director.

As it happens, the most lucrative parachute went not to an edged-out CEO, but to a second-ranking executive. After fourteen months as Disney's president, Michael Ovitz was informed he was not up to the job. In return for his resignation, he was given at least $70 million in cash and stock options. Assuming that he put in eighty hours throughout those sixty weeks, his good-bye gift paid him an extra $14,583 for each hour he had been at Disney. (We may assume that Disney keeps the rights for turning this antic into a film.)

In theory and in fact, every CEO's compensation is decided by the board of directors. And virtually all of those boards have a compensation committee, charged with reviewing top-level salaries and benefits. Almost never does a chairman request a raise or specify the actual amount he expects to receive. Indeed, he leaves the room during the discussion of his compensation. The protocol is to wait and act surprised when the figures are announced. In some cases—albeit rarely—he will insist that he not be given a raise or will perhaps signal willingness to take a cut, since the company had a bad year.

Corporate boards vary, but it is still largely accurate to say that most members are nominated by the chairman and are beholden to him. The Chase Bank has been paying its directors almost $90,000 a year. Pepsico also gives them $30,000 in stock each year, and most firms throw in pensions as well. All told, General Electric's directors come away with about $132,000 for attending nine meetings a year.

Since chairmen prefer passive boards, it makes sense to keep on directors who will not make waves. They also favor people who don't do the necessary homework and hence cannot ask informed—or embarrassing—questions. In this regard, an ideal director would be someone like Vernon Jordan, who has accepted invitations from ten corporate boards, ranging from American Express and Sara Lee to Xerox and JC Penney. Another example is Ann McLaughlin, who receives more than $400,000 a year for occupying nine board seats, including for such corporations as Kellogg and Host Marriott, Nordstrom and General Motors. Most companies have about ten board meetings a year, for which directors are sent binders containing upward of two hundred pages of data. People familiar with the corporate world attest that even an experienced executive can at best do justice to two directorships. Thus far, no company has set such a limit, which is hardly surprising, since amateur overseers are generally amenable to management.

And how do boards' compensation committees decide what a CEO should be paid? A common recourse is to approach a consulting firm for advice. Such firms know full well why they have been called in and prepare elaborate reports showing that their clients fall behind comparable firms in pay and benefits. With these documents in hand, boards lift their CEO just enough above the norm to show that they are ahead of the pack. After all, no company wants it to appear as if it cannot pay its top people the prevailing rate. So here, too, the aim is not to find out what your man is worth, but to affirm the image of the company by the zeros on his check.

People who embark on corporate careers generally come from modest origins, and few start out with dreams of big money. Here is where some of the top CEOs were born: Valley City, North Dakota (population: 7,163); Laurel, Montana (5,686); Anna, Illinois (5,408); and Benson, Minnesota (3,656). Most of them attended public universities or lower-tier private schools, where they were more likely than not to study science or engineering. Of the current heads of the one hundred largest corporations, only eleven attended Ivy League colleges. Yet even there, half majored in science or engineering, rather than choosing the more leisurely liberal arts route. Most entered the corporate world directly from college; indeed, few began with dreams of a CEO's desk. Colleagues who knew them at that time will tell you that they hoped to end up comfortably middle class, in suburbs with a good school system, so their own children might go to Stanford or Princeton.

It can easily be argued that top-level compensation comprises a very small item in total company costs. Few companies have more than four or five people at the million-dollar level, even though they have many thousands on the payroll. General Motors has more than 700,000 employees, while Sears, Ford, Kmart, and AT&T all have at least 300,000. The wages and benefits of the mass of employees make up most of the budget and shape the firm's ability to compete. Of course, slicing top salaries could save several million dollars. But for significant bottom-line gains, a much broader swath must be cut. For instance, if all 300,000 employees were made to contribute $500 more toward their health benefits, the overall savings would amount to $150 million a year.

There is also the matter of appearances: Should CEOs get huge packages at the very time they are slashing their firm's payroll? Robert E. Allen, the chairman of AT&T, had his compensation tripled to $20 million just as he was announcing 40,000 layoffs. Albert Dunlap dismissed 20 percent of Scott Paper's workers—over 11,000 men and women—and a little later sold the slenderized company to Kimberly-Clark, netting $100 million for himself by exercising his awarded stock options. As CEOs, Dunlap and Allen say their principal obligation is to their shareholders, whose company it is. These investors put their money into the firm looking for good dividends or appreciation of stock value, and not because it furnished employment for a certain number of people. One of America's major stockholders is the fund that provides pensions for California's public employees. It feels a duty to secure its firefighters and librarians comfortable retirements. Thus it keeps a close watch on corporations such as Scott Paper and AT&T since, as one of its managers said, "there are companies that are fat and

America's Corporate Elite

CEOs of the 100 Largest Companies in 1995

Average Annual Pay, 1991–95		Stock Owned in Their Companies	
Under $1 million	5	Under $1 million	5
$1–$2 million	21	$1–$5 million	22
$2–$3 million	29	$5–$10 million	31
$3–$4 million	17	$10–$20 million	19
$4–$5 million	12	$20–$50 million	9
$5–$10 million	13	$50–$100 million	4
Over $10 million	3	Over $100 million	10
Median: $2.8 million		Median: $8.4 million	

Years with Their Companies		Years as Chief Executive	
30 or more	44	More than 20	5
20 to 29	24	10 to 20	16
10 to 19	16	5 to 9	29
Under 10	16	Less than 5	50
Median: 28		Median: 5	

	Current Age	When Made CEO	
60 or over	31	5	Recruited as CEO from outside the company: 13
55 to 59	42	21	
50 to 54	19	40	Insiders: 80
Under 50	8	34	
Median:	57	52	CEO founded company: 7

Undergraduate Education		Undergraduate Degrees	
Ivy League	11	B.S. 57 B.A. 28 Other 10	
Other private	37	Graduate Degrees	
Public colleges	43	MBA 25 L.L.B 10	
Foreign	4	Ph.D. 8 M.A. 14	
None or not given	5		

have not taken a good look at the number of employees they need." Of course, part of the pared-away fat may be some of those librarians' husbands and those firefighters' daughters who work at companies in which the pension fund owns stock.

A recurrent theme throughout this book has been that our kind of economic system—or at least America's variant of it—has never made the creation of jobs its first priority. Jobs come into being as and when enterprises need them and disappear when tasks no longer need to be done. Two well-known American firms illustrate this process. Corning Glass, founded in 1851, has long engaged in manufacturing in the United States, and it currently employs approximately 43,000 American men and women. In 1995, it had earnings of $279 million on revenues of $4.8 billion, and it is the kind of company that investors find attractive. Another company, named Nike, was started in 1971, and in 1995 it had earnings of $299 million on sales of $3.8 billion and is also considered a good investment. However, not a single one of Nike's products is made in the United States. Every one of its shoes is made abroad, almost all in less developed countries where labor costs are low. Nike does have 9,500 employees in the United States, whose jobs are largely in sales, design, and promotion, plus, of course, preparing contracts for the foreign manufacturers.

The moral of Nike vs. Corning is straightforward: one company can be just as profitable as the other, even a little more so, with less than a quarter of the number of U.S.-based employees. Nike has never engaged in large-scale firings, nor is it constantly looking for ways to reduce its payroll. But then it doesn't have to. Unlike Corning, it decided not to hire Americans to make its products, so the issue of downsizing does not arise. Of course, it has been known to lay off workers, but they live in places like Taiwan and Malaysia and Brazil.

Most companies that begin as family enterprises soon find they need new capital to expand and in so doing must sell a share of the ownership to the public. As of 1995, Michael Dell owned 21.3 percent of Dell Computer, while Philip Knight held 33.9 percent of Nike and Bill Gates retained 23.9 percent of Microsoft's stock. As the table on page 117 indicates, there are founders, such as Frederick Smith of Federal Express and Bernard Marcus of Home Depot, who own considerably less. Presumably they have decided that what they have retained is quite enough. Indeed, both of them rank among *Forbes* magazine's four hundred wealthiest Americans, with Smith's fortune estimated at $415 million and Marcus's at $840 million.

Among heirs who now sit in CEO's chairs, Willard Marriott owns only 7.5 percent of the company his father founded, and Arthur O. Sulzberger has 7.1 percent of the New York Times Company, which now has holdings well beyond the newspaper. On the other hand, a great-grandson, William Wrigley, still holds 17.8 percent of the chewing-gum empire. August Busch III's share of the family firm is a fractional

Chief Executives: Who Owns How Much			
Founders	**Company**	**Stock Owned**	**Average Compensation***
Philip Knight	Nike	33.9%	$1,378,000
William Gates	Microsoft	23.9%	$370,000
Leslie Wexner	Limited	23.1%	$2,036,000
Michael Dell	Dell Computer	21.3%	$573,000
Charles Schwab	Charles Schwab	20.0%	$4,457,000
Frederick Smith	Federal Express	8.5%	$884,000
Bernard Marcus	Home Depot	3.1%	$2,591,000
Founders' Heirs			
William Wrigley	William Wrigley	17.8%	$1,457,000
Donald Graham	Washington Post	16.0%	$606,000
Willard Marriott	Marriott	7.5%	$1,482,000
Arthur O. Sulzberger	New York Times	7.1%	$1,419,000
August Busch III	Anheuser-Busch	0.5%	$3,891,000
Employed Executives			
Anthony O'Reilly	H. J. Heinz	1.6%	$23,829,000
Sanford Weil	Travelers Group	1.3%	$39,935,000
Roberto Goizueta	Coca-Cola	0.7%	$11,917,000
Michael Eisner	Disney	0.6%	$46,549,000
John Welch	General Electric	0.03%	$9,080,000
John Smith	General Motors	0.01%	$1,988,000

*Average of total payments for years 1991–95.

0.5 percent. But that should not occasion surprise, since the company was formed in the 1860s, and the ownership is dispersed among hundreds of heirs as well as the investing public. Even so, even a fractional stake in the country's premier beer company can go a long way; in 1995, Mr. Busch's shares maintained a market value of $81.8 million.

In some of the nation's top companies, the founders or their heirs retain sufficient holdings so that the company remains private. One example is the Continental Grain Company, which has revenues of $15 billion. Another is MacAndrews and Forbes, which in 1995 took in over $6 billion by mixing perfumes and cosmetics with book publishing. Unlike firms that sell shares to the public, these and other privately held enterprises do not have to disclose their executives' salaries and stock holdings to the Securities and Exchange Commission.

The world of investment banking becomes relevant here, since some of the major firms are public corporations, while others are fully owned by their partners. What both have in common, though, is that the principal participants can make huge amounts of money. Indeed, skilled arbitrageurs and acquisition experts, often with minuscule staffs, have made more than CEOs who manage companies having a hundred thousand employees. Among the public investment banks, Bear Stearns's chief executive has averaged upward of $13 million during his tenure, while Morgan Stanley's CEO has been averaging $7 million. It will be recalled that among the current heads of the one hundred largest corporations the median pay package is still under $3 million. In contrast, there are the private Wall Street firms, where Lazard Frères's top earner made $38 million in 1995, and Smith Barney's chairman received $35 million.

Goldman Sachs, the most profitable private firm, shows how earnings can be dispersed. In 1993, while its CEO was being given $46 million, each of the other 160 partners averaged $11 million as their share of the profits. (Even those who had just been promoted to partnerships averaged $5 million.) Earnings in investment banking come from two major sources. The first is a firm's own pool of capital, which is deployed in diverse financial markets, where good timing and shrewd judgment can bring impressive profits. Investment banks also launch stock offerings, assist with mergers and acquisitions, and find buyers and sellers for all kinds of securities. In 1994, for example, Lazard Frères advised on 116 corporate mergers or acquisitions, which had an aggregate value of almost $130 billion. Since the customary commission for this counsel is 1 percent of the assets being exchanged, the firm had close to $1.3 billion to distribute among its partners. With fees like these, it isn't difficult to see how seven- and eight-figure incomes become possible. In 1996, a notable year for salaries and bonuses, the consensus among those who watch paychecks was that at least fifteen hundred people on Wall Street received a minimum of $1 million.

In firms where effective ownership remains with founders or their families, there can be little objection to their paying themselves what they please, just as the proprietor of a local delicatessen can decide how much he will take from the till. (Henry Ford told an underling, "Never forget, my name is on this building.") Yet the compensation they take can be quite modest. Frederick Smith of Federal Express averaged $884,000 between 1991 and 1995, while Michael Dell took $573,000 and Bill Gates of Microsoft settled for $370,000. However, it hardly needs to be noted that these men are millionaires many times over, and whatever walking-around money they need comes from dividends or cashing in some capital.

In our time, fewer of the owners of corporate America are people, which is to say, sentient human beings. The dominant shareholders are now investing institutions, which are presided over by trustees and salaried administrators. If CEOs are accountable to their companies' owners, then they are answerable not only to individual investors, but to banks and brokerage houses, mutual funds and pension funds, as well as insurance companies and occasionally other corporations that have spare cash to invest. A good case in point is Time Warner, the media giant that produces movies and television programs, publishes magazines and books, and has a huge stake in the music industry. Who owns Time Warner? Two of its leading owners are banks, Wells Fargo and Bankers Trust, which used funds entrusted to them by depositors to buy Time Warner shares. If you have a savings account at Wells Fargo, they are obliged to take care of your money, but they don't have to ask your consent if they want to use it to purchase a piece of Time Warner. Another institution that operates in a similar manner is the College Retirement Equities Fund, a pension fund for professors, who remit monthly contributions toward their eventual retirement. Once CREF gets the money, it decides how to use it, which may include pressing for changes within companies in which it invests. Among the fastest-growing financial institutions are mutual funds, which have literally millions of owners. If you buy shares in a Vanguard fund, you probably know that the fund already has shares in Time Warner and may use your money to buy some more. However, all that stock has been bought in the name of Vanguard, which is only obliged to send you an accurate share of the dividends from its stock portfolio.

Back in 1952, a young economist named John Kenneth Galbraith wrote a book entitled *American Capitalism: A Theory of Countervailing Power.* In that opening year of the Eisenhower era, Galbraith found the system safeguarded by an equipoise among corporations, labor unions, and a watchful government. There is little likelihood that he would repeat that argument today. Unions are shadows of their former selves, and there is widespread sentiment for curbing the powers of regulatory agencies. Galbraith could not have known a new source of countervailing power would arise in investing institutions. What we do know today is that they wield a double-edged sword. On the one hand, they have been among the strongest critics of excessive payments to executives. In one case involving the W. R. Grace Company, pension funds demanded that a dismissed CEO return most of an outsize severance package.

On the other hand, the very same institutions insist that firms generate high earnings, as well as turn in a performance that will increase the value of their stock. These are the pressures behind the waves of downsizing, which have shortened thousands of corporate careers. A similar strategy calls for replacing permanent employees with contingent workers, who have no settled place on the payroll. Hence we see the increasing use of temporary workers, who can range from receptionists and typists to legal researchers and civil engineers. A parallel trend is outsourcing, where firms have components manufactured or services performed by outside companies, where the work is done by people who are paid markedly less than were their own employees. Indeed, an airline once even arranged for inmates of a women's prison to handle telephone reservations, which brought the added dividend of being heralded as a rehabilitation project. Each day, a New York–based insurance company gets a mountain of mail, which must be dealt with quickly and efficiently. While the envelopes are ostensibly mailed to a Manhattan address, the zip code in fact sends the letters directly to the John F. Kennedy airport. The sacks are then flown overnight to Dublin, where they are opened and processed by Irish clerical workers, who transmit all the information back to

New York by satellite. More and more firms are using sophisticated services abroad; thus architectural firms are having blueprints drafted by college graduates in Bombay.

The position of chief executive officer is no longer confined to business enterprises. Another hallmark of our time is that other organizations are emulating the corporate model. Museums and foundations, hospitals and colleges, public television stations and opera companies, are increasingly headed by executives who are not easily distinguished from their profit-seeking counterparts. Of course, the spheres are legally separate. Still, even Planned Parenthood and the American Heart Association will tell you that they need people of proven administrative skills. The Boy Scouts of America and the United Negro College Fund will undoubtedly add that it isn't easy to get people who have a talent for raising large sums of money. So we see organizations that have goals other than financial gain giving generous six-figure salaries to their chief executives.

And yet one might ask why the Ford Foundation felt compelled to bestow $839,139 on its presiding officer. It is unlikely that he is besieged with offers from Exxon or Du Pont and that only a hefty check will induce him to stay. It is not as if the Ford Foundation needs a fund-raiser. It already has $6 billion in the bank, so its only job is to hand out grants, which doesn't call for extraordinary skills. (Nor does investing that amount of money require special talent; one need only spread it around the Dow Jones stocks.) As the table on page 122 shows, at least four universities paid their chief executives more than $500,000 in 1995. And does Tulane University really need to pay its president $397,612, or does New York University have to provide $410,832? After all, like most heads of colleges, they started as members of the faculty, and they didn't enter the field of education for the money. At Tulane, the average full professor gets $74,900; and at NYU, where the cost of living is higher, the figure is $96,800. So if their boards of trustees added, say, $20,000 to what their professors get, Tulane's president would have a salary of $94,900 and NYU's would get $116,800. One would like to think that they care about their institutions and did not aspire to its top office for monetary reasons. Perhaps hospitals and schools, symphonies and museums, charities and foundations, would not be able to fulfill their purposes if they did not give their leaders with lavish salaries. If this is in fact the case, it conveys a lot about our age.

Doing Well by Doing Good: How Philanthropy Pays

Sloan-Kettering Medical Center	$1,002,716
Ford Foundation	$839,139
Carnegie Corporation	$617,249
Rockefeller Foundation	$589,015
Metropolitan Opera Association	$471,000
Mayo Clinic	$456,230
U.S. Olympic Committee	$444,331
Boy Scouts of America	$419,742
American Heart Association	$360,108
Metropolitan Museum of Art	$281,789
Smithsonian Institution	$280,284
Los Angeles Public Television	$267,645
New York Public Library	$265,691
Planned Parenthood	$251,538
United Way of St. Louis	$247,377
Art Institute of Chicago	$242,309
United Negro College Fund	$226,212
National Wildlife Federation	$194,754
Mothers Against Drunk Driving	$129,252

Ivied Executive: What Presidents Are Paid

Universities		Colleges	
Howard	$800,318	Morehouse	$425,030
Boston University	$565,018	Smith	$392,680
Stanford	$527,533	Amherst	$280,825
Adelphi	$523,636	Williams	$234,649
Vanderbilt	$478,489	Wellesley	$217,396
New York University	$410,832	Wesleyan	$216,913
Chicago	$404,022	Mount Holyoke	$211,815
Tulane	$397,612	Kenyon	$208,570
Yale	$387,138	Spelman	$201,418
Princeton	$341,842	Oberlin	$199,810
Columbia	$338,838	Haverford	$196,031
Duke	$315,821	Middlebury	$187,124
Cornell	$294,687	Kalamazoo	$172,329
Harvard	$278,659	Simmons	$167,948
Michigan	$260,923	Transylvania	$143,000
Brown	$229,956	St. Olaf	$111,718
California (Berkeley)	$201,315	Siena	Nothing

Annual salary plus benefits, but does not include free housing. Of the Howard amount, $676,980 was a severance contract; at Stanford, $156,643 was relocation repayment; at Adelphi, $149,200 went into deferred compensation.

CHAPTER SEVEN

M.D.s, J.D.s, Ph.D.s

Medicine has been America's best-paid occupation for most of this century. This is not to say that many physicians become inordinately wealthy. When it comes to stratospheric salaries, they are far outpaced by currency traders and investment bankers. For one thing, doctors are essentially paid by the hour, so the clock and calendar set ceilings on the amounts that most of them can earn. They also lack a counterpart to the shares of settlements and damages that make some lawyers millionaires. Indeed, in that arena, more than a few physicians have augmented the wealth of their brothers-in-law.

What has been unique about medicine is that virtually anyone who has a medical degree and who has completed a residency could count on finding a position that promised $100,000. Apart from a handful of MBAs coveted by Wall Street firms, no other profession starts people at that level. As the table on page 124 shows, three-quarters of private practitioners net more than $100,000, and a third make at least double that amount. But the important story is that the 1990s marked the end of an era in which medicine had a special dispensation. Each year since 1993 has seen a decline in physicians' incomes. The reason can be simply stated. In the past, "third parties" had agreed to whatever fees doctors filed; today, these payers are specifying how much they are willing to provide. Of every $100 that physicians now take in, only $17 comes from personal checks that their patients write. The rest is paid by insurance plans, government programs, and—increasingly—health maintenance organizations, which either set ceilings for reimbursement or decree what kind of treatment will be allowed.

Moreover, the table giving income ranges covers only private practitioners. As it happens, they total about 275,000 and account for only

Health, Justice, and Higher Education

Physicians (private practice net)

Over $400,000	5%
$300,000–$400,000	5%
$200,000–$300,000	23%
$150,000–$200,000	17%
$100,000–$150,000	27%
Under $100,000	23%

Medians

Private practice	$176,000
All physicians	$150,000

Lawyers (all)

Over $100,000	31%
$80,000–$100,000	13%
$60,000–$80,000	19%
$40,000–$60,000	15%
$20,000–$40,000	11%
Under $20,000	11%

Medians

Law firm partners	$135,000
All lawyers	$72,100

Professors (all ranks)

Over $100,000	3%
$80,000–$100,000	5%
$60,000–$80,000	16%
$50,000–$60,000	19%
$40,000–$50,000	23%
Under $40,000	34%

Medians

Full professors	$65,400
All ranks	$43,800

four of every ten men and women who possess medical degrees. About three-quarters of them are "sole proprietors" (as they are classed by the Internal Revenue Service), which simply means that they own and operate a business. The rest are either in partnerships or they have found it advantageous to turn their practices into corporations and allocate themselves a salary out of the proceeds. From an economic standpoint, those with their own offices have been an elite group. After fifteen years of practice, a self-employed physician will typically make $175,000. In fact, as will be seen, the medians for some specialties are considerably higher. The downside is that because of the duration of residencies, it is not possible to open—or even join—a practice until in one's early thirties. Not to mention the medical school loans that young doctors need to repay.

Still, of the 693,000 active physicians counted by the Bureau of Labor Statistics in 1995, no fewer than 417,000 were employed in salaried positions, where the median income was an unprepossessing $59,280. This is partly due to the fact that a quarter of them are recent graduates who hold low-paid residencies on hospital staffs. While the work is grueling and exploitative, most physicians look back on those years as the most exciting in their lives. The federal government employs some 23,000 civilian physicians, whose average salary is $81,505. Some oversee clinics on Indian reservations, while others conduct research at the Centers for Disease Control. Many physicians prefer public service or a nine-to-five schedule, even if it means settling for a modest salary.

A growing group of doctors are signing on full-time with health maintenance organizations. Their base pay tends be from $100,000 to $150,000, with the possibility of bonuses linked to the firm's bottom line. Medical school professors average about $140,000, although that figure is inflated by the much higher remuneration given to those who bring in research grants or attract affluent patients. Medical schools are now largely research centers, which makes teaching a secondary func-tion. At last count, their salaried faculty outnumbered students by a margin of 90,017 to 66,970. During the 1994–95 academic year, Cor-nell gave four of its top medical professors over $1 million, while Columbia had three at that level, and Stanford and the University of Pennsylvania have had at least one faculty member at the seven-digit tier. At other schools, salaries surpassing $500,000 are not unusual.

Rewards for Healing

In 1995, the number of physicians in the country totaled 693,000, more than the adult population of Indianapolis, our twelfth-ranking city. They are the best-paid professionals, with self-employed practitioners netting a median income of $176,000. Here are the medians for specialists in fifteen fields of private practice:

Orthopedic surgeons	$304,000
Cardiologists	$295,000
Radiology	$282,000
General surgeons	$242,000
Anesthesiologists	$220,000
Pathology	$215,000
Ophthalmologists	$215,000
Urology	$213,000
Otolaryngology	$207,000
Obstetrics-gynecology	$200,000
Emergency medicine	$185,000
Internists	$150,000
Psychiatrists	$137,000
Family-general	$122,000
Pediatricians	$113,000

The physicians who make the most tend to be associated with medical schools, although this does not necessarily mean they spend most of their time teaching students. Here are the top checks at twelve leading institutions:

Cornell	$1,762,083
Columbia	$1,560,500
Stanford	$1,133,832
Pennsylvania	$1,129,000
Tulane	$722,092
Miami	$698,943
Vanderbilt	$673,872
Georgetown	$671,737
Yale	$554,520
Johns Hopkins	$539,550
Chicago	$516,097
Howard	$461,930

One of the most fascinating facets of medicine is reflected in the disparities in incomes among specialties, or between those who specialize and general practitioners. The table on page 126 shows that earnings of orthopedic surgeons are almost more than triple those of pediatricians. Lay-people want to believe that the specialties with impressive titles must be extremely intricate, calling for unusual intelligence and skill. Such sentiments are fostered by the fact that the rest of us haven't any idea what highly paid specialists actually do. And even if we could watch them at work, we wouldn't know if what they did was easy or difficult. In fact, there is no evidence to show that cardiologists are smarter or more dexterous than, say, internists or psychiatrists. While we allow ourselves to be entranced by the mysteries of medicine, none of us really knows whether orthopedic surgery is any more complicated than overhauling a transmission. We know that police officers deliver babies with no ill effects, and on at least one occasion a submarine corpsman has performed a successful appendectomy.

Much of medicine now depends on high-tech equipment, which most of us wouldn't know how to plug in. As it happens, doctors are just as baffled by it. Many must deal with machines and procedures that hadn't been invented when they were in medical school, such as tissue plasminogen activators, noninvasive pulse-oximeters, and percutaneous transluminal coronary angioplasties. So they must take workshops and seminars where they are shown how the apparatus works. In these sessions, they are often taught by technicians, many of whom are only high school graduates who helped in designing and manufacturing the instruments. These technicians have also been asked to be present when the machines are used on patients, to show the physicians how they actually work. After all, having earned a medical degree is not necessarily evidence of technological proficiency. And in some cases, these high school graduates had to take over aspects of an operation, because they were the only ones in the room who understood the intricacies of the procedure. This meant, of course, that they were practicing medicine, not only without the specified training, but in violation of state and federal laws.

The advent of high-tech medicine also explains why some fields pay so much better than others. Through the 1950s, the incomes of both specialists and general practitioners were not far apart, and that is still generally the case in Europe. In the 1960s, an array of mysterious machines made their appearance, and hospitals began to look like aerospace laboratories. The simple scalpel, while still in use, no longer symbolizes the physician's skills. Complex machinery has taken its place: visualize doctors twirling knobs, watching dials, and checking images on screens. At that point, specialists started raising their fees, citing the wondrous procedures only they understood. In largest measure, the incomes of specialists are related to the apparent complexity of the equipment they are prone to employ. And small wonder that pediatricians, psychiatrists, and family practitioners, whose ministrations are more conversational, are at the bottom of the list. Health insurers accepted the specialists' explanations, as did the federal agencies that pay for work done under Medicaid and Medicare.

Undergirding the payment system are volumes listing thousands of procedures, with each assigned precise points on a "relative value" scale, which gauges the amount of skill and the intricacy of the equipment. Thus a high-tech esophagectomy performed by a gastroenterologist rates 63.67 points, which Medicare translates into a $3,378 payment. On the other hand, an internist who may need forty minutes to give a full physical examination gets 2.34 points. Since delivering babies tends to be a mid-tech routine, it only goes as high as 28.93. But that at least moves obstetricians nearer the middle of the income ladder. (In fact, they spend much of their time on prenatal care, which has lower point ratings.)

As was noted earlier, not many doctors break through the million-dollar barrier because most work on a fee-per-service basis, and there are just so many hours in a day. Still, some have set up impressive assembly lines, with patients prepped and waiting in sequential rooms. This obviously entails overhead. A study by *Medical Economics* found that plastic surgeons had to gross $454,000 to take home $228,000. But there are other medical routes to wealth. Some have set up radiology enterprises, buying their own CAT and MRI equipment, and operating them as profit-making businesses. Others have turned serving as an expert witness into a full-time sideline, netting better daily fees than they could get with a stethoscope. And still others take retainers from class-action attorneys, finding that almost everyone who is sent to them has a litigable malady.

The real road to wealth has been through HMOs, although not by treating patients. Physicians have been prominent among those heading these corporations. One is William McGuire, whose pay as head of United Healthcare averaged $6.5 million between 1991 and 1995. Another is Health Systems International's Malik Hasan, who averaged $5.3 million. Dr. Hasan's holdings in his company were valued at $137 million in 1996, putting him slightly behind Norman Payson, the physician who founded Healthsource, whose stock was worth $161 million. As hardly needs recalling, their HMOs are enterprises intent on a profitable balance sheets. But before registering shock, we might recall that medical practices have long been businesses, so what doctors took home were proprietor's profits. The change is that physicians who participate in managed care either receive salaries or are given flat fees for each of the patients on their lists. Just as most pharmacists no longer own their own drugstores, so growing numbers of physicians will find themselves employed by corporate organizations.

Between 1960 and 1995, the number of physicians practicing in the United States tripled, rising from about 230,000 to 695,000. If the size of the profession had simply kept pace with the population growth during that period, which was about 47 percent, we would have had 340,000 doctors in 1995. But during those thirty-five years, an additional 355,000 physicians were added to the rolls, so on a per capita count, we now have more than twice as many practitioners. In theory, this should have caused us to be a much healthier society. We needed more practitioners, we were told, because the earlier number could not attend to all the ills that beset Americans; with more entering practice, that shortfall would be remedied. By some aggregate measures, more of us are healthier than we were in 1960; longevity is up and infant deaths are down. But it is not self-evident that it was having more physicians that led people to stop smoking, use condoms, and buckle up. Nor can they be credited for the infrastructure changes— purer water, waste removal, food refrigeration—that account for most of the improved measures of health. Despite all of our musings about preventive medicine, doctors devote most of their energies to doing repair work after something goes wrong.

A report released in 1994 by the Johns Hopkins University School of Public Health noted that at current rates of graduation, the United States will have 165,000 superfluous physicians by the end of this century. Or, to put it more precisely, there will be no positions for them, given the changing structure of health delivery. In particular, less

129

money will be available for specialists, since managed care will allow fewer of their procedures. But not all of those who keep their jobs will be able to count on familiar forms of practice. Some, for example, will be taken on by HMOs that have contracts to provide medical services to prison inmates.

Even now, evidence suggests that we have more doctors than we need. Or, more candidly, not enough of them have enough to do, at least under the current system. In 1994, the most recent figures at this writing, doctors spent $126 million on advertising, largely in the *Yellow Pages* of metropolitan areas. In Manhattan's directory, the nation's largest listing of physicians spreads over seventy-nine pages. But fifty-six of them are devoted entirely to display advertisements, many of which occupy an entire page. If doctors had their appointment books filled, they wouldn't be pleading for more customers. Not only that, the most widely advertised offerings are cosmetic surgery, treatments for baldness, even removal of tattoos, which may count as medical procedures but are not generally critical to good health.

Over the past thirty-five years, the number of lawyers in the nation has more than quadrupled, rising from 213,000 in 1960 to 894,000 in 1995, a period during which the general population rose by somewhat less than 50 percent. The United States now has more attorneys than the adult inhabitants of Atlanta, Pittsburgh, and St. Louis taken together. Bills for legal services increased at an even faster pace: more than four times the figure for the rest of the economy, even after allowing for inflation. Thus far, the expansion of the profession has not depressed its earnings. Rather, the country is cutting expenses in other areas—or cutting back on growth—so it can pay the bills of its lawyers.

Law differs from medicine in at least two important respects. To start, it is requires a much smaller investment. Fledgling physicians must submit to a decade-long regimen renowned for its unyielding rules. Indeed, they must devote their college years to what is essentially a vocational program, then spend their late twenties as round-the-clock residents. The result is that few physicians leave their profession. Nor do many want to. Most have enjoyed their work and it has provided generous incomes. Still, too much was put in to allow an easy shift to another calling. (The few who do leave tend to go into medical administration.) It will be instructive to see what will happen if, as predicted, there will not be enough paying positions for everyone with a medical degree.

Becoming a lawyer is relatively easy. Colleges do not have rigid prelaw programs, and just about anyone who wishes can gain admission to some law school. Fees for three years of legal study might total around $60,000, which is not an immense investment of time or money. Thus when individuals find that they do not like practicing law, or are not succeeding at it, they avail themselves of opportunities in other occupations. These departures suggest that among the current total of 894,000 lawyers, perhaps as many as a third will in time find themselves doing something else.

The second difference rests with their clienteles. Doctors always have individual patients. That is to say, they cannot care for people in or as groups. (An exception may be psychotherapy.) Even if they work in clinics, treating college students or prison inmates, they deal with each person's condition, one at a time. Consequently, this limits their incomes to whatever sources are willing to pay for each individual they treat. Lawyers, on the other hand, can practice on behalf of corporations and business associations, as well as undertake class actions involving large numbers of litigants. That kind of work permits more lawyers than doctors to attain $1 million incomes. (True, one can get nice fees from people who are rich, but this is a fairly limited clientele.)

In 1995, the Bureau of Labor Statistics located a total of 894,000 actively employed lawyers, of whom 379,000 were solo practitioners or partners in firms, while the other 515,000 had salaried positions in law firms or with other employers. In 1993, the Census Bureau's most recent study of occupations computed that the median income for all attorneys was $72,144. And in 1994, the Internal Revenue Service received "sole proprietorship" returns from 231,416 lawyers, with an average net income of $46,995, which suggests that some may be practicing part-time and will soon be leaving the profession. The IRS also received returns from 28,990 partnerships, which had a total of 138,855 partners, and these lawyers reported a net average of $135,020, substantially more than their solo colleagues. The median for the 515,000 salaried practitioners was $58,200, breaking into $60,892 for the 360,000 men and $49,816 for the 155,000 women.

Recent years have seen law schools turning out some forty thousand graduates each year, all of whom are eager for employment. Given the

size of this pool, public service agencies find they can get able applicants for quite modest salaries. Here, according to the *National Law
Journal*'s 1995 survey, is what recent graduates are offered. On the
prosecution's side, Florida's Broward County starts its people at
$25,000, while the Texas attorney general's office begins with $30,492.
Chicago's novitiate public defenders get $32,772, which is at least
more than Western Kentucky Legal Services' $24,200. Law clerkships
for the 846 federal judges, generally coveted positions, pay $36,426
during the first year. With these salaries, a requisite would be a rent-
sharing roommate.

But other salaries in the legal profession run considerably higher. For
example, full professors at the University of Michigan law school average $142,750; seventh-year associates at the Los Angeles firm of Latham
& Watkins make as much as $185,000; and the chief justice of the
United States receives $171,500, while his eight associates get $164,100.
Of course, business pays better. The median compensation for chief legal
officers came to $222,000 in 1995. However, many were well above the
median. The general counsel at Avon Products made $405,768; Camp-
bell's soup gave its top lawyer $625,209; and Johnson & Johnson paid out
$873,375. Near the top was Philip Morris's attorney, with $1.3 million;
and even higher was Viacom's chief counsel, whose $860,000 salary was
augmented by a $2.2 million bonus. The best government pay goes to the
attorney general, who receives $148,400, which turns out to be $100 more
than the prebonus salary of a sixth-year associate in New York's Chad-
bourne & Parke firm. (The attorney general isn't allowed bonuses,
even in a good year.) A total of 24,699 "general attorneys" work for federal agencies, and their salaries average $68,271. The navy's judge advo-
cate general gets a base figure of $118,145, with another $13,442 available
for housing and related expenses.

In 1993, the Census Bureau counted 158,000 "legal establish-
ments," which ranged from one-person offices (with or without a secretary) to the Baker & McKenzie firm with its 2,281 lawyers and as
many supporting personnel. The typical law office had 6.2 persons on
its payroll, and their average pay came to $41,912, but that includes the
secretaries. A private survey of 555 large law firms, completed in 1994,
found that fifth-year associates, who tend to be in their late twenties,
typically made $75,830. Partnerships are usually awarded at the end of
one's seventh year. Nationally, the median compensation upon getting

that promotion is $93,294 and rises to $206,118 after about twenty years as a partner. The median compensations for partners in the 555 firms that were studied was $168,000, ranging from $145,019 in Colorado to $187,964 in Florida.

At the summit are the nation's one hundred wealthiest firms, which are analyzed each summer by *American Lawyer* magazine. Taken together, these one hundred partnerships had revenues of $16.2 billion in 1995, which was almost one-seventh of the nation's legal billings. The firms had 38,156 attorneys on their payrolls, of whom 13,131 were partners with ownership stakes in their firms, while most of the other 25,025 were salaried associates. The typical firm thus had 131 partners, and their average share of the year-end profits came to $446,000. Of course, that average conceals a wide range, not least because the one hundred firms are spread among twenty cities. At the top was New York's Wachtell, Lipton, whose members averaged over $1,595,000. Coming in last was Cleveland's Arter & Hadden, at $170,000.

Not surprisingly, New York leads the list by a comfortable margin. The 1,059 partners in its ten wealthiest firms averaged $1,043,201 in 1995. The 1,125 in the top ten firms in Washington, D.C., averaged $418,480. Next come the 1,263 in the San Francisco Bay Area, at $339,418. Perhaps because Chicago's top ten firms are larger, with a total of 1,808 partners, the average income per partner is a more modest $311,446.

The table on page 134 lists the compensation per partner in the twenty best-paying firms in twenty cities, as well as the highest salaries for starting associates in some of the same cities and several others. One fact that comes across right away is that variations in pay among the associates are less pronounced than for the partners. In fact, if we look at the cities that are on both lists, it appears that what associates are paid relates quite closely to the average earnings in each area. (The Bureau of Labor Statistics charts wages by metropolitan areas since there is a lot of commuting between cities and suburbs.) While firms may say that they must make good offers to get the people they want, they do not go beyond two and a half times what is typically made by residents of their areas.

More often than not, the associates that the top firms recruit move in from out of town, so much of their compensation will go for housing. Still, beginning lawyers are expected to put in a lot of night and weekend work, so they may not have to spend much on leisure diver-

Lawyers: Partners and Starters

Profits per Partner in City's Wealthiest Firm

New York (Wachtell, Lipton)	$1,595,000
Chicago (Kirkland and Ellis)	$685,000
Los Angeles (Latham and Watkins)	$635,000
Washington, D.C. (Williams and Connolly)	$635,000
Boston (Hale and Dorr)	$490,000
Atlanta (King and Spaulding)	$485,000
San Francisco (Wilson, Sonsini)	$480,000
Miami (Greenberg, Traurig)	$460,000
Houston (Andrews and Kurth)	$435,000
Cleveland (Jones, Day)	$425,000
Philadelphia (Morgan, Lewis)	$405,000
Detroit (Honigman Miller)	$320,000
Tampa (Holland and Knight)	$320,000
Milwaukee (Foley and Lardner)	$310,000
Richmond (Hunton and Williams)	$300,000
Pittsburgh (Kirkpatrick and Lockhart)	$290,000
Baltimore (Piper and Narbury)	$275,000
Seattle (Perkins, Cole)	$260,000
St. Louis (Bryan, Cave)	$255,000
Minneapolis (Dorsey and Whitney)	$220,000

Salaries of Starting Associates

New York (Chadbourne and Park)	$85,000
Los Angeles (Latham and Watkins)	$78,000
Washington, D.C. (Dickstein Shapiro)	$74,000
Chicago (Bell, Boyd)	$70,000
Houston (Andrews and Kurth)	$63,500
Milwaukee (Godfrey and Kahn)	$63,500
Miami (Greenberg Traurig)	$63,000
Philadelphia (Blank, Rome)	$63,000
Cleveland (Benesch, Friedlander)	$60,000
Stamford (Cummings and Lockwood)	$60,000
Cincinnati (Taft, Stettinius)	$58,000
Indianapolis (Ice Miller)	$58,000
Dallas (Hughes and Luce)	$56,000
St. Louis (Lewis, Rice)	$56,000
Winston-Salem (Womble Carlyle)	$56,000
Phoenix (Brown and Bain)	$55,000
New Orleans (Jones, Walker)	$53,000
Rochester (Nixon, Hargrave)	$52,000
Austin (Clark, Thomas)	$50,000
Buffalo (Phillips, Lytle)	$50,000

sions. When it comes to partners, the picture is quite different. Since they have completed their apprenticeships, they now leave the office earlier and thus have more time for expensive activities. But this does not explain why the relative incomes of attorneys in New York are almost twice those of Chicago and Los Angeles, or triple those for Philadelphia and almost five times the figure for St. Louis. One reason, which will be discussed shortly, is that some New York law firms have a mystique that persuades clients to pay their prices. But there is another reason, which extends beyond the legal profession.

By and large, the average earnings in any area reflect its general cost of living. Indeed, the relation is reciprocal, since lower wages allow prices to be lower. Housing is markedly cheaper in some parts of the country, but so are the salaries people are paid. (Most of the doctors who fall below the $176,000 median live in regions where everyone makes less.) An area's cost of living is computed by entering the prices charged locally for a standard "basket" of goods and services. One problem—and there are many—is that the same collection of items is used everywhere in the country. True, tank tops and corn flakes are national commodities. So the contents of the official basket probably reflect the needs and tastes of most Americans, including junior attorneys. However, at higher pay levels, a more sophisticated index may be required.

How Well Do Lawyers Live?
Compensations as Multiples of Average Earnings

	Average Area Earnings	High-Pay Partners	High-Pay Associates
New York	$39,933	39.9	2.1
Chicago	$31,339	21.9	2.2
Los Angeles	$31,831	20.0	2.5
Washington, D.C.	$33,949	18.7	2.2
Miami	$26,493	17.4	2.4
Cleveland	$27,927	15.2	2.2
Houston	$30,349	14.3	2.1
Philadelphia	$30,519	13.3	2.1
Milwaukee	$26,958	11.5	2.4

Compensations for the top-paid partners in New York, Chicago, Los Angeles, and Washington, D.C.—all averaging above $600,000— reflect what might be called the high-status cost of living in their areas. These cities and their surrounding areas offer a wide range of expensive purchases and diversions, the partaking of which becomes integral to the definition of an appropriate life. So a New York basket might include $140 opera tickets, Chicago's could contain smoked sturgeon at $50 a pound, while Los Angeles's would have nursery school fees totaling $12,000. As it happens, everyday items are not conspicuously cheaper in Milwaukee or St. Louis. The big difference is that they have fewer high-price attractions to lure one's money. Thus $255,000 goes a long way in St. Louis, indeed further than twice that pay goes in New York. After all, it doesn't have restaurants where the bill can total $600 for a party of four.

Another well-compensated segment of the legal profession consists of attorneys who specialize in filing suits against corporations for dangerous or defective products, employment discrimination, and other actions that can produce staggering verdicts or settlements. About ten of these lawyers win as much as $10 million in a good year, although such cases are usually only resolved after years of litigation. And for every victory, there can be strings of losses. These lawyers tend to have modest overhead expenses, sometimes with only a dozen associates. Perhaps not surprisingly, Texas has been the most fertile ground for this kind of practice. Some of America's wealthiest attorneys work from offices in towns such as Beaumont and San Antonio, where if $600 were paid out at dinner, it could feed everybody in the restaurant.

In the worlds of music and motion pictures, a "star system" exists. In any given season, a fairly small number of performers rise well above the rest. During their time at the top, they command public attention and win universal recognition. (Of course, universes vary. Some incline toward Kurt Masur, while others hitch their wagons to Hootie and the Blowfish.) In some cases, stars are unusually talented; in others, personal magnetism accounts for their popularity. Their ascent may also be due to their being expertly packaged and sold. But what makes the system work is that the rest of us apparently have a need for the kind of firmament they represent.

A similar system may be found in the professions. The fields of pediatric surgery, liability litigation, and deconstructive criticism have stars, too. Here, the rosters tend to be short, partly because potential clienteles cannot be expected to remember many names, but also because the premise of creating stars is that there will be only a few of them. The professions have a further presumption of specialized knowledge, which laypeople cannot or are not allowed to fathom. Thus a great deal of stress is placed on rewarding "the best" persons within particular callings. Certainly, by monetary measures, we may presume that the New York law firm of Wachtell, Lipton, Rosen & Katz ranks among the very best in its profession. Why else would its clients accept a scale of fees that in 1995 netted its partners an average compensation of almost $1.6 million? Nor can we doubt that the Cornell medical school has one of the nation's best cardiothoracic surgeons, since patients—or other parties—consented to fees that yielded him a one-year pay package approaching $1.8 million. A bit behind, but still well ahead of his peers, was a star professor of electrical engineering at the Massachusetts Institute of Technology, whose compensation in a recent year came to $321,967. Stars also shine in other academic disciplines. Brandeis University pays $173,992 to a much sought professor of classics.

All of these cases carry the same message: some individuals and organizations want "the best" that may be available and are willing to pay whatever those at the top of their fields may charge. Of course, it is beyond the capacities of most of us to assess the quality of cardiothoracic surgeons and corporate litigators. Still, enough clients and patients take high fees as evidence of a practitioner's competence. According to this logic, if they are paid that much, they must be at the summit of their professions. The rest of us are not untouched by this kind of reasoning. How many of us would go to a dentist whose full charge for a half hour's work was $10?

By some numerical measures, the United States is the best-educated nation in the world. We have more institutions of higher learning (3,632), more enrolled students (16.1 million), and more full-time faculty (553,000). True, about 40 percent of the colleges are two-year schools, some 35 percent of the students attend part-time, and an increasing share of the instruction is handled by 275,000 part-time teachers. At best, a few dozen schools are difficult to get into. Even well-known colleges such as Lehigh and Southern Methodist take 70 percent of their applicants. Most admit virtually everyone who applies. Indeed, many now advertise in an effort to fill their dormitories and classrooms. Not all students complete their courses of study. Of the current crop of 12.3 million undergraduates, only half will eventually receive a bachelor's degree.

The academic world may be the most isolated of professions. While we may not understand what physicians do, in most of our dealings we meet with them face-to-face. But after ending their student days, few adults are in a position to assess what professors actually do. That reason alone makes it difficult for outsiders to draw conclusions about their compensation. So it would be best to begin with the numbers.

According to the Bureau of Labor Statistics, the median salary for the 553,000 full-time faculty members comes to $43,836, which breaks down into $48,932 for the 325,000 men, and $38,220 for the 228,000 women. But these figures cover all academic ranks at all kinds of institutions. More precise information can be culled from the annual surveys done by the American Association of University Professors. While confined to some 1,500 institutions, they cover all with national reputations and supply details on pay patterns for 220,000 college teachers. Thus the assistant professors at Stanford average $55,100, while the full professors at California Lutheran University average $52,400. At UCLA, the 159 men at the rank of associate professor make $57,900, while the figure for the 83 women is $54,700.

The table on page 124 noted that 3 percent of all full-time faculty members—a total of 6,068 professors—made at least $100,000. And as the table on page 139 indicates, there are five institutions where the average for all of their full professors exceeds that figure. What college teachers have in common, whether they are Arizona State University's $27,500 instructors or Harvard's $107,000 professors, is that they need to be on their campuses for a surprisingly small potion of the year. Courses are usually scheduled for thirty weeks, including examination periods. And most professors arrange their classes and office hours for two or three days on the campus. In short, the basic work year for college faculties adds up to 90 days, not counting sabbaticals, which allow them every seventh year off. Most other Americans are expected to spend 250 days at their place of employment.

Needless to say, professors will respond that they put in long hours

Average Salaries for Full Professors, 1995–96

Main State Campuses

1.	New Jersey	$90,800
2.	California (Berkeley)	$86,500
3.	Michigan	$85,000
4.	Connecticut	$82,400
5.	Virginia	$81,400
6.	Delaware	$79,700
7.	Pennsylvania	$77,600
8.	New York (Albany)	$77,100
9.	Maryland	$76,600
10.	Ohio	$76,400
11.	Texas	$76,100
12.	North Carolina	$75,900
13.	Illinois	$75,200
14.	Iowa	$74,300
15.	Minnesota	$73,000
16.	Indiana	$72,400
17.	Colorado	$71,900
18.	Nevada	$70,800
19.	Hawaii	$70,600
20.	Massachusetts	$70,500
21.	Wisconsin	$70,400
22.	Nebraska	$70,300
23.	Washington	$70,200
24.	Arizona	$69,100
25.	Alaska	$68,700
26.	Georgia	$68,500
27.	Missouri	$68,400
28.	Utah	$68,000
29.	Kentucky	$67,600
30.	Florida	$66,000
31.	South Carolina	$65,800
32.	Rhode Island	$65,300
33.	Tennessee	$65,100
34.	New Hampshire	$64,300
35.	Alabama	$63,800
36.	New Mexico	$63,700
37.	Kansas	$63,300
38.	Vermont	$63,100
39.	Oklahoma	$62,700
40.	Mississippi	$61,600
41.	Oregon	$60,900
42.	Arkansas	$60,400
43.	Louisiana	$59,200
44.	Wyoming	$58,100
46.	West Virginia	$58,100
47.	Idaho	$56,100
48.	South Dakota	$50,600
49.	Montana	$49,600
50.	North Dakota	$47,900

Private Universities

Harvard	$107,000
Stanford	$103,100
Cal Tech	$103,100
Princeton	$101,400
Yale	$100,500
MIT	$96,900
NYU	$96,800
Chicago	$96,500
Columbia	$93,000
Northwestern	$92,000
Duke	$91,700
Georgetown	$91,200
Notre Dame	$86,800
Johns Hopkins	$84,800
Dartmouth	$83,700
Cornell	$82,200
Brown	$80,000
Rochester	$78,500

Liberal Arts Colleges

Pomona	$78,400
Smith	$78,400
Barnard	$77,900
Bowdoin	$77,300
Wesleyan	$77,300
Amherst	$77,200
Williams	$77,000
Colgate	$75,000
Bates	$73,300
Carleton	$67,600
Colorado College	$66,100
Reed	$63,900
Oberlin	$63,400
Beloit	$57,600
Earlham	$53,300

Historically Black Institutions

Cheyney State	$73,300
Howard	$67,600
Spelman	$57,300
Hampton	$56,000
Florida A&M	$55,400
Xavier	$51,100
Grambling State	$49,000
Alcorn State	$47,600
Shaw	$35,000

at home preparing their classes, and in laboratories or libraries conducting research. Some undoubtedly do. But most only marginally revise their courses, and the majority of senior people have long ceased producing all save for an occasional book review. And the bulk of what does get published is read by small circles of colleagues, since citing each other's work is the key to building scholarly careers. Or they will allude to the countless hours they spend on committees. In fact, this mode of resolving issues is carried to extremes on campuses. Where else do grown men and women meet for so many afternoons to deliberate on the most trivial of topics?

But what really differentiates the academic profession is the policy known as tenure. In theory, it began as a way to protect teachers who espoused unpopular views. However, when put to the test, it turned out to be a fragile shield. Certainly, during the 1950s, when the loyalty of many Americans was being questioned, tenure did not prevent administrators and legislators from ending the careers of many professors. Today, academic tenure assures faculty members that they will have job security for the rest of their lives. About the only causes for dismissal are conviction of a felony or egregious displays of moral turpitude. While schoolteachers and civil servants often have similar protections, they can be removed for incompetence, even if it requires a costly series of hearings. Professors can stay on as long as they like, especially since colleges are no longer allowed to set a retirement age.

One result of lifetime security is that many faculties look like inverted pyramids. Duke's full professors comprise 53 percent of the teaching staff; at Yale, it's 57 percent; at Stanford, 64 percent. Because of their top-heavy pay, senior professors consume so much of the college budget—in some schools, three-quarters of instructional costs—that little remains to hire junior people. Thus every every full professor who refuses to retire is preventing several young scholars from beginning their careers. Law firms, by way of contrast, can force the resignation of unproductive partners.

A well-kept academic secret is that faculties make mistakes. Tenure is usually given to people in their midthirties who give signs of scholarly promise. In all too many instances, that potential never blossoms, perhaps never existed. Every college and university, even those with national reputations, has professors of whom no one has heard, for the simple reason that they have long since stopped contributing to scholarly endeavors. Were they to seek employment elsewhere, no other school would want them. Yet under the shield of tenure, they, too, can stay on for as long as they like, unless they neglect to show up for their classes, and even then allowances may be made. Indeed, these protected professors often share in annual raises, perhaps due to collegial solidarity or as a way of denying that a mistake has been made.

In common with medicine and law, the academic world makes much of its stars. The $1 million packages of top medical professors not only head the list, but are far ahead of their colleagues in private practice. Still, Northwestern University pays one of its accounting professors $294,194, Princeton gives $233,546 to a star psychologist, while Cal Tech sets aside $199,045 for a professor of physics. In these cases and others, schools seek recognized scholars because their presence adds to the luster of the campus. Every institution wants people who are esteemed within their own disciplines, and it's even better if their names are known beyond the Ivied world. Hence the periodic raids, the recurring flirtations, the matching of offers to keep people from straying. Just as MGM was MGM because its roster included Clark Gable, Norma Shearer, and Jean Harlow, so Harvard is Harvard because it can point to having Laurence Tribe, Stephen Jay Gould, and Henry Louis Gates.

So professors are not altogether immune from market forces. The most popular major today is business, attracting close to a quarter of all undergraduates, and colleges must compete for people to teach those courses. Full professors of business average over $75,000, with many in the $100,000 group, compared with $55,000 going to their colleagues in philosophy. (In fact, the latter salary could be considered generous, since less than one-half of 1 percent of current students major in philosophy.) But what raises the bidding for business professors is not that there is a shortage of people who have had experience in the field. On the contrary, many men and women have had impressive entrepreneurial and corporate careers, and possess personalities suited for classroom teaching. Quite a few might like the change of pace and would do it for token salaries. The obstacle is the academic rule that to be granted full faculty status, professors are expected to have a doctorate, and business is not an area where many people are moved to pursue a Ph.D. As a further irony, business schools could find their accreditations at risk if too many of their faculty members came straight from the business world.

But where colleges compete most vigorously is in that realm of education called intercollegiate athletics. The head football coaches at Florida State University, Bobby Bowden, has received a compensation package worth $975,000. In fact, not all of that sum comes from the school itself, since Bowden's straight salary was more in the vicinity of $150,000. However, his position as a highly visible figure could be counted on to bring him offers of payments for endorsements, which in a recent year exceeded $600,000, plus additional sums for speaking engagements. Of course, coaches are not the only academic employees who can use their status to advantage. Prof. Laurence Tribe receives a mere $160,000 from Harvard Law School, but the prestige of that affiliation had to have something to do with the $2 million he received in a recent year for advising corporate clients.

The star system shows no sign of waning in higher education, since money can generally be found for acquiring a luminary. And most current incumbents will be allowed to keep their slender work schedules and lifetime-tenure guarantees. As has been seen, they are continuing to give themselves annual raises, even while junior people are being dismissed or not being hired at all. But, as with medicine, the profession is changing. States are slashing their support for public universities, and there are fewer federal funds for private schools. Nor does alumni support fill the gap. (If it did, Dartmouth would not be billing its students $21,950 simply for sitting in classes.) So the salad days of the academy are coming to an end. Just as the coming generation of physicians are unlikely to have independent practices, so new professors will enjoy little or no job security. Colleges are already hiring more part-time teachers, especially for introductory sections, who can shoulder a full load of courses at a fraction of the old cost. Most of these adjuncts are graduate students. Their low wages—typically $7,000 a semester—are excused on the grounds that they are learning to teach. Here they share something with medical residents, who are said to practice on their patients.

In fact, all three professions face similar futures. Far fewer lawyers will be promoted to partnerships. And more of those who are will find themselves edged out if they do not augment the firm's profits. Still, as has been noted, many people who begin with legal careers have always moved into other occupations, and that pattern will persist. Physicians face a bleaker future. Not only will more patients get their care through health maintenance organizations, but these groups will also decide how many doctors they need. The prospect of unemployed physicians is real, most certainly for recent graduates but also for others in their middle years. Among young academics, this experience is not new. Since the early 1980s, their profession has been overloaded with senior people, who have shown scant concern for those who will follow them. On the contrary, they have continued recruiting graduate students to fill their seminars and assist with teaching and research, even as they knew there would be no positions for them.

The professions flourished during most of the postwar period for a simple reason: an abundance of money. Public funds were showered on higher education, increasing the perquisites of professors, ranging from frequent sabbaticals to reduced teaching loads. Federal money also spurred the growth of medical schools, turning them into huge research centers with budgets for expensive new technologies. Employers, in their turn, were willing to pay whatever fee physicians billed for treating employees. And companies seldom questioned the invoices submitted by their law firms, which allowed a generous attitude on promotions to partnerships.

But those days have passed and are unlikely to return. The stars will continue to shine, and some will even set records for annual earnings. But law and medicine and higher education will offer fewer of the well-paid careers that earlier generations could take for granted.

CHAPTER EIGHT

OUTCASTES
AND IMMIGRANTS

If the United States were truly a color-blind society, then black and white Americans would show much the same distribution across the income spectrum. Quite clearly, they don't.

In 1865, at the close of the Civil War, this country had its chance to welcome emancipated slaves as full citizens. Instead, it chose to replace bondage with a caste condition, under which descendants of slaves would be kept subordinate and segregated. And caste is an appropriate description, since it means a hereditary social classification that will restrict every aspect of a member's life. America has perpetuated this condition for well over a century, never giving its citizens of African descent opportunities equal to persons of other ancestries, including recent immigrants.

But, we often hear, race isn't the only reason for the discrepancy between the incomes of black and white Americans. If two groups vary in income, the disparity could be due to other factors, such as marital status, level of education, or commitments to careers. Only if these are factored into the equations can we begin to talk meaningfully about the impact of ancestry. Of course that can and should be done, and it will be done here. Yet before we begin, it is worth asking why these additional disparities exist. It could well be that because they are members of a caste, black Americans will have a lesser likelihood of steady employment, comparable schooling, and stable marriages.

Let's start with a few words on the place of race in the world's oldest democracy. Some have assailed the very concept of race. Dividing humanity into "races" is an artificial exercise, with no basis in genetics, let alone common sense. That is absolutely true. Yet the fact remains that America has accepted the notion of race for close to four centuries: since the first slaves were brought to Virginia in 1619. And while slavery was ended 246 years later, its legacy persists in an unwillingness to view its descendants as fully equal Americans. This record has resulted in the country's principal constituents—those whose ancestors came from Europe and persons with African forebears—being seen and defined as races. So even if the division is artificial, it remains embedded in millions of minds, and that gives it a reality.*

The chief task in this chapter will be to analyze variations in income, wealth, and occupations to ascertain whether they have a basis in race. Attention will also be paid to changes that have taken place over the past several decades, to see how far the country has moved toward equity and equality, or if there has actually been retrogression.

The figures in the table on page 147 tell a curious—and disturbing—story about what has occurred within and between the races during recent decades. In 1975, black households were arrayed in a classic pyramid, with over half relegated to its two lowest tiers. White families had already transformed themselves into an inverted pyramid with a smooth and continuous slope. For every $1,000 received by white families, black households were making do with $605. In fact, the 1975 ratio represented an all-time high. In 1960, it had been $554, up from $542 a decade earlier, showing that what passes as racial progress moves at a glacial pace. In 1975, black men and women were seldom considered for managerial jobs, in part because comparatively few of them had college credentials. Indeed, they were only about a third as apt as whites to have bachelor's degrees. Yet well over half maintained two-parent households, which generally meant a man's wage was coming in, and in

*Not all Americans are encompassed by the racial division. An omnibus group called Asians embraces people from Osaka, in Japan, to Istanbul, in Turkey. Individuals from China, Korea, and Japan were once combined as "Orientals," but that term is rarely used today, nor are allusions to a "yellow" race. Hispanics are another expansive group, among whom may be found black Cubans, blue-eyed Argentines, indigenous Indians, and every conceivable permutation of these origins. There are even Asian Hispanics, such as Alberto Fujimori, the president of Peru. By and large, Asians and Hispanics, along with American Indians and immigrants from the Middle East, have chosen to sit on the sidelines while the racial drama plays itself out. While a few may use the "white" option, most acknowledge that adopting a racial identification brings more trouble than benefits.

many families the wife also worked. The problem was that black men and women were paid the lowest possible wages, so even with two sets of earnings they were well below the national norm.

By 1995, the white pyramid not only remained inverted, but had taken an unprecedented shape. Four out of ten of the nation's white families were making more than $50,000. The distribution for black

	Black and White Families: Changing Configurations **(in 1995-value dollars)**	
White	**1975**	**Black**
33.2%	Over $50,000	13.9%
23.8%	$35,000–$50,000	16.4%
16.3%	$25,000–$35,000	17.0%
15.1%	$15,000–$25,000	21.0%
11.6%	Under $15,000	31.7%
$39,356 ($1,000)	Median Income (ratio)	$23,806 ($605)
White	**1995**	**Black**
44.0%	Over $50,000	21.3%
19.4%	$35,000–$50,000	15.9%
14.0%	$25,000–$35,000	14.3%
12.9%	$15,000–$25,000	18.3%
9.7%	Under $15,000	30.2%
$45,018 ($1,000)	Median Income (ratio)	$25,970 ($577)
Diagrams above are not necessarily to scale.		

households is also unique. The growth of the black upper-income stratum has been a much hailed hallmark of our time. Liberals cite it as proof that their social programs have worked, opening the middle class to people hitherto denied entry. Conservatives say it shows that black Americans can make it, so there is no more need for special aid. To what extent the expansion of this group has been a result of affirmative action will be explored later in this chapter. What can be said for sure is that more black Americans have been investing in their own education, and the margin between the races is now discernibly smaller. Even more than with whites, the top black group drew recruits from the slightly lower tiers.

Yet what stands out is that the 1995 median ratio for black families—that is, what they were making for every $1,000 received by white families—is actually lower than the 1975 figure. In any scheme of history, something like this should not happen. Twenty years should have contributed at least a few digits toward closing the racial gap. The black distribution, while no longer a pyramid, retains the wide bottom base it had two decades earlier. In 1975, that level had many homes with two earners, who stayed afloat by pooling their wages. Today, the households with the lowest incomes are more apt to be headed by single mothers, many of whom work while others get by on public assistance. Income distribution among black Americans has thus changed more markedly than it has among whites, with its two largest tiers now at the top and the very bottom.

Several years ago, the Census Bureau tried to estimate what black incomes might be if some of their attributes paralleled those of white householders. If educational levels were equal, black income would rise by about 15 percent. And if both groups had the same percentage of two-parent families, black income would increase by slightly over 22 percent. Indeed, more recent figures show that black married couples where both spouses work earn $920 for every $1,000 made by their white counterparts, which is quite close to parity. However, less than a quarter of black families are in that favored situation. At the end of their analysis, the Census found if "incomes of blacks are standardized on the basis of white characteristics," their income ratio would rise to $780 per $1,000. This is a considerable step, but it leaves a long way to go. So the racial money gap arises from more than variations in characteristics such as education and family composition. The Census simply concluded that "other factors are clearly at work." Perhaps, as a civil service agency, they found it prudent not to delve into what those other determinants might be. Or, as statisticians, they may believe that prejudice and discrimination cannot be entered into equations in a reliable way.

One way to determine what other factors contribute to the racial income gap is to identify some groups of people who appear to be comparable in relevant ways. The 1990 Census has specific income information on the 134,599 black and white lawyers who were then between the ages of thirty-five and thirty-nine. Since they had all completed college and law school and were in the same age range, we can look for economic differentials and then ask why they exist. The Census found that black men earned $745 for every $1,000 made by their white colleagues. How to account for the $255 per $1,000 discrepancy, which amounted to $20,453 a year at the time of the Census count? Could the cause be race-based discrimination, one of those "other factors" that is not measured in the numbers? Some people may respond that not all educations are equal, and that the white men were more apt to have attended Harvard Law School, while the black men may have done their legal studies at Howard University. However, the individuals we are examining are at least a dozen years from law school, and by that time practical skills should outweigh what you once did in a classroom.

The candid answer seems to be that black men are not as likely to be offered better-paying positions. Thus the Census also found that more take salaried jobs, since fewer are awarded partnerships or have the

	134,599 Lawyers		
	Average Earnings of Attorney, Age 35 to 39		
	White	**Black**	**Race Ratio**
Men	$79,838	$59,385	$745
Women	$52,339	$48,443	$926
Sex Ratio	$656	$816	
Salaried	59.3%	74.6%	

resources to set up practices of their own. Of course, it is hard to prove racial bias, especially when lawyers say that subtle judgments come into play with hirings and promotions. Many of these assessments turn on whether the candidate looks like "our kind of person" or if he will "fit in" with the firm and its clients. Even though law firms rarely acknowledge it, or might even be unaware of it, a job candidate's passing as acceptable requires his being "white." Needless to say, every firm will insist that they hope to find black partners who meet their criteria. Perhaps they are looking for a fledgling Colin Powell with a legal degree.

Black women lawyers are as likely as black men lawyers to have attended Howard or comparable law schools, yet their incomes come a lot closer to parity when compared with those of white women. But then, as the Census findings show, white women only earn $656 for each $1,000 made by white men. Most women are relegated to a lower tier of legal practice, and at that level a person's race is less of a factor. Indeed, in every organization, the number of black faces dwindles as one moves into higher ranks. In any event, since the law and other occupations seem to have concluded that black women are as capable as white women, one may wonder why they have not made a similar judgment about black men. Because they are disinclined to do so, a Johnnie Cochran had to build his career on police brutality cases since he did not pass the "fit in" test at elite Los Angeles firms.

Young black Americans are often exhorted to stay in school, as that is the only realistic way to break the cycle of prejudice. Here we may again look at somewhat comparable individuals, in this case black and white men and women aged thirty-five to forty-four. At first glance, education does seem to pay off. Black men who get bachelor's degrees make $1,865 for every $1,000 earned by black men who only finished high school. For black women, the contrast is an impressive $2,033 per $1,000. Yet those computations only make the comparisons *within* the black community. What also emerges is that if black men make the effort to finish college, by the time they are between the ages of thirty-five and forty-four, they are still getting only $739 for every $1,000 going to white male college graduates.

As it turns out, black women who have finished college receive even more than their white female counterparts: their ratio is $1,104 per $1,000. The chief reason is that black women devote more years to their careers. Nor should this be surprising, since they are more likely to be single or, if married, cannot count on having a husband with high earnings. What should be added is that if and when organizations feel compelled to hire more black workers, they generally prefer to take on black women rather than black men. Black women, like all women, are perceived as being less assertive and more accommodating than their male counterparts. Hence employers hope that they will show less resentment or hostility and will be less apt to present themselves as "black" in demeanor and appearance. In addition, black and white women tend to mingle more easily in workplace settings than do black and white men. This is partly because women tend to feel less tense about race. But there is also evidence that women can ignore racial lines in acknowledging common experiences, at least to a far greater extent than white men and black men are willing or able to do.

The table on page 152 provides a sampling of where black workers tend to be found in the employment force. Occupations where they have the strongest showing are not necessarily menial. Still, they do more than their share of janitorial chores and cleaning up after others, which have been traditional "black" positions. As the tabulations show, the positions where blacks have greatest representation tend to be jobs that whites are reluctant to take (hotel maids and nursing aides) as well as at lower governmental levels (corrections officers and postal clerks). They are also used for repetitive tasks (telephone operators and pressing-machine operators) and work in fields where the clienteles have become disproportionately black (bus driving and social work).

Even at the end of the 1990s, after more than a generation of civil rights legislation and rhetoric about equal opportunity, less than 2 percent of the nation's dentists and geologists, or cabinetmakers and dental hygienists, are of African descent. Nor is the record much more auspicious in architecture and advertising. For many decades after the Civil War, white patrons were pleased to have their meals served and drinks prepared by black waiters and bar attendants. Today, they prefer that those services be performed by persons of their own race.

The showing hardly improves when we look at the changes that have occurred in the past third of a century, as reflected in the table on page 154. That there are more black firefighters reflects the changing composition of urban populations, while retail sales is now more of a minimum-wage occupation due to the growth of superstores. It is instructive that black workers are being hired as telephone operators,

Black Occupational Representation★

Greatest Overrepresentation

Nursing aides and orderlies	30.4%
Postal clerks	29.3%
Hotel maids and housemen	29.1%
Corrections officers	28.2%
Bus drivers	27.9%
Telephone operators	26.0%
Pressing-machine operators	24.9%
Social workers	23.7%
Security guards	23.4%
Textile and apparel workers	20.3%
Janitors and cleaners	20.1%

Closest to Parity

Retail salespersons	11.4%
Bank tellers	11.0%
Aircraft mechanics	10.4%
Elementary school teachers	10.1%
Hairdressers	9.9%
Actors and entertainers	9.8%

Greatest Underrepresentation

Engineers	4.7%
Waiters and waitresses	4.5%
Designers	4.2%
Lawyers	3.6%
Realtors	3.4%
Architects	2.5%
Advertising executives	2.3%
Bartenders	2.0%
Dentists	1.9%
Tool and die makers	1.7%
Cabinetmakers	1.6%
Dental hygienists	1.0%
Geologists	0.5%

★Black workers comprise 10.6% of the total employment force.

secretaries, and aircraft mechanics at a time when those livelihoods are declining in numbers with the advent of laborsaving technologies.

Equally revealing are the positions where black representation has declined. Janitors and cleaners were once protected by unions and tended to earn a good blue-collar wage. Now employers prefer to hire recent immigrants, who are willing to work for less. The same holds for household jobs, which are now rejected by black Americans, not least due to their memories of having been demeaned in such positions in the past. For their part, employers turn to persons recently arrived in this country, who are willing to accept conditions that longtime citizens would never tolerate. As for hairdressers and chefs, a greater sophistication, including an international ambience, has come to be associated with coiffure and cuisine. As a result more whites and immigrants have entered these fields, bringing about a displacement of blacks.

Affirmative action has become a national watchword, stirring aspirations and resentments, accompanied by appeals to principle from both its defenders and opponents. In fact, no one can say for sure how many of the shifts within the workforce should be imputed to these programs. As has been noted, hiring black secretaries and telephone operators did not result from race-based preferences, but from the movement of whites away from those jobs. On the other hand, more black accountants may have been hired simply because more of them now have the credentials for professional positions.

Even apart from its emotional overtones, affirmative action can mean various things. Some see it as an extra effort to diversify a workforce, either willingly or in response to official pressure. Some companies, such as Corning Glass and Motorola, have hired and promoted minority workers without court orders or investigations by public agencies. But in the view of many people, such programs may entail a lot more. What worries them is that the "action" part demands results, to the point of placing unsuitable people in jobs. Thus they complain that candidates with lesser qualifications are favored over persons who are better prepared. A recurring question in the affirmative action debate is how best to measure merit. A case in point arose in Memphis where several hundred patrolmen took a test required for promotion to sergeant. There were seventy-five openings, ostensibly to be awarded on the basis of scores. However, only a few black officers

Black Representation in Occupations
More than Doubled

	1960	1995
Telephone operators	2.6%	26.0%
Firefighters	2.5%	15.3%
Retail salespersons	2.4%	11.4%
Aircraft mechanics	4.6%	10.4%
Secretaries	2.4%	8.7%
Accountants and auditors	1.6%	8.4%
Electricians	2.2%	5.5%
Lawyers	1.3%	3.6%

Increased at a Lesser Rate

	1960	1995
Painters	7.7%	8.4%
Automobile mechanics	7.4%	7.8%
Librarians	5.1%	7.6%
Skilled metalworkers	5.0%	6.5%
College teachers	4.4%	6.2%
Physicians	4.4%	4.9%

Decreased

	1960	1995
Janitors and cleaners	38.5%	20.1%
Chefs and cooks	24.9%	17.6%
Household servants	54.3%	16.7%
Hairdressers	12.7%	9.9%

placed in the top seventy-five, so another nineteen were promoted, even though this meant displacing white candidates who had higher scores.

On first reading, this looks like a classic affirmative action case. One of the issues was that the promotions were originally going to be based on the results of a pencil-and-paper test with multiple-choice questions, an "objective" method, used to prevent political and personal favoritism. Yet another consideration was that Memphis's population is more than half black, and it is likely that residents of that race make up a high proportion of those in contact with the police. For the city to have effective law enforcement, it would be prudent to have a strong black presence at supervisory levels. But to obtain those officers, the department would have to reduce the importance of multiple-choice test scores. This said, it can and should be argued that what was done in Memphis was not so much affirmative action as an attempt to create a more effective police force.

Ambiguous situations such as this one beset any attempt to ascertain which individuals, and how many, have been aided by affirmative action. Still, some answers can be inferred by analyzing Census records. The table on page 156 gives distributions by race and gender for various occupations in 1970 and 1990. (Only the ten-year counts provide information in this detail.) The most noticeable fact is that white men have lost much of their dominance. They now comprise less than half of the workforce, less than two-thirds of all physicians, barely half of college faculties, and are now a minority among journalists. While there are variations among occupations, for the most part, white men have been supplanted by white women, Asians, and black women, essentially in that order. Except for two blue-collar trades—electricians and sheet-metal workers—black men have had smaller gains than members of other groups. In many spheres, black women have moved further and faster than black men. The most depressing reason for this trend is that fewer black men now have jobs of any sort, and those who do are outnumbered by black women.

Affirmative action has clearly contributed to the growth of a black middle class. While merit has always existed among black workers, but was usually ignored, some professions have been taking extra steps to find people who have it. Yet when the results are tallied, it turns out that the most determined efforts have been made in the public sector, most prominently the military and the postal service, and also health and education and social services. The nonprofit sector has shown a similar vigor. The Ford Foundation has had a black president, as have Planned Parenthood and National Public Radio, the College Board and TIAA-CREF, the last a pension fund for college professors. These organizations have tended toward the liberal side of the political spectrum and have pressed for more diverse staffing on moral grounds. Somewhat more pragmatic, the armed forces have found it prudent to

Racial Representation in Occupations (per 1,000 in field)							
	1970	**1990**	**1970**	**1990**	**1970**	**1990**
	All Workers		**Physicians**		**Lawyers**	
White men	562	426	880	653	930	710
White women	331	353	87	147	45	211
Black men	52	49	18	23	11	19
Black women	42	54	4	12	2	15
Asians	—	28	—	108	—	14
	College Faculty		**Engineers**		**Journalists**	
White men	689	501	961	787	578	443
White women	265	338	16	68	381	445
Black men	19	24	11	28	11	22
Black women	16	24	1	7	10	30
Asians	—	69	—	70	—	20
	Computer Analysts		**Electricians**		**Sheet-Metal Workers**	
White men	824	591	942	840	940	795
White women	136	247	17	13	17	36
Black men	19	29	29	55	30	48
Black women	9	24	2	3	2	8
Asians	—	72	—	16	—	21

Totals add to less than 1,000 since other racial groups are omitted. Hispanics are included with the race they chose. Asians were not specified in the 1970 occupational totals.

mount a visible display of black admirals and generals. It is businesses that have been least likely to promote black employees to supervisory positions. Here one must be wary when relying on official figures. The Bureau of Labor Statistics reported in 1995 that black men and women made up 7.2 percent of all persons classed as "executives, managers, and administrators." This is an all-time high, and a manifest advance over their 2.3 percent share in 1970. However, the last twenty-five years have seen a surge in title inflation, and more than 17 million Americans are now in this category, which runs all the way from corporate chairmen to night-shift supervisors at Burger King, including a lot of people who don't oversee anyone at all. The median salary for this group is $35,568—so half make less than that—which is not usually what we regard as executive compensation.

In 1993, the most recent breakdown available at this time, black managers were paid at a ratio of $868 for every $1,000 made by whites. That, too, is an advance over 1970, when the ratio was $672 per $1,000. However, the most striking racial gaps appear at levels carrying more responsibilities and higher pay. Among the white managers, 31.1 percent earned over $50,000, and 6 percent exceeded $100,000. However, only 13.5 percent of their black colleagues made more than $50,000, and a scant 2.2 percent earned over $100,000. Most of the black managers were considerably below the salary median, suggesting that they were several steps down the chain of command.

While we cannot say precisely to what degree the growth of a black middle class has been due to affirmative action, we do know that the policy's adoption by government agencies has played an important role. If we look at Americans earning $40,000 or more a year, a decent middle-class income, less than 20 percent of the whites are on public payrolls. So the white middle class is largely a private-sector creation. However, over forty percent of blacks who earn more than $40,000 are employed by government, and the proportion grows to more than half if we add quasipublic positions in health and education and social agencies. This should not be surprising since, as has been noted, these are the areas where affirmative action has been most energetic. In fact, were it not for this commitment, there would not be much of a black middle class. (This also helps to explain why black managers make less than white managers: fewer black managers are in private business, where $50,000 and $100,000 paychecks are more common.)

Of course, business is where the big rewards are. A realistic measure of black promotions comes from the Executive Leadership Council, which says it limits its membership to the "nation's most senior African-American corporate executives." Its 133 members come from 104 corporations, a ratio that itself tells us that most of the 104 firms have a single black manager in a senior position. Only 5 of the 104 corporations—Sears, Xerox, Mobil, Kraft, and Merrill Lynch—can point to three or more black persons at that level. Currently, hardly a handful of black corporate executives head operating divisions. More commonly they hold positions in charge of "community relations," "corporate diversity," and "market development," the last usually referring to promoting products among black customers. Only in one of the top one thousand corporations does a black executive have a corner suite. He is Richard Parsons, the second-in-command at Time Warner who has responsibility for the music and entertainment divisions.

The *Forbes* annual roster of the four hundred wealthiest Americans has cited more than a thousand different men and women since it began in 1982. Of this number, five—less than one-half of 1 percent— have been black. Two of the earliest were Berry Gordy of Motown Records and John Harold Johnson of *Ebony* and *Jet* magazines. A later addition was the late Reginald Lewis of Beatrice Foods, who was estimated to be worth $400 million at the time of his death in 1993. The 1996 listing contained Oprah Gail Winfrey, whose holdings were put at $415 million; William Henry Cosby Jr. was on the 1995 roster with $335 million.

Because of this nation's way of designating races, all of the Americans from the countries in the left-hand column in the table on page 159 are regarded as being equally and uniformly white, even if some ancestries tend to be blonder and others tawnier. In light of all the analysis given to the race-based white-black division, it is revealing that so little has been said about differentials in achievement within the white sector. There has been no shortage of writing celebrating the immigrant experience: immigrants' vibrancy, their perseverance, their struggle to preserve an identity. We rarely hear media pundits pondering aloud why the Irish lag so far behind the Greeks in median income, and why all four Scandinavian nationalities fall in the bottom half of the European roster. Most of the people whose incomes are reflected in the statistics in the left-hand column of the table have been here for at least three generations, so it cannot be claimed that they are still being treated as outsiders. Indeed, in view of all the advantages that derive from being identified as white, it could be concluded that some members have been less than a credit to the Caucasian strain. But it has been deemed best not to accentuate distinctions, and rather to reserve remarks of that sort for members of another race.

Region of Ancestry: Median Household Income

Europe		Other Countries	
Russia	$45,778	India	$44,696
Latvia	$38,586	Philippines	$43,780
Austria	$38,278	Japan	$41,626
Romania	$37,452	Israel	$40,242
Greece	$37,212	Armenia	$36,860
Scotland	$36,810	Iran	$36,813
Wales	$36,515	China	$36,259
Italy	$36,060	Lebanon	$35,721
Lithuania	$35,916	Argentina	$35,202
Estonia	$35,818	French Canada	$33,702
Switzerland	$35,531	Barbados	$33,480
Hungary	$35,200	Thailand	$31,631
Poland	$34,763	Jamaica	$30,461
Belgium	$34,598	Ecuador	$30,383
Ukraine	$34,474	Trinidad-Tobago	$30,305
England	$34,117	Korea	$30,184
Portugal	$33,936	Vietnam	$29,772
Denmark	$33,882	Colombia	$29,171
Sweden	$33,881	Cuba	$27,741
Germany	$32,730	Brazil	$27,309
Slovakia	$32,352	Nicarauga	$25,717
Norway	$32,207	Haiti	$25,547
Northern Ireland	$32,106	Guatemala	$24,569
Bulgaria	$31,850	El Salvador	$23,729
Irish Republic	$31,845	Mexico	$23,694
Czech Republic	$31,800	Eskimo	$21,891
Finland	$31,142	Puerto Rico	$21,056
Croatia	$30,991	Dominican Republic	$20,006
Netherlands	$30,929	American Indian	$19,900
France	$30,696	Cambodia	$18,837

It is in the interest of the United States to open every possible avenue to immigra-
tion from abroad. Ingenious and valuable workmen in different arts and trades,
listening to the powerful invitations of better price for their labor, would flock to the
United States.

So wrote Alexander Hamilton in 1791. It would be hard to find such strong support for immigration today. The reasons why so many Americans oppose immigration are by now familiar. Newcomers either take jobs from citizens or depress prevailing wages because they are willing to work for less and are more apt to accept unpleasant working conditions. Immigrants are accused of being a burden on social services, ranging from kindergarten classes to emergency-room care, not to mention the costs of crime and prison cells. Apart from the economic impact of immigration, there remains the worry that America's national identity is eroding, as we become a potpourri of alien religions, customs, and tongues. Hence the demand that the gates clang shut, walls be raised, and welcome signs retired. Even if that were done, many say, we are overstrained and imperiled by those already here. This attitude leads to calls for more serious surveillance of immigrants, electronic identity cards, even mass deportations.

The remainder of this chapter will show where immigrants stand on the income spectrum, and what this tells us about what they do when they get here. The table on page 161 gives the median earnings for fully employed men of twenty-nine different races or origins. Those who are identified as black or white, or Eskimo or American Indian, are all or for the most part native born, as are at least two-thirds of all Japanese-Americans and Mexican-Americans. Most of the Puerto Ricans and Hawaiians were born on those islands, whether under commonwealth or territorial or statehood status. Those in the other twenty-one groups, identified by their country of origin, are primarily foreign born.

A few generalizations may be hazarded at the outset. One is that the farther a country is from the United States, the more likely will its immigrants be to secure higher-paying employment. Clearly, it takes more resources, either financial or personal, to get here from India or the Philippines than, say, Mexico or the Dominican Republic. Similarly, Argentina and Chile call for more of a trek than does Central America. Also, immigrants from Argentina and Chile tend to come with experience of a modern economy, whereas Central American cultures are still

Earnings of Fully Employed Men
(medians by race or national origin)

Japan	$37,334
India	$36,185
China	$31,746
White Americans	$30,764
Argentina	$30,708
National Median	$29,237
Korea	$28,256
Chile	$26,609
Venezuela	$26,446
Hawaiian Americans	$26,438
Philippines	$26,094
Panama	$25,660
Thailand	$25,261
Eskimo Americans	$25,076
Cuba	$24,671
Vietnam	$24,258
Colombia	$22,347
Peru	$22,325
Puerto Ricans	$22,197
American Indians	$22,005
Black Americans	$21,691
Ecuador	$21,677
Dominican Republic	$18,954
Mexico	$18,847
Cambodia	$18,552
Honduras	$17,574
Nicaragua	$17,489
Laos	$17,296
Guatemala	$15,722
El Salvador	$14,954

more strongly Indian. Cuba and Vietnam are in the middle of the table for similar reasons, as both combine rather disparate groups of immigrants. The first wave of Cuban refugees brought middle-class backgrounds and skills, while later arrivals were less prepared for work in the United States. The Vietnamese group contains both persons of Chinese origin who were middle class, and indigenous Vietnamese who have found it less easy to adjust to the demands of American employment. Least prepared of all have been the Laotians and Cambodians, most of whom were rural peasants. They were airlifted to the United States toward the end of the Vietnam War, hardly realizing where they were going or what they would find once they arrived here. After two decades, many are still on local welfare rolls.

Have immigrants taken many jobs that were once held by, or would otherwise go to, American-born workers? There is no doubt that they have, and as often as not because of business decisions made by American employers. This is especially apparent when a business decides to recast its workforce, often by contracting out jobs it once kept on its own payroll. One example is the food we eat aloft, which airlines once handled for themselves, where wages were negotiated under union contracts. Now service companies get the meals prepared at lower costs, by using nonunion immigrants at much lower pay, thus raising the earnings of both the airlines and the contractors. In Los Angeles, building maintenance used to be the preserve of local black employees, whose wages helped to create a stable working class. Those jobs are now given to Mexican- and Central American immigrants, just as hotels are choosing Filipinos for their service staffs, in both cases for considerably less pay. Annual medians of $18,847 for Mexican-American men and $17,574 for Hondurans mean that employers are supplanting blue-collar pay scales with a domestic equivalent of Third World wages. Not only large firms prefer immigrant help. Professional families looking for domestic servants, including nannies for their children, prefer people with foreign roots. The reasons for this preference are not only economic. Both the firms and the families find that immigrants are dependent on their jobs and so are more likely to do as they are told and less apt to complain or show resentment.

In other areas, the displacement is more problematic. For example, the nation has seen a resurgence of sweatshops, where immigrants receive minimal wages for sewing garments with brand names that are present in many of our wardrobes. A generation or so ago, the United States had a thriving garment industry, staffed either with union members in the North or unorganized workers in the South. What shuttered many of those sources of employment were imports from low-wage countries and American companies' choosing to have their goods made abroad. Domestic sweatshops may have to pay somewhat more than Third World wages, but they can fill orders quickly and make on-the-spot changes in models and styles. If they were shut down, the jobs would be shifted not to American workers, but to others in the real Third World.

Still, the most widespread employment for immigrants has been in work that native-born Americans are not willing to do. Outside the South, this is generally the case with domestic service, as it is with washing dishes and mopping floors in restaurants. Few people born in this country are prepared to stoop all day picking vegetables. Nor will they sit all day in a saddle herding sheep and cattle; so virtually all of today's cowhands are Latin American. Indeed, many cities would not have sufficient taxicab service if they had to rely on native citizens for their drivers. As consumers, Americans have benefited mightily from immigrant labor. Imagine how much more office cleaning would cost, or how much more you would have to pay for an avocado or a steak, or a taxi ride or a meal out, were Americans to be given optimal wages for performing these and other services. And let's not forget about that bargain-priced sweater from the Gap and the women who care for the children of busy dual-career couples.

In the view of many Americans, immigrants exploit the easy access to this country. Some come on visitors' visas, overstay the specified period, and then disappear into the general population. Given the limited number of Immigration and Naturalization Service inspectors, along with opportunities for appeals for those who are caught, the odds of actual deportation are small and well worth the risk. Others get here as grandparents or cousins, under indulgent "family unification" provisions. And still others arrive illegally, relying on security gaps in thousands of miles of border, or even by ships that leave them on isolated beaches.

Once here, many if not most are willing to work for wages on which no American could survive. More than a few come on their own, leaving their families behind, so they live in cramped and crowded quarters, often on mattresses laid side by side. All in all, it has been argued that they are exploiting an easygoing system, taking advantage of the ease of entry and a job market that does not ask too many questions. Yet, others argue that the immigrants themselves are exploited, enduring living and working conditions barely different from those they had before coming here.

At issue here is how much and what this country owes to individuals who come here voluntarily. Hence questions arise about whether undocumented immigrants should be entitled to a free attorney and full due process in contesting deportation. Or should aliens who come here legally claim the full range of public services, ranging from expensive medical procedures to low-cost higher education? And what about the constitutional presumption that any child born here—even to a mother who only crossed the border an hour before—must automatically become an American citizen? (This practice is by no means universal. European countries do not confer their citizenship on infants with alien parents.) Does the United States owe immigrants a specified level of compensation, living and working conditions, or every legal guarantee, beyond protection against indentured servitude or, say, enforced prostitution? The point is that individuals who decide to emigrate know the score before they come. They are aware that they will not really be welcomed and may face hostility or worse. Indeed, they come with quite realistic expectations, aware that they face a decade or more of arduous toil. And like immigrants a century ago, they know that opportunities to move up and out of poverty are better in the United States than in any other country in the world.

It would be a grave mistake to regard all immigrants as unskilled laborers, performing chores that call for only sweat and muscle. For one thing, that Pakistani driving your taxicab may have an engineering degree, and the woman taking your dry cleaning might have taught high school in Manila. Companies such as Intel and Microsoft, Texas Instruments and Hewlett-Packard, have hired thousands of skilled immigrants because there aren't enough native Americans with the knowledge and experience they need. Taiwan and Korea, and more recently Russia and Ukraine, are key sources of physicists and mathematicians.

Take a more mundane case: New York's subway system is the oldest and largest in the nation, and the most challenging to operate. While some of its cars are state of the art, they must function in tunnels that have been in use for close to a century. Indeed, the system only works— and it really does—because it has at its disposal a sophisticated staff of engineers. Much of a subway engineer's job requires working under-ground, with high-speed trains shrieking inches away on darkened tracks. But the Metropolitan Transit Authority, which manages the subways, found that American engineering graduates were less than attracted to subterranean careers. So the Authority let its needs be known at engineering schools in Calcutta and Bombay. (Green cards could be arranged, since these were jobs Americans did not want.) And unbeknownst to the 2 million daily riders, their trains make their runs on schedule due to the equations and calibrations of Indian-born engineers.

If America was the first country to embrace capitalism's tenets, immigrants arrive here every day hoping to make good on that promise. Indeed, evidence suggests they are more avid to start enter-prises of their own than are longtime residents. Thus *Inc.* magazine has estimated that one in eight of the nation's most profitable small busi-nesses is headed by immigrants. Most are providing innovative ser-vices, ones that many Americans now find indispensable. Here are several examples, the first set in the New York City area and others tak-ing place across the country.

For many New Yorkers, especially those with modern tastes, the city's food markets were oblivious to their needs. One was a desire for fresh fruits and vegetables, aesthetically presented, accompanied by a speedy checkout. Korean newcomers to the city, somehow sensing that stores of this sort would be welcome, filled this niche. That immi-grants from a distant continent had this intuition is itself instructive. Where, it might be asked, were homegrown entrepreneurs, who missed this chance to provide for their compatriots?

Today Korean stores continue to thrive, not least because they antici-pate the needs of new clienteles. Fusing the interest in fresh foods with the pace of urban life, the stores installed salad bars, where one could mix a customized take-out lunch or take-home dinner. Here, too, immigrants sensed the kinds of ingredients—avocados, arti-chokes, sushi rolls—that would appeal to American palates. They also concluded that Americans would pick up modest bouquets of flow-ers—simpler than those carried by professional florist shops—so these were displayed alongside the pyramids of apples.

One more development deserves to be mentioned. When the Korean stores first opened, the menial tasks were given to recently arrived relatives. They could be seen stacking oranges, washing lettuces, and tying asparagus in bunches. However, this is no longer the mise-en-scène. It would seem that the Koreans ran out of nephews and cousins who were willing to stack and wash and sweep. So the owners looked for others to take their places. In the end, they settled on a group even newer to America than themselves: Central American immigrants, largely of native Indian stock. Thus one sees Koreans giving orders and Salvadorans carrying them out, the lingua franca being English, a language native to neither employer nor employee.

How, it may be wondered, have immigrants from India achieved earnings higher than those of white Americans? In New York, like the Koreans, they identified services that were not being supplied. One consisted of sidewalk newsstands, many of which are open round-the-clock. Matching them were magazine stores, carrying hundreds of titles, covering subjects ranging from woodworking and windsurfing to summaries of soap opera plots and journals in several dozen languages. Before this Indian innovation, one might have to scour the entire city for a publication on motorcycle repair. Now it is likely that it is on sale in your neighborhood.

In hundreds of towns dotted across the South and Southwest, Indian immigrants own and operate small motels. In most cases, they were sold to them by Americans who had grown weary of having to be available twenty-four hours a day, and clean rooms and make beds when employees fail to show up. While motels are hardly an innovation, travelers need a place to spend the night, and only the arrival of Indian immigrants saved motorists from miles of No Vacancy signs. Entering the motel business was not simply a matter of finding a niche. In many cases, the motel owners would be the only Indian family in the town, their children the only ones of Indian origin in the schools, and their closest place of worship several hundred miles away. Moreover, this isolation might be one's lot for half a dozen years, until one had amassed enough capital to move on to a larger community with more Indian immigrants. (How many Americans would be willing to start such new careers as, say, the sole American family in a Malaysian village?) Of course, families who make this choice are aware of what they are getting into. They are betting that long hours and isolation will be the first step toward a new and prosperous life in a new homeland. Census statistics on Indians' income and earnings suggest that this is by no means an impossible dream. But if they attain this prosperity, it is because they are providing a needed service. Were it not for those immigrant-lighted Vacancy signs, a lot of Americans would be sleeping in their cars.

One reason immigrants open their own enterprises is that they are unsure whether they would be allowed to succeed in corporate careers. Our largest firms have been quintessentially American institutions, until recently preferring personnel of Anglo-Saxon stock. Yet there are signs that this attitude is changing. Even in 1979, no fewer than twenty-one of the chairmen of the eight hundred largest companies had been born outside the United States. By 1995, their number had increased to fifty-six. True, most of them hailed from Canada (12), England (8), France (6), Germany (5), and Australia (3). But also on the list are such names as Samir Gibara (born in Egypt), who heads Goodyear; Malik Hasan (India), of Health Systems International; Mory Ejabat (Iran), of Ascend Communications; Ray Irani (Lebanon), the chairman of Occidental Petroleum; and Roberto Goizueta (Cuba), who has long presided over Coca-Cola.

Between 1970 and 1994, while the number of bachelor's degrees granted in the country rose from 839,730 to 1,169,275, the number of graduates who majored in the physical sciences dropped from 21,439 to 18,400; those majoring in mathematics fell even further, from 24,937 to 14,396. Still, the shortfall in high-tech personnel might have been a lot worse. Some of the defections from science and engineering have been countered by young immigrants from Asia, who are eager to take the places that Americans have abandoned. Were it not for students of Asian origin, schools such as Cal Tech and MIT would either have empty seats or would have been forced to lower their standards to fill an entering class. Most relieved are professors in such fields as physics and mathematics, where oversize faculties were facing a shrinking pool of students. With no Ph.D.s to supervise, prestigious professors might have had to return to teaching introductory courses. But that is no longer a worry. Articles in scientific journals are increasingly bearing bylines with Asian names. And in the elite high schools, the lists of Westinghouse Science Award winners primarily consist of students with Chinese, Indian, and Russian surnames.

The high incomes of many Asian households reflect that both spouses hold jobs, usually well beyond the nine-to-five norm. What often makes this regimen possible is that a grandparent lives with them, serving as a full-time baby-sitter and doing the shopping and preparing meals. To this extent, the "family reunification" provision in the immigration laws has been a good economic investment. The same may be said of government programs that enable elderly people to remain in their own homes, rather than going into nursing homes. The costs are a lot lower, and individuals can retain their self-respect. Of course, the home-care alternative requires having attendants who will come in for short or long periods, depending on what needs to be done. On the East Coast, such home care is only available because Haitian women are willing to do this work for quite modest pay.

Filipinos have provided a disportionate share of America's nurses and physicians. Filipino physicians have been willing to settle in small towns across the country, often where older practitioners had retired and young graduates showed no interest in settling. Filipino nurses were recruited so hospitals could keep beds available at a time when Americans were choosing other professions. Most of these nurses came as single women on their own, often to forbidding inner cities or to centerless suburbs. Still, they could earn salaries of $40,000, much of which they sent home to support large, impoverished families. Cutbacks in hospital stays, due to tighter reimbursement rules by insurance companies and the use of more outpatient and office procedures, have cut down on the need for nurses. Or if not the need, then the money necessary to provide positions for them. This may mean that nurses from the Philippines will be informed that they had better return home, since the gap they once filled no longer exists.

Few Japanese-Americans should be classed as immigrants. The majority are at least third-generation, most of them descended from agricultural laborers who had been brought to California and Hawaii at the turn of the century. Today, considerable numbers are in well-paying professions, with their median household earnings well ahead of all the European ancestral groups except the Russians. What makes this ascent all the more notable is that California Japanese-Americans—by far the largest group—were confined for most of World War II in barbed-wire prison camps, from which they left in 1945 with barely more than the clothing on their backs. (Hawaii, on the other hand, which was much closer to the combat zones, allowed its Japanese-American residents total freedom.) Yet they set about rebuilding their businesses

168

and careers, with a determination to which their current income attests. Still, as the immigrant status of Japanese-Americans has receded, so has much of their drive. One indication is that younger Americans of Japanese descent are now less likely to attend college than those of Chinese and Indian origin.

In large measure, the lower incomes of immigrants from Mexico, Puerto Rico, Central America, and the Dominican Republic can be explained by the ease of entry these groups experience. Since Puerto Rico is an American commonwealth, its residents can come and go without passports or visas or official approval. Mexicans comprise the largest pools of both legal and illegal immigrants, since they are just a boundary line away. And the Dominican Republic is connected with the United States by cheap and frequent airline service. As a result, these immigrants can engage in a good deal of shuttling back and forth and hence make less of a commitment to North American ways.

Low incomes and earnings may stem in part from discrimination and lack of expected skills. But they also reflect ambiguous feelings of individuals about whether to settle here for good. In fact, fewer entrants from Mexico and the Dominican Republic end up applying for citizenship than do immigrants from the more distant nations China and Korea. Also revealing is an inclination by many of these immigrants to describe themselves as "Latino," to convey that a large part of their identity remains south of the Rio Grande. Some learn no more than workday English, and some take a casual attitude toward their children's education. In this regard, they have at times been abetted by liberal Anglo-Americans who support preserving homeland cultures with bilingual programs in schools and separate residential halls in colleges. Efforts to keep Chicano and Cambodian customs alive may be well intentioned. After all, this country has a long history of erasing earlier immigrant identities. Yet endangered cultures are much like endangered species: to protect them calls for creating reservations, where undermining influences are kept from intruding. In our ideological times, it is understandable that some securely assimilated Americans wish to atone for their own complicity in the nation's homogenization. But it is quite another matter to limit the lives of today's immigrants in order to comfort one's own conscience. For an example of what happens when this type of protection of cultural identities is attempted, we need only examine the effect—economic and otherwise—of reservation life on America's Indians.

Alexander Hamilton's case for immigration was that, in every generation, the nation would be invigorated with new ideas and new energies. The last great surge, largely from southern Italy and eastern Europe, occurred during the first ten years of this century. In those years, close to 9 million legal immigrants arrived, raising the nation's population during that decade by almost 10 percent. But the next forty years saw a sharp decline in immigration, due to legislated barriers, two world wars, and an international depression. The table on this page shows that immigration quadrupled between the 1950s and 1990s. In fact, the new arrivals in the 1990s added only 3 percent to the

A Half Century of Immigration

1951–60	2,515,000
1961–70	3,322,000
1971–80	4,493,000
1981–90	7,338,000
1991–2000	10,000,000 (estimated)

Ethnic Composition of the United States

	1995	2030 (projected)
Whites	73.6%	60.5%
Blacks	12.0%	13.1%
Latins	10.2%	18.9%
Asians	3.3%	6.6%

Current Fertility Rates

Needed for replacement	211
Mexican-Americans	317
Puerto Ricans	252
Black Americans	243
Total USA	205
Asian Americans	194
White Americans	176

population. However, current newcomers are notably visible, since they are mainly from Latin America, Asia, and the Middle East. Which means that their complexions tend to be other than "white."

This difference accounts for forebodings that their presence will alter the essential character of America. The Census Bureau has projected that by the year 2030, the white part of the population will be down to 60 percent. Even now, whites account for less than half of California's residents. Still, we would do well to recall that at the turn of the century, similar misgivings were heard about the arrival of darker-hued Greeks and Italians and Jews. Yet with remarkable rapidity, those immigrants and their children adapted to the Anglo-American model. In return, it was agreed that a darker tone would not debar them from ranking as fully "white." As a testament of having assimilated, many now join their compatriots of northern European origin in decrying the influx of immigrants from other continents.

The arrival of immigrants is not the only reason why the white proportion of the population is declining. Whites have made their own contribution by having fewer children. Demographers agree that if a population is to replace itself, every 100 women must bear 211 surviving children. (The extra eleven are to make up for the five or six girls who may not reach reproductive age.) Currently, each 100 women in the country are having 205 children, which would mean a slightly smaller population for the next generation. But, as the table shows, white Americans are not replacing themselves, and their reproduction rate is even lower higher on the income scale. Asians are also curbing childbearing. As was noted in an earlier chapter, the chief reason for having fewer offspring is that children are extremely costly, if one adds up the amenities and experiences that today's youngsters are expected to have. But every country needs at least modest population growth, if only to muster the taxpayers needed to support an increasing cohort of the aged, who can also be very expensive. If white baby boomers want their nursing-home bills paid in the decades ahead, they will need the goodwill of the children of Mexican-American immigrants.

In fact, despite all of the murmurings about a "multicultural" America, the majority of immigrants intend to spend the rest of their lives here. While older adults may not adapt to American customs and styles, parents know they cannot shield their children from the lures of fun and freedom that pervade American life. A country that can count Henry Kissinger and Arnold Schwarzenegger as full-fledged Americans and has Samir Gibara and Mory Ejabat on its corporate roster is agreeing that it wants and needs the talents and vigor that newcomers bring. And if immigrants and their children show they can outearn residents of longer tenure, that, too, is a lesson worth pondering.

CHAPTER NINE

FOUR SISTERS

As has been emphasized from the outset, actual people stand behind all the figures in this book. This chapter introduces several individuals whose lives personify the complexities of our times. In fact, the persons portrayed here are fictional, created to illuminate the decisions modern women face. All the statistics used in these depictions come from official sources and are based on people much like the four we are about to meet. Getting to know them personally will also add a human dimension to the themes to be considered in the next chapter.

Meet the four Sloan sisters, all currently in their thirties. While perhaps not a typical set of siblings, together they sum up much about the economic status of women today. They were born at a time when having four children was close to the norm. For one thing, raising children was a lot simpler and cheaper. During the Eisenhower and Kennedy eras there was also a sense of optimism about the nation's future: few worried about the kind of world their daughters and sons would know. That, too, has changed.

SARAH SLOAN: NO INCOME OF HER OWN

Sarah, the eldest, is just a few months away from turning forty. Along with some 10 million other women, she has no income she can call her own. Since we live in the 1990s, we must be careful about calling Sarah a "housewife," so suffice it to say that she is married to a wage-earning husband, has two children, and by her own choice does not do any work for pay. (Indeed, on the family income-tax form, she is listed as a "dependent.") As it happens, this is the case in about a quarter of the nation's 54 million marriages. Often, the wife chooses to stay at home with young children. But in almost half of these instances, the wife is an older woman who has never worked and is disinclined to start at her present age. There are still some husbands who don't want their wives to work ("Don't I make enough to support us?"), often in an effort to retain their dominant status. Indeed, as the table on this page shows, considerable numbers of wives remain at home even when their spouses have quite modest earnings. Among the wives who work, most do so part-time or tend to have "jobs" rather than "careers." As can be seen, in those marriages where the husband makes between $50,000 and $75,000, the median paycheck for working wives is a modest $13,786.

Sarah's husband is one of some 2 million husbands who make more than $100,000, and at that bracket 41 percent of wives do not work. "Not work? You've got to be kidding," is Sarah's riposte. "My husband puts in at least a seventy-hour week, and managing a home for someone at his level is a full-time job." She cites two recent occurrences. Last week, a company crisis forced him to fly to San Francisco with barely an hour's notice. He called Sarah at home, asking her to pack a bag for him and meet him with it at the airport. "This is not something

Dual-Income Marriages			
Husbands' Earnings	Couples Where Both Spouses Work	Average Earnings of Wives	Wives' Share of Combined Income
Over $100,000	59.1%	$18,514	★
$75,000–$100,000	67.8%	$12,296	12.3%
$50,000–$75,000	74.7%	$13,786	18.1%
$40,000–$50,000	77.7%	$19,708	30.5%
$30,000–$40,000	80.0%	$18,252	34.3%
$20,000–$30,000	78.0%	$15,954	38.9%
$10,000–$20,000	73.8%	$13,698	47.7%
Under $10,000	65.9%	$12,304	71.1%

★Cannot be calculated, since bracket is open-ended and husband's earnings could go into the millions.

a secretary or a housekeeper could have done. I'm the only one who knows exactly what he'll need." On another occasion, an important client from Australia was coming to town with his wife. Would Sarah show her around during the day, while the husbands did their business, after which the four of them would have dinner? "She didn't know anyone here, and without me she might have sat all day in the hotel." Instead, the Australian wife had a splendid time, which may have helped Sarah's husband to clinch the Sydney deal.

"So I do work," Sarah says with a bittersweet smile. "And there is *no* way hired servants or a service could do what I do." But she gets no cash compensation, not even the minimum wage, unless we count sharing in her husband's year-end bonus, which was due at least in part to services she herself had performed. As it happens, her husband did buy her an expensive coat, one he knew she had been eyeing. "In fact, I really wish he had given me the money," she told a close friend. "It can be scary, not having something to put away that you can call your own."

We can take as a given Sarah's attention to her two children, which ranges from chauffeuring them to endless activities to serving on PTA committees and being at home when they return from school. But now that they are both in their midteens, she has quite a bit of time on her hands. So she occupies herself with projects such as decorating a new house, which is now possible on a rising executive's income. In the final analysis, though, Sarah's contributions to the net domestic product—whether within her own home or the nation as a whole—are largely psychological and emotional. In particular, she sees it as her job to inspirit her husband, girding him for each challenge in his demanding career. So she cheers his successes, consoles him during disappointments, and commiserates when he needs an attentive ear. Given the competitive arena Sarah's husband must enter each day, support on the home front is important in his life. Thus she spends much of her time keeping current with his world of work. Indeed, comforting words are only a start; she must also be informed and provide practical counsel.

Most will agree that Sarah's life is largely supplementary, not to mention self-effacing. After her husband responds at length to her question "How was your day, dear?" he shows little inclination to afford her equal time, let alone listen to her reply. Indeed, how can she challenge the presumption that what he does is more important? Not so long ago, she remarked to a friend, "I could write a whole book about him, but I doubt if he could fill a few pages about me." Of course, in return for receiving no income, she gets to share a purchasing power that is enjoyed by only a minor fraction of the nation's households. At the same time, she is forever aware that what she spends is her husband's money. So even when he asks her to plan their vacation, and she feels it would be relaxing to fly business class, she must first get his approval.

Has Sarah any misgivings? More than a few, since these are after all the 1990s. For one thing, her fourteen-year-old daughter—not at a very tactful age—has said she has no wish to "waste" her life as her mother has done. At social gatherings, Sarah has no ready reply when asked what she "does." Clearly, "housewife" doesn't have the right kind of ring in the kind of suburb where she lives. People start glancing around the room when she mentions her volunteer work. (In fact, she won honors in her art history major at college and occasionally leads tours at a local museum.)

Although Sarah is an intelligent individual who has put as much of her life into a vocation as, say, a woman her age who has been practicing medicine, she frequently finds herself on the defensive, which she regards as unfair. Indeed, she is always aware that her status and security derive from her husband's career. Now that she is about to turn forty, it is not too late for her to reconfigure her life. But, as with those vacation plans, must she ask her husband's permission?

SALLY SLOAN: A $389 MONTHLY CASH STIPEND

Sally, the youngest sister who just turned thirty, was the family rebel. Bored by school, she ran around with a fast crowd and is now on her own with two young children. Sally lives in New Mexico, where she is enrolled in what used to be called the Aid to Families with Dependent Children program, but has recently been redubbed Temporary Assistance to Needy Families. (Most people still refer to it as "welfare.") Each month, she receives a check for $389 as the principal support for her household of three. As it happens, New Mexico's stipend is the median payment at the start of 1996 among those granted by the fifty states. Apart from Alaska and Hawaii, Vermont has been the most generous, with a monthly grant of $656 for a family of three. Were Sally to reside in Alabama, she and her children would have to get by on $164 each month.

Currently, one in every seven of families with children is receiving public assistance, so it is not as if Sally's case is unusual. Still, it is worth recalling that a quarter century ago, in 1970, only one family in fifteen was on the rolls.

Until recently, Sally was legally "entitled" to this type of income. She could show up at a government office with proof that she had one or more children, and the agency would be obliged to start sending her checks. In several ways, Sally is typical of the 5 million mothers who are still on the welfare rolls. Contrary to popular impressions, three-quarters of the recipient families have one or two children, and only one in ten has four or more. Still, welfare's days seem to be coming to an end. Cash stipends and supplements such as food stamps are no longer federal entitlements, and the states need not replace such assistance. During the 1996 presidential campaign, the principal candidates agreed that mothers like Sally could no longer look forward to subsisting on public funds.

Like close to two-thirds of single welfare recipients, Sally has never been married. In the nation as a whole, about half of unwed mothers have been receiving welfare assistance, a large part of the reason why public sentiment has turned against the program. Many Americans believe that the likelihood of government support has encouraged the creation of children who should not have been conceived or born. Of the fathers of Sally's children, one sends no support at all and the other infrequently provides a fraction of the agreed-upon amount. Here, too, her situation is common. Despite efforts to collect from defaulters, less than one in eight "deadbeat dads" is found and forced to pay up. Still, such "welfare fathers" face less scorn than the women who end up bearing and raising their children.

Sally offers no apologies for receiving public assistance. "Look, I'm raising two kids," she says, "and I think I'm a pretty good mom." One of her children is a toddler of three and the other, who is seven, has just entered second grade. At these ages, she believes, youngsters need the presence of a parent. "In many ways, I'm like my sister Sarah, who chose to stay at home with her two." Even if they're miles apart financially, both are strong adherents of family values. "I want my kids to turn out right," Sally adds. "And the best start is a loving atmosphere at home." In fact, both sisters are "dependent": one on her husband's earnings and the other on public funding. Sally doesn't feel that she is being paid for doing nothing. "Someone has to raise the next generation, especially when everyone knows there's a shortage of reliable husbands." She believes she is performing a public service.

Actually, no one can raise two children on a welfare stipend, whether it is Vermont's $656 or Alabama's $164. Hence the food stamp program, which brings Sally another $214 each month to help pay her grocery bills. She has also been getting another $185 a month from two other government programs to put toward the rent she pays to a private landlord and for her heating bills. Together, the stipend and subsidies give Sally the equivalent of $788 a month. To this may be added the value of the free school lunches her second-grader receives. Even so, her family is well below the 1995 poverty threshold of $995 a month for a household of three. Welfare was never intended to allow people to live well, or even at a modest American standard. While it is perceived as a "liberal" program, welfare's primary purpose is to spare the public from having to see people in utter destitution.

It has been argued that Sally is better off than many working people, due to her access to the health care system known as Medicaid. According to the most recent estimate, its benefits add $465 to her monthly budget—altogether, $5,580 a year—which is measurably more than her cash stipend. Sally and her children have access to free dental care and prescriptions and appliances, for which they pay no deductibles. It is true that a family looking to purchase a private policy offering this kind of coverage might easily pay $5,580 a year. But it isn't as if Sally is getting this money. That sum represents what the government pays to providers and says nothing about the quality of care that Sally will end up receiving. During the first half of the 1990s, Medicaid programs averaged about $120 billion a year, of which $30 billion was for welfare recipients. (Almost as much—some $25 billion—went to nursing homes, where the clienteles are largely middle class.) Not surprisingly, most AFDC recipients go for health care close to where they live, which often means harried emergency rooms or outpatient clinics, where they may be treated each time by a different trainee resident.

Thus the major beneficiaries of Medicaid are physicians and dentists, hospitals and nursing homes, laboratories and pharmacies, plus the companies that sell drugs and anesthetics and all the paraphernalia of the health-care industry. True, one of Sally's children might someday need a complex operation, for which the doctors and the hospital could bill Medicaid to the tune of $100,000. But would we then say that her income for that year was $109,456?

The concern over welfare is not primarily financial. Most Americans find the presence of a supported class unseemly; it runs counter to the way we as Americans are supposed to organize our lives. The presumption is that welfare promotes the promiscuous production of babies that society does not need and who would be better off not being born. Yet, another group of husbandless mothers are being supported by a public program that evokes scarcely any comment. They are younger widows who still have school-age children and whose husbands had held steady jobs and contributed to a Social Security account. These women do not have to apply for welfare, nor are they urged to become self-supporting. Currently, almost three hundred thousand American women are supported under this provision, and in 1995 they could receive as much as $29,676 a year, almost six times the average AFDC stipend. These payments are not viewed as undeserved, since they are seen as derived from a husband's years of employment. In fact, that is only partly true, since what he paid into Social Security accounts for only a small fraction of what his widow and children will be receiving.

SANDRA SLOAN: EARNINGS OF $17,000

What would happen if welfare was wholly dismantled? Liberals say the result would be increased homelessness and crime, more signs of malnutrition, as well as other personal and social dislocations. Conservatives claim that women would cope: they would find jobs and learn to live on their earnings. They might want to put Sandra Sloan on their posters, although it is doubtful she would seek that attention.

Whether due to pride or conscience or conviction, Sandra has not applied for public assistance. She is now thirty-five and was recently divorced after an eleven-year marriage that produced one child. "My husband had a better lawyer, who persuaded the judge that I could support myself," Sandra says. "So I was denied any alimony and all he sends is two hundred and fifty dollars a month in child support." As it happens, this is the national average for fathers who actually pay. A more practical reason why Sandra did not ask for welfare is that she resides in Arkansas, where the stipend for a mother with one child is $162 per month. In fact, inadequate allowances have long been part of a Southern strategy to keep people off welfare, and many conservatives would like to use that approach as a national model. Since few families can survive on a welfare grant, the states have a ready pool of women to work at a minimum wage as household servants, motel maids, and in food-processing plants. "While I hadn't much of a résumé, I did have a year of college," Sandra says, "so I thought I could do better than stand on my feet all day cutting up chickens." Even so, the best she could do was taking telephone reservations for a commuter airline, which pays $7 an hour or $14,000 a year, to which she can add the $3,000 she receives in child support.

And who looks after her child? Liberals say that when welfare is ended, elaborate child-care services will have to be created, preferably staffed by well-paid professionals who are sensitive to the needs of disadvantaged children. But this could be extremely expensive, costing even more than many mothers earn. (Yearly fees at Kindercare, a national chain noted for individual attention, range from $7,500 to $10,250, depending on the child's age.) However, the idea that poor youngsters need a good start has lost much of its popularity, so legislators cannot be counted on to subsidize the costs of quality child care. When the supervisor at a poultry plant was queried on what mothers did with their children while they were at work, he replied, "They manage, we don't ask." According to a 1993 Census study of working mothers, less than a third used "organized child-care facilities." The remainder relied largely on relatives or left the children in other people's homes, where they often spent most of their time watching television. Another argument for making mothers work is seldom stated: if they come home weary from a demanding job, they will be less inclined to produce more children.

Sandra has no need for child care, since she performs her job at her home. The airline installed a terminal in her bedroom, and callers are routed directly to her. For Sandra, this is actually an advantage: "I can put in my hours at night, when my child is asleep." What does the future hold for Sandra? On the domestic front, she agrees with her sister Sally about the scarcity of dutiful men. In no small measure, both sisters are where they are due to the advent of what one commentator has called "men's liberation." This phrase does not refer to a heightened sympathy for women's rights, but rather the freedom husbands now have to leave their wives and children, with little or no social censure and at minimal cost. Men are also more likely to remarry, as Sandra's husband has, which often produces a second round of children and allows men to claim that they cannot do much for the offspring of their first marriage.

Sandra's income of $17,000 puts her near the $17,170 median for the households headed by single women who hold down jobs. As can be seen from the table on page 182, more than two-thirds of these families are trying to get by on less than $25,000 a year, which is not easy given the cost of breakfast food and up-to-date sneakers. But the table also shows that one in six of these self-supporting women brings in at least $35,000, and one in sixteen surpasses the $50,000 mark. "Sure, I don't take welfare checks like Sally, but I don't have the kind of drive you can see in Samantha," she says, alluding to her third sister. In theory, Sandra could return to college and upgrade her skills, as many women have. In fact, she admits to being not very ambitious, a trifle disorganized, and lacking any serious ideas about what she wants to do with her life. Sandra is a good person and a loyal friend, but she does not have that extra edge that is needed to succeed in the American arena. Nor do all men have that trait.* Still, until recently, fewer men had to settle for receiving $7 an hour, since their gender was presumed to entitle them to what was deemed a "man's wage."

SAMANTHA SLOAN: $190,000 AND RISING

According to a 1995 Census survey, 1.4 million working women had annual earnings exceeding $75,000, placing them in the top 2 percent of the female workforce. Samantha Sloan, thirty-seven years old and a

---

*Or even the desire. No fewer than one in five men polled by the *New York Times* said that they would just as soon take care of the house and children. At the same time, three-quarters of working women were telling *Newsweek* that they would still want to work even if they didn't need the money.

Incomes of Families Headed
by Single Women Where She Has a Job

Over $50,000	6.0%
$35,000–$50,000	9.7%
$25,000–$35,000	15.0%
$15,000–$25,000	25.2%
Under $15,000	44.1%

Median income: $17,170

---

corporate vice president, is highly placed in this group. The merchandising division she heads employs 110 people and is one of the top earners for her company. Samantha feels she can count on a bonus this year, which would lift her total pay above $190,000. "I came to this firm at just the right time," she freely admits. "It was in the early 1980s, and they felt pressured to hire more women. I've been told that they took me ahead of some very good men." Still, Samantha had superior credentials. She ranked close to the top of her class, both as an undergraduate and at business school. She impressed the recruiters, not least because she showed she had studied their company carefully before her interview. "But they didn't promote me to head this division because I am a woman," she takes pains to emphasize. "Affirmative action stops when there are big responsibilities at stake." Here, with no doubts about merit, Samantha got the job over several men. Indeed, among her talents is the care and stroking of male subordinates.

Samantha takes home a full briefcase every night, even when she leaves late. She also works smart, discerning opportunities and anticipating trends. And this includes her own career. Samantha has accepted a variety of assignments, ranging from running a regional office in Kansas to starting distributorships in Korea. She recalls reading about Mary Jo Meisner, who became editor of the *Milwaukee Journal-Sentinal* at the age of forty-three. Ms. Meisner had honed her skills and proved her worth at papers in Wilmington, Philadelphia, San Jose, and Fort Worth. Have laptop, will travel. Men have long accepted that stricture. So has Samantha.

No, she isn't married, and she can't see herself having children.

"Combining marriage and a career can only work when you both stay in one place," Samantha points out. "But I'm with an international firm, and they've talked about sending me to Prague for a two-year stint." Her longtime boyfriend finally turned to someone who had more time to spare, and she is currently involved with a married man. Occasionally, Samantha envies Sarah's husband. "He has an accepting spouse who provides him with sex and supper and sympathy." Indeed, men who ascend the executive ladder make fewer sacrifices and get more home-front support. Samantha has no illusions about how far she can rise. Her problem is that a company can have only one CEO, who in many ways personifies the firm. At this point, the directors don't seem ready to have a woman in that position.

Samantha is amused that many companies have created divisional "presidencies," perhaps so they can say that they are putting women in corner offices. Thus in 1996, Brenda Barnes was president of Pepsi-Cola North America; Geraldine Laybourne had that title at Disney-ABC Cable Networks; and Karen Katen was president of Pfizer's U.S. Pharmaceuticals Group. But only in a few fields have women reached the summit. As of 1996, only two women presided over companies on the Fortune 1000 list. One was Jill Barad, the chief executive at Mattel, the toymaker; the other, Linda Wachner, headed Warnaco, a women's apparel company. (Their respective compensations were $6.2 million and $11.2 million, which put them ahead of the average for their male counterparts.) But Samantha isn't counting on this happening to her. So her plan is to rise as high as she can in her current company, then leave to start her own firm, as some of her women friends already have, so she can make her own rules.

CHAPTER TEN

THE GENDER GAP:
CONTOURS AND CAUSES

American women are still far from economic parity. In some spheres progress has been made, and those gains will be documented here. There can be no denying that these advances are long overdue and far from sufficient. Yet the story is not wholly one of improvement. An unhappy fact of our times is that in some ways women are worse off than they were in the past.

While the typical woman's wallet is fuller than ever before, it is still measurably thinner than the typical American man's. And while it is now true that when men and women hold the same jobs, they tend to be paid the same wage, women still have less chance of reaching the highest earnings levels. What's more, even though more women are entering occupations traditionally held by men, once they get there, the positions start to decline in prestige and pay.

But the world of work offers only a partial view of the economic disparities between the sexes. So it makes sense to look at the population as a whole. In 1995, the median income for the 92.1 million adult men was $22,562, while the midpoint for the 96.0 million women was $12,130. This means women receive $538 for every $1,000 going to the men. This is not an auspicious ratio. Indeed, it could be construed as society's verdict that women's needs and contributions amount to half of those of men. But even that figure can be viewed as evidence of progress: as recently as 1975, American women received a paltry $382 for each $1,000 received by men.

However, this aggregate comparison has limited meaning, because most men hold full-time jobs, whereas the majority of women have no earnings from employment or work only part-time. Indeed, almost 10 million women told the Census Bureau in 1995 that they had no incomes at all, or at least none that came to them in their own names. Most of these women are nonworking wives, ranging from blue-collar homemakers to the spouses of top executives. Their lack of a personal income pulls down the gender ratio. And when we examine marriages where both partners work, the typical wife emerges earning only $418 for each $1,000 made by her husband. (Few wives have investments of their own that yield them comfortable independent incomes.)

So marriage is the chief cause of the income gap and will remain so as long as it relegates more women than men to tending to the home and caring for the children. In fact, over 40 percent of at-home wives either have no children or all of their youngsters are grown. Like Sarah Sloan in the previous chapter, most of these women never developed careers, and few have shown much interest in entering the workforce. There are still husbands who declare that they do not want their wives to work, and not all are affluent executives who want their mates available to pack their suitcases and entertain business clients. In the households where only the husband brings home a paycheck, his earnings are often quite modest. Over a third of these breadwinners make less than $30,000 a year. Thus many families still rank what they see as domestic values ahead of whatever material benefits additional earnings would produce.

Far fewer Americans are married today than at any their time in our nation's history. This social change has an upside as well as a downside when spreads in income are computed. More people are postponing marriage until they are older, and more marriages are breaking up. Even after allowing for remarriages, a larger portion of the population is now single at any given time. Among women in their early to mid-thirties, almost 20 percent have not yet been married, three times the proportion of thirty years ago. Virtually all of these nonmarried women work; more of them than ever before have serious careers. This cohort comes closest to parity with men. Indeed, a 1993 Census study found that "never married" women who work at full-time jobs earn $1,005 for every $1,000 made by comparable men.

Some of these women live alone, and others have live-in room-mates or partners. Indeed, this is a major reason why there are fewer intact marriages today; many people now spend several years—or more than several—in what is essentially its equivalent. They are part of a growing group of people whom sociologists have dubbed DINKs: Double Incomes with No Kids. Composed sometimes of married couples and many who are not, most of whom are straight but many of whom are gay, this stratum is notable for its discretionary spending, which is indispensable to a high-consumption economy.

But the downside of the decline in marriage is that while most Americans eventually give it a try, about half of these unions end in divorce or permanent separation. And not everyone has the opportunity or the desire to undertake it again. As it happens, men are more apt to remarry, partly because they are not adept at living alone and also because they have a wider choice of possible mates. In addition, more women now have higher expectations for a partner and have not yet found a man—or at lease one who is available—who meets their standards. This has become especially evident among black women, who are now only half as likely to marry as white women. As a result, more single women than ever before are deciding to have children. Indeed, they now give birth to over 30 percent of all babies. True, many are becoming mothers while in their teens and without giving much thought to the future. However, one in six is over the age of thirty and has presumably deliberated about the decision. For these and other reasons, each year finds more women supporting offspring on their own. In most cases, their living standards will be lower than they would have been had the women been married or kept their marriages going.

So while the fact that more women are working has increased their income relative to men, the fact that more are on their own has had a countervailing effect. Today, over one-fifth of all families are headed by single women. And in more than a third of these households, the mother has never been married. Some of the single women heading families receive public assistance, which is intended to keep them alive but below the poverty line. And while over half find work, their median income is only $17,170, and fewer than a third have incomes that exceed $25,000 a year.

PROGRESS TOWARD PARITY?

Interestingly enough, the first signs of progress toward economic parity between men and women came during the still traditional 1950s. This was supposed to be a period when women eschewed paid employment and instead opted for early marriage and a procession of children. Yet as the table on this page shows, the pay ratio of women who were working rose by 25 percent, from $486 to $607, the largest increase of any postwar decade. Several reasons for this stand out. To start, women were abandoning what had been one of their principal occupations, and an ill-paid one at that: domestic service. Back in 1940, 2.4 million women cleaned and cooked and cared for children in other people's homes; by 1970, only half that number were so employed. It appears that the women who chose to work were expecting more from their jobs, including better pay. Even if many women were still secretaries, the corporate world was remaking its own image. The sassy gum chewers of Hollywood such as Joan Blondell would not fit in with the new carpeted corridors. At this time, also, two other major occupations for women began to pay more, for the classic economic reasons. Nurses and schoolteachers were in short supply because so many women were staying at home. In the suburbs, the future-oriented middle class was willing to pay for quality education and health care. Starting in the world of "women's" work, a ripple effect caused women's expectations to rise even in the domesticated Eisenhower era.

	Cause for Applause?	
Year	Percent Working	Pay Ratio to Men
1950	31.4%	$486
1960	34.8%	$607
1970	42.6%	$594
1980	51.5%	$602
1990	57.5%	$716
1995	58.7%	$714

But progress came to a halt. The pay ratio reached by 1960 remained essentially the same in 1970 and 1980. Hence, the slogan "59 Cents!" that was emblazoned on protest placards in the early days of the women's movement, often accompanied by a popular ballad of the time: "Fifty-nine cents for every man's dollar; fifty-nine cents, it's a low-down deal!" These laments were not unavailing, since during the 1980s the ratio rose from $602 to $716. One stimulus was that lawyers and judges began applying the hitherto somnolent Equal Pay Act of 1963, which said that at jobs that called for "equal skill, effort, and responsibility," there could be no gap in "wages to employees of the opposite sex." Also significant was that fewer women were becoming secretaries and nurses or teachers, just as an earlier generation had abandoned domestic service. If we total up these traditionally "female" occupations, in 1970 they had absorbed 28 percent of all employed women, but by 1995, only 18 percent. Indeed, in 1995, the workforce had 700,000 fewer secretaries than in 1980. An obvious reason is the advent of word-processing equipment, which facilitates copying and correcting. Also, in many organizations the position has been retitled "assistant." And, as a further sign of our times, just as women were less willing to do routine typing, men were adapting to the keyboard as it was the only way to communicate with a computer. And in a reverse twist, the number of household workers began to rise in the 1980s, reflecting a demand for nannies in two-career families.

Statistics also indicate that women have been been investing their time and effort in ways that augment their economic value. Postponing marriage and children is one route to a higher income; additional education is another. In 1994, the most recent figures at this writing, women accounted for well over half—54 percent—of those awarded bachelor's degrees, compared to 43 percent in 1970 and 35 percent in 1960. Even more graphic has been their entry into professional programs. As the table on page 190 shows, in 1964 they were barely visible in engineering, dentistry, and business administration, and received well under 10 percent of degrees awarded in architecture, law, and medicine. Today, apart from engineering, women have made substantial strides in most professional programs. In the 1995 entering classes at Yale, Stanford, and Johns Hopkins medical schools, they outnumbered men.

But an increased presence in many occupations and professions does not necessarily lead to greater equity in earnings for women. The table on page 191 presents a mixed picture. The Bureau of Labor Statistics only began releasing pay differentials in 1983, but that at least allows comparisons across a twelve-year period. While some occupations have witnessed modest progress, in none have women's earnings breached the 90 percent mark, and in many they are still below 70 per-

Proportion of Degrees Awarded to Women		
Professional Programs	**1964**	**1994**
Architecture	4.0%	36.6%
Engineering	0.4%	16.4%
Business (MBA level)	2.7%	36.5%
Dentistry	0.7%	38.5%
Medicine	6.5%	37.9%
Law	3.1%	43.0%
Pharmacy	13.9%	66.8%
Academic doctorates	10.6%	44.1%★

★American citizens only.

cent. Even more disturbing is the finding that in some fields women's remuneration has actually dropped relative to men's. Among salaried lawyers and physicians and high school teachers, women comprise a large share of those recently entering those professions, which may account for their lower wages. But among health technicians and electronic assemblers, the proportion of women has actually been dropping, which means another explanation is needed.

THE LAW ADDRESSES ANATOMY, SOCIOLOGY, AND PSYCHOLOGY

The last few decades have witnessed a series of court cases addressing conditions women confront in the world of work. Two from the mid-1980s are worth recalling, since they sought to give a judicial answer to Sigmund Freud's question "What does a woman want?" The first case involved the kind of issue that law professors love. Would the rule that all workers must be treated equally be violated by requiring extra benefits for women workers who become pregnant?

The federal Pregnancy Discrimination Act of 1978 simply stated that there cannot be any discrimination against women if they decide to have a child. They shall, this law reads, "be treated the same for all employment-related purposes" as others on the payroll who are "sim-

Women's Earnings (per $1,000 received by men)		
Occupation	**1983**	**1995**
More Than 10 Percent Improvement		
Chefs and cooks	$711	$885
Realtors	$683	$794
Production inspectors	$563	$649
Waiters and waitresses	$721	$822
Public administrators	$701	$786
Computer analysts	$773	$860
Less Than 10 Percent		
Journalists	$782	$855
Retail sales	$636	$693
Insurance adjustors	$651	$691
Financial managers	$638	$674
Education administrators	$671	$708
Janitors and cleaners	$810	$844
Engineers	$828	$862
Accountants	$706	$734
College faculty	$773	$781
Deterioration		
High school teachers	$886	$881
Health technicians	$839	$813
Electronic assemblers	$857	$808
Lawyers	$890	$818
Physicians	$816	$649

ilar in their ability or inability to work." However, our federal system sometimes allows states to amend national statutes. In this vein, California's legislature added a proviso that women who give birth may take an unpaid leave and that their jobs (or a similar one at the same rate of pay) must be held for them when or if they wish to return.

A Los Angeles savings and loan association challenged the state law, arguing that it required "every employer to have a disability leave policy for pregnancy even if it has none for any other disability." The special provision for pregnancy could be construed as moving well beyond equality because it accorded a preferred status to women, providing no counterpart for men. Thus a man who had a heart attack could not demand his job back when he recovered.

Not surprisingly, many other employers sided with the savings and loan association. But what added interest to the case was that the National Organization of Women also chose to oppose the California law. "What we women have been saying all along is we want to be treated equally," was the view of Dianne Feinstein, who was then San Francisco's mayor. "I don't think the work market has to accommodate itself to women having children." Another feminist group contended that making pregnancy a special category represented "a resurgence of the nineteenth-century protective legislation which perpetuated sex-role stereotypes and which impeded women in their efforts to take their rightful place in the workplace."

Those who held this view should not be accused of being callous. Opponents of special provisions for pregnancy worry that if women are defined as a different class of workers, then they will continue to be vulnerable to discrimination. Protections geared to their gender have a long history. Under what was once deemed to be progressive legislation, women were not allowed to work at night or to lift heavy loads, allegedly for their own good, or to protect them from exploitation. Now many women feel that such laws are demeaning and prejudicial.

More than that, these safeguards can easily become barriers to women when it comes to hiring and promotions and salary parity with men. For example, the United Parcel Service specifies that all of its delivery people must be able to lift fifty-pound packages. There are women who can do this—just as there are many men who can't—and they don't want well-intended "protections" to disqualify them from a well-paying job. In another sphere, our armed services expect candidates for the ranks of admiral and general to have combat experience. Thus women officers who have not faced an armed enemy cannot get to the top. Most women who choose military careers do not want a separate "track" that keeps them behind the battle lines.

One gender-blind solution is to get rid of maternity benefits altogether and replace them with "parental" provisions that do not specify "disability." Thus fathers or mothers, or both together, could be allowed specified periods to care for an infant while their jobs were being held. Not surprisingly, the Swedes are sensible on this score. More than a quarter of eligible fathers take parental leave at the time of childbirth. Swedish law also permits employees to stay at home to care for sick children, with almost as many fathers as mothers taking on this task. If for medical reasons a mother should take time off before or after a birth, that part of the leave could come under generic surgical benefits, which would also cover, say, a prostate procedure for a man.

When it was being debated in the U.S. Senate, one of the sponsors of the Pregnancy Discrimination Act said that the major reason for "this legislation is to guarantee women the basic right to participate fully and equally in the workforce, without denying them the fundamental right to full participation in family life." Even so, that federal law failed to address the fact that men can be full family participants without missing a day of work. Hence the feeling in California for frankness about a basic sexual distinction. Many believed that to have equal prospects in employment, women must be regarded as different from men. On this premise, the U.S. Supreme Court rejected the views of Dianne Feinstein and the National Organization of Women. Rather, it upheld the California law since it "allows women, as well as men, to have families without losing their jobs."

If pregnancy is essentially a matter of anatomy, another case considered sexual differences from a cultural standpoint. In *Equal Employment Opportunity Commission v. Sears, Roebuck & Co.*, a federal judge was asked to decide whether bias may be presumed if women are found to be underrepresented in certain kinds of jobs. In Sears's retail operations, there were two types of selling positions: salaried salespersons and those on commission. In practice, the latter group made considerably more money.

As it happened, the EEOC had no actual complainants, nor did they produce any witnesses who said they detected discrimination at Sears. Instead, its lawyers introduced statistics showing that women held 75 percent of the salaried posts, but only 40 percent of those eligible for commissions. This imbalance, the agency argued, was evidence of bias. Both the EEOC and Sears hired academic historians, both of them women, who prepared supporting briefs.

Sears's expert, Rosalind Rosenberg of Barnard College, first sought to show that women tend to be put off by the competitive ambience of commission sales. Moreover, she went on, they tend to prefer "jobs that complement their family obligations over jobs that might increase and enhance their earning potential." While many people hope that these sentiments will change, Rosenberg cited research studies that found that these are "values that have been internalized by women themselves." The charges against Sears, she concluded, were based on the incorrect assumption that "women and men have identical interests and aspirations regarding work."

Alice Kessler-Harris of Hofstra University, who supported the EEOC, chose a rather different approach. Women's attitudes toward employment, she said, depend on the temper of the times. These moods are mainly shaped by men, as are attitudes about the kinds of work deemed suitable for women. Kessler-Harris noted that "where opportunity has existed, women have never failed to take the jobs offered." Thus, prior to the Civil War, women were employed in what might seem to be "men's" industries, ranging from bookbinding and whip making to mixing gunpowder and assembling clocks. In Philadelphia, cigar making was a male preserve, while in Detroit it was considered women's work. Throughout World War I, women performed ably as streetcar conductors, but the job resumed its status as "men's work" once peace was declared.

Kessler-Harris granted that on the surface it might seem that a majority of "women have conformed to notions of domesticity." She argued, however, that these preferences are not innate or even ingrained. Rather, the historical record shows that attitudes about who does what in the workforce tend to reflect "employers' assumptions and prejudices about women's roles." And Sears, she said, was such an employer. The men who ran Sears had the power to decide how big a part gender would play in determining work assignments. Firms such as Sears could go a long way toward changing the culture. They could actively recruit women and make a point of encouraging them to apply for jobs with higher pay, more responsibility, and greater prospects for advancement.

In her rebuttal, Rosalind Rosenberg wondered how far the EEOC position allowed for freely made decisions, given Kessler-Harris's claim that "women's choices are so controlled as not to be choices at all." There seemed to be a contradiction here. On the one hand, the commission's stance appeared to be that women willingly take "men's jobs" when they are available, often venturing into new kinds of careers. However, a similar willingness is not attributed to those opting for "women's work," since they are assumed to have done so because their choices were conditioned by a male-dominated culture.

Also at issue was whether statistical disparities should be accepted as evidence of discrimination. Can conscious bias be deduced from figures showing that women were only half as likely to get the better-paying jobs? On occasion, even conservative judges have been willing to pay attention to percentages. In one civil rights case, a court discerned discrimination in the paucity of black members in a sheet-metal union. The union sought to explain the low figure by contending that blacks seldom applied, implying they weren't interested in sheet-metal work. Of course, such a defense should not be dismissed out of hand. After all, not many Asians or Jews aspire to be firefighters. Still, in the case of sheet-metal work, the court found the statistics a sufficient sign that the union's barriers were racially based, refusing to accept the union's argument that blacks had been "socialized" away from sheet-metal work.

Sociologists are familiar with the arguments in the Sears case. The brief submitted by Rosalind Rosenberg generally adhered to a "socialization" model, while the one by Alice Kessler-Harris emphasized a "structural" approach. The first focuses on how attitudes are shaped, stressing that women tend to adopt aspirations deemed suitable to their gender. A structural analysis posits that since men create and control most major institutions, they delineate the choices open to women.

In fact, the conditions of real life do not always reflect either of these hypotheses. A woman may be raised to expect that motherhood will be the center of her life. Yet a divorce and the necessity for her to provide most of the support for her children can counteract what she had earlier absorbed. Indeed, many of these women are finding that they like working and that chances for advancement are greater than they ever realized.

Yet women who really want to succeed may be reluctant to take advantage of benefits tailored to their gender. One study of women in management found that those who were married felt that it was in their interest to act as if they did not have a home life. While colleagues will listen politely when male executives allude to their wives, no one wanted to hear about a woman's husband. In a similar vein, while unmarried men might talk at length about their afterwork activities, single women found it prudent to remain silent. In short, women "have to find a balance between work and family that is never required of men." An American Management Association survey found that women executives were "more willing to work long hours" and "give up activities at home if work activities conflict." Indeed, they only got as far as they did by being willing to make those sacrifices. Some biases may sound trivial, but taken together, they are not. If women inflect their voices, it is often construed as a lack of confidence, just as a readiness to smile or to listen closely to subordinates may be taken as a sign of weakness.

So arguments over equality and opportunity go beyond pregnancy and parenthood. Also at issue is whether women should settle for the standards by which men are judged and judge themselves. One study of successful women discovered most had never been married or no longer were; and a majority had never had children. This price that some working women paid signals more than a statistical shortfall. Recall Samantha Sloan, for whom being childless was not something she had planned, but was a constraint brought on by her career, one that few if any men have had to confront.

SEXUAL SEGREGATION

By most measures, the last quarter century has seen steady moves by women into positions traditionally reserved for men. As the table on page 197 shows, the advances have been real in fields as varied as medicine and meat cutting and bartending. But in some cases, progress may be less than it first appears. In 1970, insurance adjustors were mainly men, and in their well-paid work they examined burnt-out buildings and wrecked cars. Today, insurance adjustors are mainly women, who sit at computer terminals entering insurance claims. Many are part-time employees, with few or no benefits. And some, like Sandra Sloan, even do their jobs from their homes. Or, to cite another example, in 1970, the typical typesetter was a well-paid union worker who set hot lead for a newspaper in a printing plant. Today, type is generally keyed in electronically by women who are paid a fraction of what their male forerunners received. Many of the new women pharmacists count out pills for mail-order services and never see a customer. Few of the incoming female physicians will have practices of their own, but will be employed—or subject to scrutiny—by health-maintenance organizations.

Indeed, it has been argued that occupations start to admit women just when a field is beginning to decline in prestige and economic standing. That happened many years ago, when men ceased being bank tellers. Sometimes, as with typesetting, new technologies recon-

Women's Shares Within Occupations

	1970	**1995**
Total workforce	38.0%	46.1%
Considerable Change		
Insurance adjustors	29.6%	73.9%
Typesetters	16.8%	67.3%
Educational administrators	27.8%	58.7%
Publicists	26.6%	57.9%
Bartenders	21.0%	53.5%
Government administrators	21.7%	49.8%
College faculty	29.1%	45.2%
Insurance agents	12.9%	37.1%
Pharmacists	12.1%	36.2%
Photographers	14.8%	27.1%
Lawyers	4.9%	26.4%
Physicians	9.7%	24.4%
Butchers and meat cutters	11.4%	21.6%
Architects	4.0%	19.8%
Telephone installers	2.8%	16.0%
Dentists	3.5%	13.4%
Police officers	3.7%	12.9%
Clergy	2.9%	11.1%
Engineers	1.7%	8.4%
Sheet-metal workers	1.9%	7.5%
Modest Change		
Hotel receptionists	51.4%	75.2%
Social workers	63.3%	67.9%
High school teachers	49.6%	57.0%
Journalists	41.6%	53.2%
Realtors	31.2%	50.7%
Computer programmers	24.2%	29.5%
Essentially No Change		
Dental hygienists	94.0%	99.4%
Secretaries	97.8%	98.5%
Registered nurses	97.3%	93.1%
Elementary school teachers	83.9%	84.1%
Librarians	82.1%	83.2%
Men Replacing Women		
Telephone operators	94.0%	88.4%
Data entry keyers	93.7%	82.9%
Waiters and waitresses	90.8%	77.7%
Cooks and chefs	67.2%	44.5%

figure the job. Moreover, women entering law and university teaching are finding the ground rules have been changed. Until recently most law partners and college professors enjoyed lifetime tenure. But now fewer attorneys can expect to become partners; and those that do can now be dismissed. Colleges, after years of being overstaffed in their top ranks, are tending to replace more of their retiring faculty members with discardable adjuncts. What may be added, though it hardly provides solace, is that young men who are also entering these and other professions will encounter the same barriers and rebuffs.

A smaller but still discernible pattern of change within the workforce has been the decision by some men to enter fields traditionally associated with women. The development began with flight attendants and then extended to nursing. By and large, these tend to be younger men who feel comfortable working with women. One has only to observe a plane's cabin crew to appreciate the symbiosis. And we are now accustomed to a male voice answering our requests for telephone numbers. The country has more restaurants with stylish pretensions than ever before, and one validation of that status is to have male waiters. Of course, many of these men view what they are doing as temporary or transitional. They may be deferring career decisions or waiting for openings in their chosen fields. Indeed, much of our service economy is predicated on the inclination of young people to remain single, to manage on modest pay, and to live and share expenses with other persons of their age.

Does the arrival of women really spell economic decline for an occupation or a profession? The task is to find if gender is the operative factor or whether other forces are at work. Between 1970 and 1995, for example, women rose from being 4.9 percent of the country's lawyers to an impressive 26.4 percent. Yet what also happened was that the head count of lawyers more than tripled, rising from 288,000 to 894,000. So a growing glut of lawyers was the principal reason for the overall decline in pay for that profession. Moreover, of some 600,000 new lawyers, only about a third were women; so they should not be blamed for a falling wage scale.

Still, because so many of them are newcomers, relatively more women will be in an occupation's lower levels. In fact, earnings for younger people of both genders have become quite comparable. Among full-time workers under the age of twenty-five, women make $950 for every $1,000 paid to men. This approach to parity is even more revealing since she is still more likely to be starting out as a teacher while he is more apt to be a better paid engineer. And if they are both beginning engineers, today their pay will usually be identical. In fact, the *National Law Journal* found that among law school students graduating in 1994, for men the median starting salary was $48,000, while the typical woman graduate began at $50,000.

It is certainly true that more women take part-time jobs, frequently because they must be—or want to be—available for family obligations. Yet it is hard to find figures to support the presumption that women give less of themselves. We do have a few measures that fill in parts of the story. For example, it might be assumed that women will choose jobs which are closer to their homes so they can attend to domestic duties or because they are less disposed to look farther afield for a better job. As it happens, the Census can provide an answer, since it collates the "travel time to work" for all employed Americans. Its most recent published study showed that the one-way journey for men averaged 23.7 minutes, while the jobs that women chose called for a 20.3 minute trip. A difference of 3.4 minutes does not suggest that women are markedly less adventuresome.

One way to hold homelife factors constant is to confine the comparison to workers who have never been married. Of course, most of these workers are younger people. It is still assumed that some single women are marking time at their jobs and have no aspirations for lifetime careers. Yet we all know older women who never married, and almost all of them have made their jobs a major part of their lives. Indeed, as was noted at the start of this chapter, the Census analysis of "never married" workers on full-time schedules found that women ended up earning $1,005 for every $1,000 made by men. So when it comes to dedication, the women are actually ahead. Moreover, current demographic data suggest that in the years ahead, more women will be foregoing marriage, which will expand the pool of women who will be able to compete with men on an equal footing.

Ascending an occupation's ladder generally requires years of experience, either within a single organization or in the field as a whole. No one will be surprised to learn that women as a group do not have as many years on their résumés. Lester Thurow stressed this point several years ago, when he said that ages twenty-five to thirty-five are the takeoff years for careers, when one gets seasoned on the job and noticed for promotion. "But the decade between twenty-five and thirty-five," he said, "is precisely the decade when women are most apt to leave the labor force or become part-time workers." Thurow is about half right. In the time period he says is crucial, 73 percent of the men are fully employed, compared with only 51 percent of the women. But there is another way to look at work experience. By focusing on age distributions within the workforce, we find that women who are twenty-five to thirty-five account for 29 percent of all fully employed women, which turns out to be exactly the proportion for men in the same age range. As Thurow says, some men may be slated for success in this "takeoff" decade. The question is why so many fewer women are put on the promotion lists.

EQUAL PAY FOR EQUAL WORK?

Of course, two people doing the same job should receive the same wage. But it isn't always easy to agree on whether identical work is being done. Nor is it easy to find statistics that assess the relative competence of men and women workers. But one way to start might be by limiting ourselves to all full-time workers who are in their early thirties, from thirty to thirty-four, a group that currently contains about 8 million men and 5 million women. The women in this cohort deserve to be taken seriously. Fully 20 percent have not yet been married, in most cases by their own decision, which suggests they have other aspirations. Another 17 percent are divorced or separated or widowed, which in most cases means they must now support themselves. And the remaining 63 percent who are married are combining full-time employment with domestic obligations. Also, at this age, about the same proportions of women and men have completed college, so the two genders look quite similar in their commitment to careers and their investments in education.

Of course, the table on page 201 cannot tell us if the men and women are performing "equal" tasks. What we do see is that the women's median earnings stand at $825 per $1,000 for the men, a relatively high ratio as current comparisons go, but still far from parity. This age group is important because it contains what should be the most promising echelon of women. Yet they are not even half as likely to have $50,000 jobs, and they are a third less apt to be in the $35,000 to $50,000 tier. In contrast, men are a third less likely to be found in the

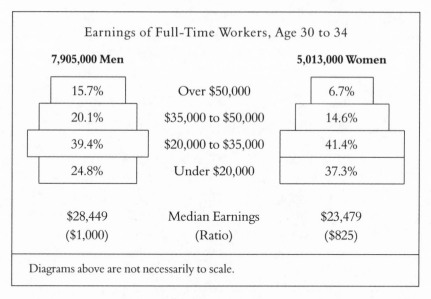

Earnings of Full-Time Workers, Age 30 to 34

7,905,000 Men		5,013,000 Women
15.7%	Over $50,000	6.7%
20.1%	$35,000 to $50,000	14.6%
39.4%	$20,000 to $35,000	41.4%
24.8%	Under $20,000	37.3%
$28,449	Median Earnings	$23,479
($1,000)	(Ratio)	($825)

Diagrams above are not necessarily to scale.

bottom bracket. The bottom line is that employers have shown much less inclination to promote accomplished women to $50,000 positions, while they seem to feel that as few men as possible should be made to take jobs paying less than $20,000. Another factor is that, thus far, women have been more likely than men to choose lower-paying professions. For example, in museums and galleries (average earnings: $18,928) or book publishing ($35,204), rather than, say, petroleum refining ($57,616) or as security and commodity brokers ($81,796).

A double standard for incomes persists not only on earth, but in the galaxies of stars. Over the years, the top moneymakers in the music industry have been all-male groups such as the Beatles, the Rolling Stones, the Eagles, Pink Floyd, and the Grateful Dead. Individual performers such as Michael Jackson, Garth Brooks, Billy Joel, and Elton John have made measurably more than the top female performers. Among authors, Stephen King, John Grisham, Tom Clancy, and Michael Crichton command larger advances than do such blockbusting novelists as Judith Krantz, Jackie Collins, and Patricia Cornwell. The men's books are then made into big-budget movies, while the women must settle for seeing theirs prepared as four-part specials for the small screen.

There is no shortage of theories to explain why this is the case. One certainly is that men have always put their stamp on art and entertainment, at the same time making sure that enough of what they produce

The Top Ten

Hollywood's Best-Paid Stars Then and Now

1934		1994
Will Rogers	#1	Harrison Ford
Clark Gable	#2	Sylvester Stallone
Janet Gaynor	#3	Bruce Willis
Wallace Beery	#4	Tom Hanks
Mae West	#5	Kevin Costner
Joan Crawford	#6	Clint Eastwood
Bing Crosby	#7	Arnold Schwarzenegger
Shirley Temple	#8	Michael Douglas
Marie Dressler	#9	Jim Carrey
Norma Shearer	#10	Robin Williams

will appeal to women. Many more women bought novels by Anthony Trollope and Charles Dickens compared with the number of men attracted to Jane Austen and the Brontës. True, women have contributed their movie dollars and television watching to Barbra Streisand and Roseanne and Oprah Winfrey. Yet while these performers have become extremely rich, they still comprise a relatively short list. Of course, plays and movies and television series all have women stars, and most men do like seeing female faces and figures. But not always for their acting abilities. Indeed, men tend to shy away from entertainment in which women have too dominant a role. Recall how every episode of Mary Tyler Moore's long-running program had her surrounded by men with strongly written scripts. And with Roseanne, one suspects that insofar as men were watching her show, it was mainly because the women in their lives insisted having the program on.

It was not always this way. Above are two sets of rankings: on the left, Hollywood's best-paid stars in 1934, and on the right, the biggest moneymakers sixty years later in 1994. Most apparent, of course, is that a majority of 1934 group were women.

It is interesting to ponder why female movie stars were popular and highly paid in the 1930s. There may be lessons that are worth resurrecting from that distant era of Janet Gaynor and Norma Shearer.

CHAPTER ELEVEN

GREED, TALENT, AND OTHER ENIGMAS

With so contentious a subject as money, we cannot ask that all issues be resolved. Especially since money—what it stands for, what it can buy—rouses so many of the foibles, frailties, and fantasies that beset the human species. On the pages that follow, the reader will be invited to explore some facets of our lives that remain mysterious. One of these is greed, a word much in common use. Yet are we so sure we know what it is, or when we are seeing it at work? Another is talent, which of course takes many forms. Here the question is whether abilities we regard as rare will always be in short supply, or if their stock can be increased.

Education also has an enigmatic side. We know that added years of schooling generally bring higher earnings. But is it so clear why spending more time in classrooms tends to enhance people's incomes? And then there is the issue of worth. All of us have a moral sense, even if at times we keep it under wraps. Still, it occasionally reminds us that some human activities benefit the world more than others. (What value would you assign to designing cigarette packages?) Or we simply have the feeling that each contribution deserves an appropriate compensation. But the way our economy rewards endeavors is another matter, along with the fact that some get no monetary reward at all. Hence the wish to infuse more rationality into the allocation of incomes and earnings. This is undoubtedly an honorable aim; the dilemma, of course, is how to achieve a consensus on what each undertaking is worth.

IS IT GREED—OR IS IT A GAME?

When investigators entered Imelda Marcos's mansion, they found closets crammed with three thousand pairs of shoes. Is this an example of what we mean by greed? Perhaps, although here we find ourselves focusing on the whys and wherefores of footware rather than money. Rupert Murdoch seems bent on becoming the prime media presence on every continent. As a result, he will undoubtedly multiply his wealth. Yet power seems more precisely to be his aim, control over the distribution of information, affixing his imprint across the globe. Surely, he would pursue this quest even if did not add more billions to those he already has. Michael Milken, when he was the shining star at the investment firm of Drexel Burnham Lambert, either asked for or did not decline a single year's pay package of $550 million. This looks more like greed, because even the most imaginative among us might wonder what one person could do with all that money.

At its most elemental, greed is wanting, getting, keeping more than you will ever need. It also evokes images of a Midas, whose dearest wish was to own all the world's gold, or of a chortling misanthrope who rejoices in the misfortune of others. Contrary to common belief, greed was *not* one of the seven deadly sins. The original litany was lust, envy, gluttony, covetousness, anger, pride, and sloth. (Try this mnemonic: LEGCAPS.) Yet as it happens, greed touches all these bases, except perhaps sloth. Gluttony stresses the physical dimension. As we are continually reminded, far too many Americans overeat, gorging ourselves well beyond the needs of optimal nutrition. Something physical also spurred Imelda Marcos to accumulate all those shoes, most of which she would probably never wear. A psychoanalytically oriented podiatrist might claim that she had projected anxieties and insecurities onto her feet. Lust is a sexual expression of greed. Hence the Don Juans who can never bed enough women, especially since a one-time seduction is what counts as a conquest. (If he finds himself wanting a second night, that shows she has gained power over him.) Others sate their desires with libidinal automobiles or one-of-a-kind designer gowns.

Media moguls covet one more network, one more newspaper, one more string of magazines. And obtaining it is all the more satisfying if in doing so they can vanquish a long-envied competitor and reach the top of the heap. Indeed, to covet literally means to lust after a person or a possession you know does not rightfully belong to you, which of course makes the triumph all the more delicious. And pride? Listen for what is really being conveyed when someone regales you with the size of his wine cellar, the splendor of his custom-built home, or the comforts of his rustic ranch.

And then, of course, there is money. That is, money pure and simple, apart from uses to which it may be put, nakedly registered in zeros and digits. Preceding chapters have detailed the record sums demanded and received by athletes and entertainers, corporate chairmen and college presidents, leading lawyers and professors of medicine. Or entrepreneurs such as Bill Gates and Warren Buffett and George Soros, for whom the money just keeps coming in. (In both 1993 and 1995, it will be recalled, Soros netted more than $1 billion.) At this point incredulity sets in: What can one possibly *do* with all that cash?

The answer is that we are asking the wrong question. Beyond a certain point, the money is not wanted or intended for spending, but for other purposes. Nor is it even to satiate desires and appetites we often associate with greed. What follows are some composite explanations from several individuals who agreed to be frank about why they have asked for or accepted more than they wanted or needed.

"Yes, I will be getting a seven-figure advance for my next book. The publisher I went with had the money and was willing to hand it over. If I took less than I thought he had, the difference that he kept would be extra profit for him, for the work I will be doing. So my pushing him to his highest offer results in the fairest division of profits."

"I started this business, and recently it has really hit the charts. The profits keep rolling in, and I just put them in my account. Sure, I could lower my prices. But people seem willing to buy what I sell with its current tab. If sales fall off, I may cut a few dollars off the price, but that isn't necessary now. No, I never expected to make this much money. But the fact that it is flowing in is quite honestly outside my control."

"True, as the chairman of this company, I am taking home what many people regard as a very lavish salary. But this money is not simply to reward me. I am at the apex of a corporate pyramid. Part of my job is to recruit the best people possible as executives, and for that we have to pay them well. In

theory, I could take less than what some of my immediate subordinates get. But it would look rather strange, and they would probably take it as some kind of message directed at them."

"To tell the truth, I think I am making good use of all those millions that have come my way. I happen to be passionate about art. And in my case, it means works not only by well-known artists, but also unknown but promising painters. In time, I will donate my collection to museums or per-haps build a gallery which will be open to the public. While I cannot say that I literally need all the money I have, I have devoted it to a pursuit which supports and sustains our culture."

"I quit my job the day my dad died, which was about twenty years ago. He left me enough so I can live very comfortably on the income from my inheri-tance. Most of my life is, well, social. You know, with friends at my level. But the point about my money is that my dad made it, as an investment banker on Wall Street. Being able to build up a personal fortune was a great incentive for him. Do you think he would have put in all that work if he knew that when he died all or almost all of it had to go to the govern-ment? So I suggest that you not focus on me, or worry about my 'idle' life. Inheritances are integral to our economy. Anyway, mine is a one generation thing. When my time's up, what I leave will be dispersed among my four kids. While it will give each of them a nice cushion, they also know they'll have to work."

"Each year I am listed in a national magazine as one of the wealthiest peo-ple in this country. Its reporters guess at how much I'm worth—they're quite accurate—and then give my relative ranking, which happens to be very high. Frankly, it means a lot to me to be up there. It's like winning an Academy Award or Nobel Prize or the Medal of Honor. And something else. When I was young, I was regarded as a nerd, especially by the girls, who wouldn't give me the time of day. They all know who I am now and what I've attained. There was one in particular . . ."

"My millions are not a mountain of dollars stashed away in some vault. This fortune, which I made, consists of the assets of the company I built up. It is an ongoing enterprise, giving jobs to people and providing the public with goods and services they have shown that they want. The issue is not whether I personally need so much money. But my firm does, if it is to keep operating and moving into new ventures. What if I sell the company and

walk away with a nine-figure check? Let's discuss that when it happens.
Just as I think my firm has contributed to the well-being of this country, so
I feel I can do something worthwhile with the money I would get if I sold it."

Thus far, drives generally identified with greed do not seem to figure strongly in these individuals' estimation of themselves. True, greed
can be subtler than in the case of a Scrooge cackling over his bank balance. Yet the fact remains that some people are notable for asking and
getting more than others who are in similar positions. For example,
presidents of top-tier universities are generally paid around $250,000.
So why, we may wonder, does John Silber of Boston University want
in excess of $500,000? In recent years, the chairmen of the country's
one hundred largest corporations have averaged around $2.8 million
in total compensation. Then why do the chief executives at Coca-
Cola, Disney, and Travelers feel they need or deserve packages ten to
fifteen times what their colleagues are getting? It is one thing to top the
list; it is another to put yourself so blatantly far ahead of your peers. At
this point, greed has to figure in the equation.

Yet virtually all people in well-paying jobs tell us that they enjoy
doing what they do, that the challenges they face give zest to their lives.
That money keeps rolling in is a nice supplement, but hardly what
sends them to their desks every day. It would be interesting to see how
many would show up and perform as ably and energetically for the
salary paid to, say, the head of the Food and Drug Administration,
which at last report was in the vicinity of $135,000. The answer is that
few, if any, would, if only because the entire structure and system has
become based on ascending levels of pay. It is difficult to imagine an
executive, or any American, responding to a salary overture, "Thanks,
but I don't need that much." Almost all of us will think up reasons why
it is appropriate to accept whatever comes our way, or for that matter,
whatever we can induce some other person to offer.

Does this mean that little is gained by asking how far greed affects
human attitudes toward money? The short answer is that even comfortably off individuals can explain why they want or need more. And
while the "more" may start as only an additional $10,000, once that
sum is in hand, the goal soon becomes another $20,000. Recall the
woes of Sherman McCoy, the antihero of Tom Wolfe's book *Bonfire of*
the Vanities, who couldn't pay all his bills on $980,000 a year. And, as has

been noted, once a certain level has been reached, adding to income or wealth becomes a way of keeping score. Perhaps in another kind of society, honorific awards could do the job instead of dollars. That, at least in our time, is not America's way. While few of us comport ourselves like Midas or Scrooge, the seeds of greed may well be in all of us. At least part of an answer lies in how each of us will react when an opportunity arises to acquire more.

TALENT: SCARCE OR UNDISCOVERED?

We may begin with what most of us consider obvious: that some individuals have gifts that others cannot hope to emulate. We can all cite artists, authors, and composers whose achievements stand far above those of any of their rivals. The same holds for small numbers of scientists, athletes, and actors who display an unusual flair. Others seem to have a genius for military strategy or neurosurgery, for building a business or teaching arithmetic to eight year olds. The list could easily be extended to include attributes that make for a good parent or an understanding friend.

But talent could be more widespread than we believe, and we may have blinded ourselves to that possibility. One reason is our penchant for ranking people and their capacities, with those lower on the lists being deemed of doubtful competence. (Would you want your child taught by a second-tier teacher?) Another reason stems from a reluctance to discover and develop abilities that in fact exist but lie dormant due to lack of encouragement. (Surely, there are potential world-class chess players in every inner city.)

It will be recalled from an earlier chapter that Derek Bok, Harvard's president for twenty-two years, argued that every society contains only "a limited supply of highly talented people." If our goals are efficiency and equity, he says, we had best "begin thinking of talent as a finite resource." Of course, it is not surprising that someone who headed Harvard thinks this way. Indeed, that institution maintains its reputation by persuading the public that very few can hope to meet its standards.

Of the thirteen thousand high school seniors who apply to Harvard in a typical year, only one in six is accepted. Given the school's well-known reputation for academic excellence, we may presume that most of the applicants had reason to believe that their records were suitable for admission. But even among this accomplished stratum, the great majority fail to make the cut. Nor were the decisions on whom to admit made capriciously. Harvard has a sizable admissions staff, whose members read folders and examine essays, conduct probing interviews, and hold numerous meetings in an effort to ensure that they are culling the very best. If any group deserves to be called "highly talented" it must be the high school students Harvard enrolls each year. Similar claims have been made by another dozen or so schools, which admit only a small fraction of their applicants. (Or just short of a dozen: Amherst, Brown, Columbia, Cornell, Dartmouth, Duke, Princeton, Stanford, Williams, Yale, and perhaps the University of Pennsylvania.)

There is only one problem with this premise. When we look at the graduates of selective colleges, say, thirty years later, the results are disappointing. Despite their presumed promise, few have carved out distinctive careers. Needless to say, most are good providers and responsible citizens. But shouldn't more be expected? One place to look is leadership in the corporate world. An inspection of the one hundred largest corporations and financial firms reveals that only eleven of their chief executives were Ivy League undergraduates, and three of them had studied engineering at Cornell.* Of course, the country has some three thousand colleges, and no one expects the alumni of a few to commandeer all the top positions. But that is not the issue here. Rather, the question is how many graduates of selective colleges make it to the top in their later lives. Considering the care those schools took in choosing them, the outcomes are not auspicious. Thus, if we take as our pool all male Ivy graduates who are now in the age range of current CEOs, it emerges that less than one-tenth of one percent of them have reached the summit of the corporate world. (Whether many more have excelled in philosophy or poetry is probably just as problematical.)

So one part of the story is that most of those supposed to be gifted

---

*Of the eleven, four attended Cornell, followed by two each from Harvard and Princeton, and one each from Dartmouth, Yale, and the University of Pennsylvania. Not one of the hundred CEOs had graduated from Amherst, Brown, Columbia, Duke, Stanford, or Williams. On the other hand, Notre Dame and NYU each produced three chairmen, and eleven state universities were able to claim two. Indeed, campuses in Kansas, Idaho, and Iowa surpassed most of the highly selective schools.

turn out not to be so, or that the aptitudes they once displayed have not proved germane in later life. Our selection mechanisms have shown to be incapable of identifying individuals with exceptional abilities. Much more prominent on the CEO roster are graduates of such state institutions as Tennessee Tech, Southwestern Missouri, North Carolina State, and San Jose State University. Or lower-tier private colleges such as Marquette, Wake Forest, Wabash, and Villanova. Indeed, it is probably not too much to say that the American economy relies on proving grounds such as Purdue and Texas Tech to supply people to make up for the Ivy League's miscalculations.

But there is also the issue of whether talent is in fact so scarce a commodity, not just in ethereal realms such as poetry, but in occupations regarded as mundane, such as hairdressers and prison guards. Several factors intertwine here, some of which have been considered in earlier chapters. One is the desire to have a small number of superstars, rather than acknowledge that many practitioners are extremely good. Another is the tendency to make occupations seem more intricate than is actually the case. Indeed, this is the hallmark of all protected professions, whether neurosurgery or preparing tax returns or teaching social studies to junior high school students.

In many cases we demand the "best" for ourselves. If your child is to have an operation, you will want her to be cared for by the hospital's top surgeon, if not the most highly rated person in the region. In fact, few laypeople have even a minimal knowledge of surgery, so we seldom pause to think what the "best" might mean. (Surgeons themselves are apt to rate their colleagues not on their skill with a scalpel, but on how many papers they have presented at professional conferences.) Still, let's suppose that one can give surgeons numerical evaluations, and then further assume that this has been done for four who are affiliated with your hospital.

You are then allowed to see the four surgeons' scores, which are as follows: 120, 100, 90, 70. Is it necessary to ask which one you would pick? But then imagine, as an alternative exercise, that you were handed this set of scores: 99.2, 99.0, 98.9, 98.7. How then would you choose? Would, in fact, a rating of 99.2 suggest to you a significantly higher competence than a 98.7? It just might, which could lead you to insist on having the surgeon who scored 99.2. If anything, we are observing how ignorance and tension can affect our judgments. In fact, all four surgeons were found both qualified and competent by standards set in the hospital. Of course, for many of us, "qualified and competent" may not suffice. We want superb, extraordinary, the very best. Yet our views about "the best" can be skewed by something as simple as the method of reporting ratings. Why did the "fourth" surgeon end up two-tenths of a point behind the one who ranked "third"? Rumor has it that one of the evaluators was put off by his humming Mozart while he stitched.

This is not to argue that all surgeons are equally proficient, but it may be suggested that almost all are sufficiently skilled to minister capably to our needs. We have been hoisted by our own petard. We become competitive, anxious, and unhappy by presuming that the skills and services we want are extremely rare and hoping that we can be among the fortunate few who are able to obtain "the best." Now let's turn to a second situation where lives are at stake.

Next Thursday afternoon, you want to fly from Chicago to Seattle. Four airlines have scheduled flights at times that suit you. Let's assume that all are charging the same price and you do not prefer one rather than another because of its frequent-flier program, the quality of the food, or what movie it is showing. So which airline do you choose? One way to start is by indicating what you will *not* do. First, you will not call each airline and ask for the name of the pilot on the flights you are considering. Nor will you then ask to speak to someone higher up, who can tell you the pilot's proficiency score when he was last rated by an observer from the FAA. (This is public information, and as a citizen you are entitled to have it.) It may take a little while, but in the end you discover that the pilots' ratings are 130, 110, 100, and 80. Will you select your flight on the basis of those scores? Perhaps you would, if you took all the pains that have just been outlined. But the point is that you don't.

Rather, we assume that every pilot retained by an airline is competent and qualified, not least because it's bad for business to have crashes. In fact, there is just as much subtlety to piloting a 737 as in performing surgery. (We seldom know how much skill is needed to get the plane down safely with wind shear on its tail.) Yet airlines have another lesson to impart. In recent years, the number of people wanting to travel has been expanding at a rapid rate. But suppose it were proposed that the individuals capable of piloting today's planes comprised, in Harvard's Bok's phrase, "a limited supply of highly talented people." Had that in fact been so, United and Delta and American would have had to bid for the services of those in that finite pool. Not only would salaries have soared; airlines would have had to limit their flights if they ran short of qualified pilots. But of course this didn't happen. Since 1970, the number of commercial pilots has almost doubled, yet no one has argued that quality in the profession has declined. Indeed, the opening of new positions has been matched by the emergence of people who have an aptitude for flying. Yet those men and women would never have displayed those capacities in a time of more constricted hiring.

Throughout history, most human talents have remained dormant because societies have lacked the capacity or interest to uncover people's fullest potential. The great migrations to America were spurred by the knowledge that this country offered opportunities for releasing abilities people sensed that they had, but could not develop in more constrained settings. The exigencies of wartime have also brought out broad spectrums of skills—including managerial talent—that people were never aware that they had. One of the most convincing arguments for affirmative action is that it compels employers to look for talents that do in fact exist within groups of men and women who were never previously recruited.

Does this mean that if a society looks hard enough, it could find another Shakespeare in its midst, perhaps some more Mozarts, and even several writers with the genius of Jane Austen? This is another enigmatic question that defies a conclusive answer. What can be said is that in periods we regard as "golden ages," an atmosphere arose that encouraged unusual displays of brilliance. Just as Florence in the time of the Medicis felt no shortage of sublime artists, so classical Athens did not lack for gifted playwrights. Perhaps it is indicative of our more mundane times that we resort to talk of shortages. Recall how, in an earlier chapter, a television executive sought to explain the low quality of comedy scripts by claiming, "There's just not enough talent to go around." That may be how it is seen at his network. Doubtless a similar plaint came from coaches at the National Basketball Association, in the days when they only took players who were white.

WHY STAY IN SCHOOL?

In today's economy, you won't get anywhere without a high school diploma. And to do more than tread water, you need a college degree. True, we can all name dropouts who have built impressive careers. Still, the belief remains that people who fail to finish high school won't make much of their lives. Hence our admonition to youngsters: stay in school.

Does this mean that our society values education? Overall, the figures certainly show that schooling adds to your income. Among men aged thirty-five to forty-four who worked full-time in 1995, those who started but never finished high school averaged $20,466 for the year, those with a diploma made $32,689, while holders of bachelor's degrees averaged $57,196. As the table on page 214 shows, moving from a diploma to a degree gave the college men an additional $749 over every $1,000 earned by the high school graduates. According to Census Bureau studies, during a working career, a typical college graduate can expect to earn $599,980 more than a person with a high school diploma. Obtaining a master's degree will add $198,120, and a doctorate averages an additional $523,470. Of course, figures vary by race and gender, along with the reputation of the awarding school. And, as the table also makes clear, a college degree today yields an even greater advantage than it did twenty years ago. Moreover, college women in this age range have fared relatively better than men. In 1975, they averaged $499 for every $1,000 earned by the men; by 1995, their ratio has risen to $645. And while the edge for college men over male high school graduates rose by 15.8 percent, college women went up 22.1 percent compared with their female high school counterparts.

Why is education so important? Having been through the schooling mill, we all have opinions. At last count, over 90 million adults had completed high school, and almost 40 million of them are now college graduates. Since obtaining these credentials required an outlay of time, and often money, most want to feel that they gained something from the experience. In addition, more than 9 million men and women owe their livelihoods to a profession related to schooling—education is easily our largest industry—which inclines them to insist on its importance. This is not to say that what they do is unnecessary. Still, the warning that youngsters should stay in school is seldom accompanied

Payment by Degrees: 1975 vs. 1995 *Average Earnings of Full-time Workers, Age 35 to 44* *(in the years' actual dollars)*		
1975		
	Men	**Women**
High school diploma only	$14,007	$7,774
Bachelor's degree only	$21,152	$10,560
Bachelor's per $1,000 high school earnings	$1,510	$1,358
1995		
	Men	**Women**
High school diploma only	$32,689	$22,257
Bachelor's degree only	$57,196	$36,901
Bachelor's per $1,000 high school earnings	$1,750	$1,658
Advantage for bachelor's: Change from 1975 to 1995	+15.8%	+22.1%

by an analysis of what education actually does to prepare young people for the challenges of employment and earnings.

The enterprise of education has a wide compass, running from show-and-tell in kindergarten to postdoctoral research in cell biology and deconstructive criticism. It also imparts specific skills, ranging from elementary arithmetic to periodontal dentistry. Or it may embrace mental stimulation for its own sake, with no thought of profit or practical application. For current purposes, we can confine our attention to the span of education that goes from nursery school through a bachelor's degree, a regimen that generally occupies the better part of two decades.

The first lesson that school imparts is that it starts at a specified time. At the age of five, the day begins with a mother's raised voice calling, *"Hurry, or you'll be late!"* Kindergarten instills in us an internal clock and anxieties over tardiness. Show-and-tell teaches us how to sense the parameters of an assignment without actually being told what they are and encourages the development of skills that may prove useful twenty years later, when your job calls for a presentation. There are field trips and laboratory exercises, as well as extracurricular activities that offer opportunities for socializing, and it is worth noting that because teachers are predominantly members of the middle class, their diction and demeanor can serve as models for youngsters from less worldly backgrounds. But the bulk of formal schooling consists of sustained sitting. From first grade through graduate school, students are assigned mainly to rows of desks or chairs, a setting unique to schools and rarely found in the world of work. How is this experience a preparation for later life?

The first answer is that school makes youngsters sit at a time when they would prefer to be doing just about anything else. In a word, school accustoms you to being in a place where you would rather not be. The fact that most of us show up at our jobs without serious compulsion demonstrates that we have learned this lesson well. Another aspect of school is essentially solitary and consists for the most part of doing assignments at home or in libraries or study halls. But today, students are setting limits on the number of hours they are willing to devote to homework. (During which time, music is almost invariably on.)

What can and should be granted is that schools do teach most youngsters to read and write, and to perform arithmetic equations that will be needed in adult life. But this is the basic job of education and hardly warrants congratulation, considering the sums the system spends to accomplish this goal. Even if only a small number of students emerge with a passion for literature, the rest are sufficiently literate to read newspapers and magazines and even some best-sellers. The majority of high school graduates can still write a functional paragraph, if given time to think through what they want to say. Since the rudiments of literacy and arithmetic can be absorbed by sitting in classrooms, that is reason enough for a teenager to remain through high school.

There is little evidence that schooling produces informed and cultured individuals. For example, millions of Americans have been "taught" poetry in high school and college. But how many of them have later dipped into a volume of verse? Adults who once took courses in history would be hard-pressed to recall the causes of the War of 1812. And except for those who embark on careers as scientists or engineers, few can remember what they learned in algebra and chemistry classes. Nor can it be shown that courses in philosophy or sociology have an identifiable impact on how graduates see the world, let alone how they will conduct themselves in later life. As a college teacher, I am flattered when former students tell me that they recall a class of mine. But this does not tell us to what extent formal education—or simply exposure to one or several teachers—is an important formative influence.

Education maintains its myths, as does every enterprise. Few assignments given in school and college classes bear much of a relation to the ways people acquire knowledge in their adult lives. While many occupations entail writing reports, few want or need the kind of footnoting required by the academic world. Or we hear it argued that being compelled to study mathematics "trains" the mind, a claim earlier generations made for memorizing Latin and Greek. However, no studies have ever shown that people who mastered calculus and trigonometry are more thoughtful or reach more rational conclusions than those who have not. The best case that can be made for mathematics is that it is a difficult subject that most students don't like. Making them suffer the rigors of a demanding discipline may be a useful regimen. August committees periodically insist that all students become expert in a foreign language, a demand untroubled by the fact that most members of such bodies cannot themselves read a foreign newspaper. As it happens, the languages common to many of the world's markets—Arabic, for example, or Chinese or Japanese—are not ordinarily taught in our schools and colleges.

Higher education has somewhat different purposes than grade and high school educations. The liberal arts account for only a quarter of all undergraduate majors. Most programs now purport to be practical training for subsequent careers. Insofar as employers want the people they hire to arrive with at least some vocational knowledge, colleges undertake to teach subjects such as accounting, just as law schools give courses in federal procedure. At the same time, all employers know they must provide in-house training, if only to show how things are done in their companies or organizations. So a residual role for higher education is to bring young people to see themselves as fledgling professionals, much as Annapolis and West Point instill in their students that they are novitiate officers.

Spending four or more years on a campus also serves a social purpose: to ensure entry into the middle class. In circles that count, having a bachelor's degree suffices for membership in that stratum. As was noted in an earlier chapter, of the chief executives of America's one hundred largest firms, only five are not college graduates, and most of these are from a founding family started their own companies. The time invested in pursuing a degree from an Ivy League college, or counterparts such as Duke and Stanford, should yield an even smoother polish and hence lead to more impressive careers.

However, anyone who has attended reunions of Ivy League graduates cannot help but be struck by how many of these alumni end up with middling middle-class incomes and quite commonplace careers. What is instructive is that so many men and women from quite modest backgrounds ascend to higher echelons, moving ahead of people who started with more auspicious credentials.

For most people, staying in school clearly pays off. Given that having a college degree yields a man aged thirty-five to forty-four an average income of $57,196, compared with the $32,689 for men who only finish high school, education is a worthwhile investment. Still, as has been stressed throughout this book, averages and medians tend to conceal many kinds of outcomes. To make precise comparisons, the table on page 218 has purposely confined itself to men aged thirty-five to forty-four who held full-time jobs in 1993.

The table posits possible ranges of earnings that might be anticipated for three educational levels. As can be seen, from 60 to 70 percent of the men are where we might expect them to be. But even more interesting are the 20 percent who have only high school diplomas who were making over $40,000, while almost 30 percent of those with graduate degrees were earning less than that amount. If these findings can be encapsulated in two phrases, they are upward mobility and downward mobility. Much attention is accorded to the former, but the latter, too, is a common occurrence in American life.

THE WORTH OF WORK

When we were students we hoped that our grades would be based on a rational system, one we could understand and accept. True, teachers

Staying in School: Who Gains How Much
Earnings of Men, Age 35 to 44

	High School Diploma Only	Bachelor's Degree	Graduate Degree
Number of persons	5,945,000	3,744,000	2,047,000
Under $10,000	763,000 (12.8%)		
$10,000–$20,000			
$20,000–$30,000	3,985,000 (67.1%)	1,077,000 (28.8%)	601,000 (29.4%)
$30,000–$40,000			
$40,000–$50,000		2,191,000 (58.5%)	
$50,000–$75,000	1,197,000 (20.1%)		
$75,000–$100,000		476,000 (12.7%)	1,446,000 (70.6%)
Over $100,000			
Average income	$27,892	$48,753	$73,034

The boxed figures suggest an expected range of earnings for the three educational levels: high school diploma, $20,000 to $40,000; bachelor's degree, $30,000 to $75,000; graduate degree, at least $40,000. The figures outside the boxes show the proportions of men making more or less than the expected earnings range.

might vary in their methods. Still, we expected that each one's criteria would yield equity and fairness. Ideally, the students would come away agreeing that their essay was in fact worth a B+, while an examination merited a C-. (One thing we learned was that the amount of time we spent preparing would not figure in the equation.)

Similar sentiments are often expressed in the world of work. The high compensation of corporate chairmen led *Forbes* magazine to proclaim on its cover, "It Doesn't Make Sense!" Much the same outburst might be heard when we learned that a local school system offers only $22,000 to its starting teachers. Of course, as stressed earlier, differences in pay can always be "explained," since "reasons" can always be found. Thus we have no problem showing why college professors receive more than kindergarten teachers.

Perhaps the most systematic approach to rational compensation is a plan called "pay equity," which is often accompanied by a variant known as "comparable worth." Underlying both these proposals is the premise that all jobs can be evaluated by standardized criteria. Those who ply this field have devised assessments that, as one proponent has written, "are based on the well-understood factors of skill, effort, responsibility, and working conditions." Here is one set of factors for inclusion in a formula or model:

Length of formal training required
Number of workers an employee is responsible for
Time spent working under deadlines
Impact on and responsibility for budget
Job-related experience
Frequency of work review
Physical stress
Time spent processing information

Once it is agreed how much weight given to these and other valuations, each position can be assigned a numerical quotient. These indices express either what is regarded as a job's intrinsic worth or where it ranks compared with other occupations. In the mid-1980s the state of Washington hired consultants to rate its civil service positions. Their report concluded, for example, that a clerical supervisor's duties, plus the training required for the job, should be assigned 305 points. In contrast, a boiler operator merited a score of only 144. In Illinois, where a somewhat different system was used, 889 points were given to accountants, against 578 for the state's electricians. To translate ratings into actual wages, each point would be multiplied by a monetary base. In Illinois, if that figure were $46.91, then the accountant's salary would be $41,703, while the electrician's 578 points would yield him $27,114.

The number of points awarded can also be based on an inherent valuation. If that approach is used, the value of an electrician's expertise would be expressed as 578 points on a scale of perhaps 1,000. Or, if a job's worth is ascertained by comparing various positions, then the contribution of an electrician is judged as worth only about two-thirds of an accountant's.

Some proponents of pay equity have agreed the state of a job market can affect the worth of an occupation. But this adds a whole new dimension to job evaluation. It is one thing to note that nursing requires rigorous training. Some evaluators may even decide to give the position extra points for its moral and social benefits. However, it is quite another matter to include within the "worth" of nursing what hospitals find they must offer to recruit the people they need. Indeed, short supply in certain occupations can end up outweighing such factors as formal training. If the state of Illinois finds that it cannot attract electricians at $27,114, it may have to raise their pay closer to the level of accountants.

By the same token, employers usually have fairly clear rules for deciding what to pay the people they hire. The first is to pay no more than they have to. Trial and error and intuition are all involved in deciding what will be the lowest acceptable rate. The same process occurs in finding what must be done to please the people you want to keep. An equally important consideration is whether paying more will threaten the survival of the enterprise. Since firms seek to keep their costs down and their prices competitive, higher salaries can only be justified if they result in higher productivity and profits.

Thus far no attempts have been made to impose pay equity on enterprises whose bottom lines are stock value and profit. Nor has anyone tried to tell General Motors that what its engineers do is "worth" $73,775, so that some on the payroll should have raises. Management's response would be that this is not the way businesses work. People are only paid what is needed to secure their services and, if their work is valued, to keep them from leaving. As a result, the pay-equity principle has been confined mainly to nonprofit organizations, especially universities and colleges.

On the premise that supervising men's and women's basketball calls for the same qualifications and involves comparable duties, state universities in Iowa, Tennessee, Georgia, and Virginia have mandated equal salaries for both coaches. The most noteworthy outcome was generous raises for the coaches of women's teams, in one case a jump from $58,000 to $97,500. Thus far, however, pay equity has not been applied on campuses where sports are a big business and the bidding for winning mentors can be extremely fierce. UCLA, for example, budgets $400,000 for its basketball coach, since winning seasons are thought to aid the university in direct and indirect ways. Should their women's coach, supposing an identical win-loss record, claim that she deserves equal pay for equal work?

"Worth" in the realm of work has three reference points: moral, technical, and what the market decrees the value of a job to be. If we use a moral measure, teachers should not make less than boiler operators. A strictly technical approach seems easier to apply, since it simply factors standardized criteria into its equations. Indeed, as was shown in Chapter Seven, such a "rationality" now governs most payments made to physicians. Public and private insurers, after consulting with experienced practitioners, have agreed on "relative value" figures that incorporate the time and skill and effort involved in thousands of procedures. Thus reimbursement for an oleoscopy is a multiple of 1.51, while the base for an endoscopy is 7.71. Of course, some actual cases may present unforeseen problems; but the chances of that happening have already been factored into the equations. Needless to say, not all physicians are happy with the system. Some say that the extra care they take with a procedure is not always reflected in its index number.

The point is not whether proposals such as "equity" and "worth" have much chance of being adopted. All indications are that they do not. On the whole, moral considerations have never had more than a marginal impact on what people are paid. And technical formulas seem too arbitrary to gain widespread acceptance. The problem is that there isn't much enthusiasm for the market alternative either. Indeed, we probably spend more time commenting on its absurdities and outrages than remarking on how equitably it works. Which is a roundabout way of showing how far we are from allocating incomes and earnings in ways that can be called even remotely rational.

CHAPTER TWELVE

MONEY AND THE WORLD
WE WANT

The period we call the postwar years actually began during World War II. The end of hostilities found this country's economy at its highest peak of efficiency; indeed, for several decades, it would have no serious competition. The war also brought about a domestic social transformation. Military service and civilian employment had entrusted millions of men and women with new responsibilities, which they now knew they could handle. Upon their demobilization, there was no diminution of their self-confidence or their willingness to seize new opportunities. This national self-assurance, which was strongly underwritten by such government initiatives as the GI Bill and Federal Housing Administration loans, contributed to the expansion of higher education, the suburban migration, and the creation of a confident middle class.

As the table on page 224 shows, the decade from 1950 to 1960 brought a rise in median family income of 37 percent in real purchasing power, an increase unrivaled in the history of this nation or any other. Between 1960 and 1970, real living standards grew by an additional 26 percent. Earnings of men in the early years of their careers increased at an even greater rate. These were halcyon years for most Americans. Families bought a first or second car, exchanged renting for home ownership, and deserted cities for the lawns and malls of suburbia. The most compelling evidence of self-assurance was the fact that families at all social levels were having three or four children, confident in the expectation that the economy would provide upward mobility for their offspring, as it had for the parents.

Income and Earnings: 1950–95 (in 1995 dollars)				
	Median Family Income	Change During Decade	Earnings of Men 35–44	Change During Decade
1950	$21,069	+37.3%	$20,656	+37.8%
1960	$28,926	+25.9%	$28,457	+30.6%
1970	$36,410	+ 6.9%	$37,164	- 0.3%
1980	$38,930	+ 5.9%	$37,046	- 6.3%
1990	$41,223	- 1.5%	$34,704	- 9.5%
1995	$40,611		$31,420	

Even though wartime advances in industrial technology meant that fewer workers were needed on factory floors, military demobilization caused no unemployment; the economy readily absorbed the 16 million young people leaving the armed services. One reason was that companies were using their new-found funds to create millions of new office and service occupations. Firms could also afford to settle generously with unions, which brought blue-collar wages and benefits to new heights.

The three decades spanning 1940 to 1970 were the nation's most prosperous years. Indeed, so far as can happen in America's kind of economy, a semblance of redistribution was taking place. During this generation, the share of national income that went to the bottom fifth of families rose by some fractions of a point to an all-time high, while that received by the richest fifth fell to its lowest level. This is the very period of shared well-being that many people would like to re-create in this country.

Yet in no way is this possible. It was an atypical era, in which America won an adventitious primacy because of a war it delayed entering and its geographic isolation which spared it the ravages that the other combatants suffered.

History usually provides hints about what is to follow. Even in the 1950s, there were signs of a reaction against generous wages. Employers were locating new facilities in Southern states, where labor costs were lower and unions were less powerful. For the period, this was the equivalent of companies' shipping jobs overseas and was a harbinger of what would happen later when China was ready to underbid America's Carolinas.

Abroad, America's erstwhile allies and enemies were rebuilding their economies, but it would take at least two decades for any of them to develop a global resonance. Before the 1970s, the goods that America imported tended to be luxury items, or curiosities such as the early Volkswagens. Not only did American companies dominate the domestic market, they also had a lot of cash to invest abroad. Each year, America movies and music, along with convenience food and leisure clothing, became more the norm across the globe.

But these rewards of war would bring about America's decline from primacy. The world was learning the lessons that the postwar years had charged us to teach. What was once only within America's power, other countries would do as well or even better. The time would come when European and Asian products would be a common presence in the American marketplace. Overseas entrepreneurs not only produced innovative and well-made products, they also showed a shrewd understanding of American tastes. From there, the next step was investment. By the 1990s, dozens of homegrown names and brands were owned by foreign firms, which have generally had the good sense not to publicize that fact. It is hard to imagine Burger King mounting British flags behind their counters, or Firestone reminding Americans who buy their tires that the profits will be sent back to Japan.

Ironically, America's quest for preeminence took a domestic toll because it was not the only nation aspiring to superpower status. Year in and year out, the United States and the Soviet Union vied for first place in military stature. For both nations, retaining an edge in weaponry, launching costly forays into space, and intervening in Vietnam and Afghanistan drained not only material resources but their sources of imagination and ingenuity as well. While these quests bankrupted the Soviet Union and had deleterious effects on the American economy, such as a skyrocketing federal budget deficit, our overseas competitors gained a distinct advantage by deciding not to incur huge military costs. Instead, they gave priority to exploring new opportunities in technology and trade. Because so much of America's creative capacity was devoted to designing sophisticated missiles and supercarriers for NASA and the Pentagon and wasn't attuned to civilian needs, businesses in such countries as Switzerland, Holland, and Sweden first sensed a demand in the American market for new kinds of products. Which is why Swatch, Heineken, and Volvo have become American household words.

A major consequence of our erstwhile allies' and former enemies' success in penetrating the American market is that their citizens are now as affluent as our own, and fewer of their people live in poverty or in prison. While these countries must still wrestle with unemployment and costly social programs, the socioeconomic problems they face are under reasonable control compared with those in the United States.

America's postwar upsurge lasted barely three decades. The tide began to turn in the early 1970s. Between 1970 and 1980, family income rose less than 7 percent. And that small increase resulted entirely from the fact that additional family members were joining the workforce. Indeed, the most vivid evidence of decline is found in the unremitting drop in men's earnings since 1970. Averages and medians, however, conceal important variations, such as that some American households have done quite well for themselves during the closing decades of the century. Those with incomes of $1 million or more have reached an all-time high, as are families and individuals making over $100,000. By all outward appearances, there is still plenty of money around, but it is landing in fewer hands. Yet it is by no means apparent that people are being paid these generous salaries and options and fees because their work is adding much of substance to the nation's output. Indeed, the coming century will test whether an economy can flourish by exporting most notably action movies and flavored water.

The term *upper class* is not commonly used to describe the people in America's top income tier since it connotes a hereditary echelon that passes on its holdings from generation to generation. Only a few American families have remained at the very top for more than two or three generations, and even when they do, as have the du Ponts and Rockefellers, successive descendants slice the original pie into smaller and smaller pieces. So if America does not have a "class" at its apex, what should we call the people who have the most money? The answer is to refer to them as we usually do, as being "wealthy" or "rich."

The rich, whom we identified earlier as the members of the 68,064 households who in 1995 filed federal tax returns that declared a 1994 income of $1 million or more, have varied sources of income. In some cases, their income came almost entirely from their compensation for that year. One such person is Philip Condit, then the newly appointed chairman of Boeing, whose first-year pay was $1.3 million and who at that time owned only $600,000 in Boeing stock. His salary warrants his being called rich, but in 1995 he was not yet *wealthy*. For present purposes, wealth may be considered holdings that would yield you an income of $1 million a year without your having to put in a day's work. Assuming a 7 percent return, it would take income-producing assets of some $15 million to ensure that comfort level.

Unfortunately, we have no official count of how many Americans possess that kind of wealth. It is measurably less than 68,064, since those households report that the largest segment of their incomes come from salaries. Indeed, among the chairmen of the one hundred largest firms, the median stock holding is only $8.4 million. (So they had better keep on working.) A liberal estimate of the number of wealthy Americans would be about thirty thousand households, one-thirtieth of one percent of the national total.

This still puts almost 90 percent of all Americans between the very poor and the wealthy and the rich. One way to begin to define this majority is by creating a more realistic bottom tier than merely those people who fall below the official poverty line. Since Americans deserve more than subsistence, we may set $25,000 a year for a family of three as a minimum for necessities without frills. And even this is a pretty bare floor. Indeed, only about 45 percent of the people questioned in the Roper-Starch poll felt that their households could "get by" on $25,000 a year. In 1995, almost 20 million families—28.4 percent of the total—were living below that spartan standard. This stratum is a varied group. As can be seen on the table on page 228, for over a third, all of their income comes from sources other than employment, most typically Social Security and public assistance. Over 43.3 percent of the households have only one earner, who at that income level is usually a woman and the family's sole source of support. The remainder consists of families where two or more members have had jobs of some kind, which suggests sporadic employment at close to the minimum wage. Whatever designation we give to these households— poor or just getting by—their incomes leave them deprived of even the more modest acquisitions and enjoyments available to the great majority of Americans.

The question of who belongs to America's middle class requires deciding where to place its upper and lower boundaries. In many larger cities and lavish suburbs, it takes at least $500,000 a year for a household to be seen as higher than the middle echelon. In those places, an income of $400,000 or so would still rank you as middle class. In smaller cities and towns, $200,000 might suffice to raise a household beyond the middle echelon. By the same token, the entry point for the middle class could be $30,000 in one setting and $75,000 in a better-off community. While it is difficult to set precise boundaries for this stratum, it is accurate to say that, by one measure or another, most Americans fit into a middle class.

Families Under $25,000		
No earners	6,915,000	35.0%
Only one earner	8,554,000	43.3%
Two or more earners	4,295,000	21.7%
	19,764,000	100.0%

While it is meaningless to classify the households in the middle of America's income distribution because this stratum is so substantial and it encompasses such a wide range of incomes, meaningful divisions can be drawn in our country's overall income distribution.

This book has sought to make clear that the prominent place of the rich tells us a great deal about the kind of country we are, as does the growing group of men and women with $100,000 salaries and households with $100,000 incomes. The same stricture applies to the poor, who, while not necessarily increasing in number, are too often permanently mired at the bottom. This noted, a three-tier division can be proposed, with the caveat that how you fare on a given income can depend on local costs and social expectations.

A corollary of this division is that no sharp edges or chasms separate the tiers. There are haves and have-nots in America, but it is not possible to specify where the possessors end and the dispossessed begin.

*   *   *

That the rich have become richer would seem to bear out Karl Marx's well-known prediction. The nation's greatest fortunes are substantially larger than those of a generation ago. Households with incomes exceeding $1 million a year are also netting more in real purchasing power. At a more mundane level, the top 5 percent of all households in 1975 averaged $122,651 a year; by 1995, in inflation-adjusted dollars, their average annual income had ascended to $188,962.

How Families Fare: Three Tiers		
Tier	**Income Range**	**Number of Families/Percentage**
Comfortable	Over $75,000	12,961,000 18.6%
Coping	$25,000–$75,000	36,872,000 53.0%
Deprived	Under $25,000	19,764,000 28.4%

But Marx did not foresee that the number of rich families and individuals would actually increase over time. Between 1979 and 1994, the number of households declaring incomes of $1 million or more rose from 13,505 to 68,064, again adjusting for inflation. In 1996, *Forbes*'s 400 richest Americans were all worth at least $400 million. In 1982, the year of the magazine's first list, only 110 people in the 400 had holdings equivalent to the 1996 cutoff figure. In other words, almost three-quarters of 1982's wealthiest Americans would not have made the 1996 list. And families with incomes over $100,000—once more, in constant purchasing power—increased almost threefold between 1970 and 1995, rising from 3.4 percent to 9 percent of the total. During the same period, the group of men making more than $50,000 rose from 12 percent of the total to 17 percent.

It is one thing for the rich to get richer when everyone is sharing in overall economic growth, and it is quite another for the better off to prosper while others are losing ground or standing still. But this is what has been happening. Thus 1995 found fewer men earning enough to place them in the $25,000 to $50,000 tier compared with twenty-five years earlier. And the proportion in the bottom bracket has remained essentially unchanged. But this is not necessarily a cause for cheer. In more halcyon times, it was assumed that each year would bring a measure of upward movement for people at the bottom of the income ladder and a diminution of poverty.

The wage gap of our time reflects both the declining fortunes of many Americans and the rise of individuals and households who have profited from recent trends. Economists generally agree on what brought about static wages and lowered living standards. In part, well-paying jobs are scarcer because goods that were once produced here, at American wage scales, are now made abroad and then shipped here for sale. A corollary cause has been the erosion of labor unions, which once safeguarded generous wages for their members. Between 1970 and 1996, the portion of the workforce represented by unions fell from 27 percent to 15 percent. Today, the most highly organized occupations are on public payrolls, notably teachers and postal employees. Only 11 percent of workers in the private sector belong to unions. For most of the other 89 percent this means that their current paychecks are smaller than they were in the past.

Analysts tend to differ on the extent to which the paltriness of the minimum wage has lowered living standards. Despite the 1996 increase, the minimum wage produces an income that is still below the poverty line. Even more contentious is the issue of to what degree immigrants and aliens have undercut wages and taken jobs once held by people who were born here. We can all cite chores that Americans are unwilling to do, at least at the wages customarily paid for those jobs. Scouring pots, laundering clothes, herding cattle, and caring for other people's children are examples of such tasks. At the same time, employers frequently use immigrants to replace better-paid workers, albeit by an indirect route. The most common practice is to remove certain jobs from the firm's payroll and then to hire outside contractors, who bring in their own staffs, which are almost always lower paid and often recently arrived in this country.

Most economists agree that the primary cause of diverging earnings among American workers has been the introduction of new technologies. These new machines and processes are so esoteric and complex that they require sophisticated skills that call for premium pay. In this view, the expanded stratum of Americans earning over $50,000 is made up largely of men and women who are adept at current techniques for producings goods, organizing information, and administering personnel. New technologies have reduced the number of people who are needed as telephone operators, tool and die makers, and aircraft mechanics. Between 1992 and 1996, Delta Airlines was scheduling the same number of flights each year, even though it was discharging a quarter of its employees. Closer to the top, there is a strong demand for individuals who are skilled at pruning payrolls. And this cadre has been doing its work well. As was seen in Chapter Two, in 1973, the five hundred largest industrial firms employed some 15.5 million men and women. By 1993, these firms employed only 11.5 million people. But this reduction in the industrial workforce amounted to more than a loss of 4 million positions. Given the increase in production that took place over this twenty-year period, it meant a comparable output could be achieved in 1993 with half as many American workers as were needed in 1973. In fact, American workers account for an even smaller share of the output, since many of the top five hundred industrial firms are having more of their production performed by overseas contractors and subsidiaries.

Still, some skepticism may be warranted regarding the knowledge and skills of the people who are receiving top-tier pay as well as the presumption that they are in such short supply that anyone seeking their services must offer outsize salaries. It can and should be granted that in our Silicon Valleys and Silicon Alleys, people are creating new and even more awesome technologies. But it would be a mistake to overstate the number of positions that call for this kind of state-of-the-art talent. Pundits are fond of claiming that half of today's jobs require a computer competence. That is certainly the case if one considers telephone operators calling up numbers and checkout clerks keying in the credits for your coupons as having computer skills. Of course, most office workers have computers on or near their desks. But they are mainly used as typewriters and for entering, locating, and transmitting information. Few operators move beyond spreadsheets and word-processing programs into the more arcane terrain of invariant analysis and mathematical models.

So what special skills do more highly educated workers have that make them eligible for rising salaries? In fact, such talents as they may display have only marginal ties to technological expertise. The years at college and graduate school pay off because they burnish students' personalities. The time spent on a campus imparts cues and clues on how to conduct oneself in corporate cultures and professional settings. This demeanor makes for successful interviews and enables a person to sense what is expected of him during the initial months on a job. Professors are paid comfortable salaries not so much for teaching subjects like history and philosophy as for being a professional presence that students can emulate.

In most cases, the new high salaries—and bonuses—are going to employees who are seen as enhancing their firm's bottom line. In some jobs, as in those on Wall Street, how much each person has brought in can be measured quantitatively. In other jobs, care is taken to identify those employees whose contributions are valued by clients. Of course, these criteria for awarding salaries have always been around. What is new is that more of today's products have an esoteric look, whether they are new kinds of investments or communications systems. But, as has been stressed throughout this book, most of the jobs relating to these products can be mastered by anyone with an average intelligence and education.

These developments help to explain the marked increase in $100,000 salaries. To ascend higher than that, the criteria become more arcane. There is now a greater emphasis on "stars." In the past, the economy had established structures. Movie studios and athletic teams were known for their performers and players, who were bound by long-term contracts. In the same vein, employees pledged their careers to a single company. Today, every arena has free agents, each open to a new and better offer. Bidding for their services are individuals and organizations intent on getting "the best" or at least the best known, qualities that are usually validated by having achieved a new high in fees or compensations.

Does America's way of allocating money make any sense at all? Any answer to this question requires establishing a rationale. The most common explanation posits that the amounts people get are set in an open market. Thus, in 1995, employees offered some 14.3 million jobs that paid between $20,000 and $25,000, and were able to find 14.3 million men and women who were willing to take them. The same principle applied to the 1.7 million positions pegged at $75,000 to $85,000, and to the dozen or so corporate chairmen who asked for or were given more than $10 million. By the same token, it can be argued that market forces operate at the low end of the scale. Wal-Mart and Pepsico's Pizza Hut cannot force people to work for $6.50 an hour, but those companies and others like them seem to attract the workers they need by paying that wage.

The last half century gave many groups a chance to shield themselves from the labor auction. Civil servants, teachers, and college professors all achieved "tenure," which made discharging them extremely difficult if not impossible, accompanied by periodic raises for reasons other than merit. Physicians performed procedures, confident that they would be paid by benefit insurers. Blue-collar unions set wage rates and job divisions that employers found it expedient to accept, as long as they could raise prices to meet those added costs. Social Security recipients used their political presence—a variant of market power—to obtain pensions larger than they could have exacted from their erstwhile employers.

But many, if not most, of these protections are no longer being renewed. The up-and-coming generations of physicians, professors, and automobile workers are already finding that they must settle for lower pay and fewer safeguards and benefits. The most graphic exception to this new rule has been in the corporate world, where boards of directors still award huge salaries to executives, without determining whether such compensation is needed to keep their top people from leaving or for any other reason. They simply act as members of an inbred club who look after one another. Only rarely do outside pressures upset these arrangements, which is why they persist.

A market rationale also presumes that those receiving higher offers will have superior talents or some other qualities that put them in demand. Some of the reasons why one person makes more than another make sense by this standard. Of course, a law firm will pay some of its members more if they bring in new business or satisfy existing clients. The owner of the Chicago White Sox wanted a highly visible star, and he had the money to offer Albert Belle a five-year contract at $11 million a year. In this equation, Belle becomes "worth" $11 million because someone is willing to pay him that much. Two roommates have just received master's degrees with distinction, one in education and the other in business administration. The former's first job is teaching second-graders and will pay $23,000. The latter, at an investment firm, will start at $93,000. About all that can be said with certainty is that we are unlikely to arrive at a consensus on which roommate will be contributing more to the commonweal.

Would America be a better place to live, and would Americans be a happier people, if incomes were more evenly distributed? Even as the question is being posed, the answers can be anticipated.

One side will respond with a resounding "Yes!" After which will come a discourse on how poverty subverts the promise of democracy, while allowing wealth in so few hands attests to our rewarding greed and selfishness. There would be far less guilt and fear if the rich were not so rich and no Americans were poor. But the goal, we will be told, is not simply to take money from some people and give it to others. Rather, our goal should be to create a moral culture where citizens feel it is right to have no serious disparities in living standards. Other countries that also have capitalist economies have shown that this is possible.

Those who exclaim "No way!" in response to the same question will be just as vehement. To exact taxes and redistribute the proceeds is an immoral use of official power since it punishes the productive and rewards the indolent. And do we want the government telling private enterprises what wages they can offer? The dream of economic equality has always been a radical's fantasy. Apart from some primitive societies, such a system has never worked. If you want efficiency and prosperity, and almost everyone does, then variations in incomes are part of the equation.

These different responses arise in part from disparate theories of human nature. Since the earliest days of recorded history, philosophers have disagreed over whether our species is inherently competitive or cooperative. Both sides can draw evidence from history to bolster their positions, although the experience of the last few centuries makes it easier to argue for the competitive position.

Also at issue is whether greater economic equality can only be achieved by giving oppressive powers to the state, either to limit incomes through heavy taxes or by setting levels of earnings. Here, too, assessments of our character influence the debate. "What is government itself," James Madison once asked, "but the greatest of all reflections on human nature?" Thus one side contends that even officials who start with well-intended policies end up distorting the ideals they once professed. One need do no more than point to the fate of Marxist regimes. Even less dogmatic states have found they have had to cut back on measures that began with egalitarian intentions. The other side takes a more idealistic approach, hoping that decisions can be made democratically and implemented with goodwill. "Nature intended man for a social animal," Thomas Jefferson wrote, "and has implanted in our breasts a love of others, a sense of duty to them, a moral instinct." While many Americans might like to echo these sentiments, the ways of today's world make them an unlikely basis for practical action.

Of course, the price that America pays for economic inequality is its persisting poverty. As was stressed earlier, much of the burden is racial. Even fourteen decades after emancipation, the United States has yet to offer the descendants of slaves the same opportunities that are accorded to recently arrived immigrants. A family just off a plane from Korea has more choice of where they may live—and send their children to school—than has a black couple whose people have been here for four centuries. Indeed, such newcomers have better chances of employment and the prospect of ascending careers. In theory, economic redress would do much to close America's racial divide, the closing of which is supposed to be a national priority. In actuality, white America has opted to retain a racial separation and to hope that the problems caused by that division will somehow disappear.

In one way or another all Americans will pay the high costs of poverty. California now spends more on its prison system than it does on higher education, and other states will soon be following suit. Bolstering police forces is hardly cheap: upward of $75,000 per officer, when overtime and benefits are added in. Being poor means a higher chance of being sick or being shot, or bearing low-birth-weight babies, all of which consume medical resources and have helped to make Medicaid one of the costliest public programs. In addition, poor Americans now represent the fastest-growing group of AIDS victims: mainly drug users and the women and children they infect. Generally, $100,000 worth of medical treatment is spent on each person dying of AIDS. The poor also have more of their children consigned to "special education" classes, which most never leave and where the tab can reach three times the figure for regular pupils.

Additional expenses are incurred by families who put as much distance as possible between themselves and the poor. Doing so often entails the upkeep of gated communities, security systems, and privately supplied guards. Yet these are expenses better-off Americans readily bear. They are willing to foot the bills for more prisons and police, as well as the guns they keep in their bedrooms and the alarms for their cars. Indeed, their chief objection is to money given to non-married mothers who want to be at home with their pre-school-age children. Virtually every such penny is begrudged, followed by the demand that these mothers take jobs even before their children go to kindergarten. While the imposition of work may make some taxpayers cheerier, it will not do much to close the income gap.

How disparities in income affect the nation's well-being has long been debated by economists. Much of the argument centers on what people do with their money. The poor and those just trying to cope devote virtually all of what they have to necessities plus the few extras they can afford. If their incomes were raised, they would obviously spend more, which would create more demand and generate more jobs. It should not be forgotten that the year 1929, which was noted for a severe imbalance in incomes, gave us a devastating economic depression that lasted a decade.

The traditional reply to critics of economic inequality has been that we need not only the rich, but also a comfortably off class, who are able to put some of their income into investments. In other words, disparities give some people more than they "need," which allows them to underwrite the new enterprises that benefit everyone. While there is obvious validity to this argument, it should be added that much of this outlay now goes to paper contrivances, which have only a remote connection with anything productive, if any at all. Nor are the rich as necessary as they may once have been, since institutions now supply most invested capital. Metropolitan Life, Merrill Lynch, Bank America, and the California Public Employees Pension Fund put substantially more into new production than do the 68,064 families with $1 million incomes.

In one sphere, the income gap comes closer to home. Most young Americans will not live as well as their parents did. Indeed, in many instances this is already occurring. A generation ago, many men had well-paid blue-collar jobs; now their sons are finding that those jobs are no longer available. In that earlier era, college graduates could enter a growing managerial stratum; today, firms view their payrolls as bloated and are ending the security of corporate careers.

This shift can be seen within individual families. Let's look at a man who was born in 1940 and is now an executive earning $100,000 with perhaps a decade to go before retirement. During the 1960s, he and his wife had three children, two of whom are now working, and the youngest is completing a graduate degree. But there is little likelihood that even two of the three children will be earning the equivalent of $100,000 when they reach their father's age. While such well-paid positions are still being created, the competition for them will be more intense than ever before. Given this prospect, most of today's children in their adult years, will have a lower living standard than they knew when they were young. If we think of orthopedic surgeons, who in the 1990s have been averaging $300,000, we can predict that their physician sons and daughters will be lucky to net $150,000—assuming that they can find places to practice in the managed-care era.

The patterns of decline prevail if the entire nation is viewed as the equivalent of family. Federal programs now award nine times as much to retirees as they do to the nation's children, so senior citizens as a group fare better than younger Americans. Twice as many children as Americans over the age of sixty live in households below the poverty line. (And as death approaches, the government is more generous: almost 30 percent of the total Medicare budget is spend on the terminal year of elderly patients' lives.) Many retired persons have come to view a comfortable life as their entitlement, and have concluded that they no longer have obligations to repay. Grandparents tend to support

---

The Cost of a Fairer Race?

A few figures tell the story. In 1995, the median income for white households was $37,178, while for black households it was $22,393. The white households taken together had an aggregate income of some $3.7 trillion. If $210 billion from that total—about 5.6 percent—were made available to black households, it would give them a median income equal to the white figure. Nor need this be done simply by handing over $210 billion in a lump sum. Rather, it could be achieved by ensuring that black Americans will have the same *range* of earnings that whites currently enjoy. Obviously, this is just a paper exercise. Even so, it suggests that in return for a 5.6 percent drop in their living standards, white Americans could remove the principal cause of racial tensions.

campaigns for the rights of the elderly, not for school bonds and bigger education budgets.

In the end, the issue may be simply stated: what would be required for all Americans—or at least as many as possible—to make the most of their lives?

Of course, philosophers and psychologists and theologians have had no shortage of suggestions. After all, that is what their jobs entail. And we can agree with them that a rewarding life must be founded on morality and character. Still, it should not occasion surprise if a book entitled *Money* assigns more than marginal importance to material well-being. This is not to argue that those with wealth always make good use of it, or that being able to make more purchases will enhance our lives. And no one will contend that money, in and by itself, will bring personal happiness. Yet having it helps.

In fact, many individuals subsist quite modestly. A Mississippi woman who spent her life taking in other people's washing donated her $150,000 savings to a university with which she had no connection. A lot of Americans are content with simple pleasures, and feel no need for more than what they have. Indeed, it is the presence of these individuals that gives our country as much stability as it has.

Poverty takes its greatest toll in the raising of children. With a few exceptions, being poor consigns them to schools and surroundings that do little to widen their horizons. The stark fact is that we have in our midst millions of bright and talented children whose lives are fated to be a fraction of what they might be. And by any moderate standard, deprivation extends above the official poverty line. In most of the United States, families with incomes of less than $25,000 face real limits to the opportunities open to their children. Less than one child in ten from these households now enters and graduates from college. The statistics are apparent to outside observers, and to the children themselves, who very early on become aware of the barriers they face. And from this realization results much of the behavior that the rest of the society deplores. The principal response from solvent Americans has been to lecture the poor on improving their ways.

No one defends poverty, but ideologies differ on what can or should be done to alleviate it. Conservatives generally feel it is up to the individual: those at the bottom should take any jobs they can find and work hard to pull themselves up. Hence the opposition to public assistance, which is seen as eroding character and moral fiber. Indeed, conservatives suggest that people will display character and moral fiber if they are made to manage on their own.

Not many voting Americans favor public disbursements for the poor or even for single working mothers who cannot make ends meet. Most American voters have grown weary of hearing about the problems of low-income people. Yet even those who are unsettled by the persistence of income imbalances no longer feel that government officials and experts know how to reduce the disparities.

Of course, huge redistributions occurs everyday. Funds for Social Security are supplied by Americans who are currently employed, providing their elders with pensions that now end up averaging $250,000 above what their own contributions would have warranted. Agricultural subsidies give farmers enough extra cash to ensure that they will have middle-class comforts. The same subventions furnish farms owned by corporations with generous profit margins.

In another example of redistribution, in a recent five-year period, the chairman of Lockheed Martin was awarded $24 million in compensation. What makes this worthy of note is that virtually all of that money came from the wallets of taxpaying Americans, since the company's chief activity is building military aircraft. Of course, Lockheed will argue that it is a business which happens to sell most of its product to the government; like any other corporation, it must pay its employees competitive salaries, but the fact remains that the federal government has taken $24 million from ordinary Americans and made it into a corporate paycheck.

In contrast, there is scant evidence that public programs have done much for the bottom tiers of American society. Despite the New Deal and the Great Society, including public works and public assistance, since 1935, share of income going to the poorest fifth of America's households has remained between 3.3 percent and 4.3 percent. Thus, if many elderly Americans have been raised from poverty, it is clear that younger people are now taking their places.

As was noted on the opening page of this book, all parts of the population except the richest fifth have smaller shares of the nation's income than they did twenty years ago. The gulf between the best-off and the rest shows no signs of diminishing, and by some political readings this should mean increased tensions between the favored fifth and everyone else. But declines in living standards have not been so severe or precipitous as to lead many people to question the equity of the economic system. The economy has ensured that a majority of Americans remain in moderate comfort and feel able to count their lives a reasonable success. Airline reservationists making $14,000 do not consider themselves "poor," and no one tells them that they are. Thus a majority of Americans still see themselves as middle class, and feel few ties or obligations to the minority with incomes less than their own.

Given this purview, why should the way America distributes its income be considered a problem? At this moment, certainly, there is scant sentiment for imposing further taxes on the well-to-do and doing more for the poor. As has been observed, there is little resentment felt toward the rich; if anything, greater animus is directed toward families receiving public assistance. Nor is it regarded as untoward if the well-off use their money to accumulate luxuries while public schools must cope with outdated textbooks and leaking roofs. Although this book is about money, about why some have more and others less, it should not be read as a plea for income redistribution. The reason is straightforward: if people are disinclined to share what they have, they will not be persuaded by a reproachful tone. Rather, _Money_'s aim is to enhance our understanding of ourselves, of the forces that propel us, and the shape we are giving to the nation of which we are a part.

How a nation allocates its resources tells us how it wishes to be judged in the ledgers of history and morality. America's chosen emphasis has been on offering opportunities to the ambitious, to those with the desire and the drive to surpass. America has more self-made millionaires and more men and women who have attained $100,000 than any other country.

But because of the upward flow of funds, which has accelerated in recent years, less is left for those who lack the opportunities or the temperament to succeed in the competition. The United States now has a greater percentage of its citizens in prison or on the streets, and more neglected children, than any of the nations with which it is appropriately compared. Severe disparities—excess alongside deprivation—sunder the society and subvert common aims. With the legacy we are now creating, millions of men, women, children are prevented from being fully American, while others pride themselves on how much they can amass.

ACKNOWLEDGMENTS AND SOURCES

Money has been a collaborative effort of its author and three Scribner editors. Edward Chase supported the initial proposal for this book and continued with encouragement during the four years of its writing. Bill Goldstein provided invaluable assistance from the earliest days until the manuscript was completed, especially in shaping a structure for its analysis and arguments. To Nan Graham, I owe special thanks: her intelligence, her enthusiasm, her vision of what this book could be, are evident on every line of every page. I have also benefited from timely suggestions by Gillian Blake, the dexterity of designer Erich Hobbing, and the keen eye of copy editor Steve Boldt, who caught what could have been some embarrassing errors.

Parts of this book have appeared, in somewhat different forms, in *The New York Review of Books, The New York Times Magazine, Working Mother,* and *Time* magazine. I am grateful to all of those publications for permission to reprint this material.

Robin Straus, my agent and friend for many years, has always been on hand with counsel and understanding, not only for this book but throughout my entire professional career.

My thanks to the following individuals for their kindness in providing advice, information, and assistance: Robert Begam, Andrew Beveridge, Philip Brickner, Peter Brimelow, Susan Chejka, Stephen L. Clark, Mary J. Cox, Graef Crystal, Paul Dexheimer, Barbara Epstein, Maryse Eymonerie, Rosemary Fogerty, Oren Jarinkes, Arthur Kaminsky, Joan Kay, Hyun Sook Kim, Stephen Koepp, Lilian Kohlreiser, Everett Ladd, Delores Lataniotis, Nicholas Lemann, Frank Levy, Nancy Macomber, James Marcus, Joyce Mercer, Polly Miller, Lorrie Millman, Paul Nadler, Terry Nuriddin, Margaret Padin-Bailo, Peter Passell, Martha Farnsworth Riche, Carl Riskin, Robert Silvers, Karen Smith, Marge Ward, Edwin L. Weisl, and Joan Zimmerman.

The information and interpretations contained in *Money* are based on hundreds of books, articles, and documents, the most important of which will be cited below. However, two sources—one public, one private—warrant special recognition. The first is the Housing and Household Economic Statistics Division of the U.S. Bureau of the Census. Each year, this office releases hundreds of pages, thousands of columns, and literally millions of figures on the incomes and earnings of Americans. These tables, which are based primarily on responses to the Bureau's annual Current Population Survey, leave it to the reader to choose and collate and then form conclusions from this Everest of data.

For a view of who has how much money at America's higher echelons, *Forbes* magazine is the preeminent source. Its reports are not only reliable, but are also notable for their sagacity and imagination. Its roster of the four hundred richest Americans, published each fall since 1982, has become a national institution. Nor is it simply a list: *Forbes* details how old and new fortunes were made, separating self-made millionaires from silver-spoon heirs. The magazine also provides annual guides to the best-paid athletes, entertainers, and attorneys. And each spring it records the latest pay for eight hundred corporate chairmen, along with their salaries and benefits over the previous five years. And here too, *Forbes* goes the extra mile, by including information like how long the CEOs have been with their companies and where they went to college.

PERIODICALS

Academe, March–April 1996.
American Lawyer, July–August 1996.
BusinessWeek, April 25, 1994; April 22, 1996.
Chronicle of Higher Education, October 4 and October 18, 1996.
Chronicle of Philanthropy, September 19, 1996.
Crain's New York Business, November 25–December 1, 1996.
Entertainment Weekly, April 12, 1996.
Financial World, July 6, 1993; July 5, 1994; July 4, 1995; October 21, 1996.
Forbes, June 9, 1980; September 13, 1982; September 12, 1983; May 27, 1991; November 6 and December 18, 1995; May 20, September 26, and October 14, 1996.
Fortune, May 1974; May and July 1993; April 18 and May 30, 1994; April 29, 1996.
Journal of the American Medical Association, July 20, 1994.
Medical Economics, September 9, 1996.
National Law Journal, July 15, 1996.
Parade, June 23, 1996.
People, November 4, 1996.
USA Today, January 18 and December 12, 1995.

U.S. GOVERNMENT DOCUMENTS

Bureau of Labor Statistics, *Employment and Earnings,* January 1996.
Bureau of the Census, *Detailed Characteristics,* 1970; *Historical Statistics of the United States,* 1975; *Studies in the Distribution of Income,* 1992; *Ancestry of the Population in the United States,* 1993; *Social and Economic Characteristics,* 1993; *Income and Poverty,* 1993; *Household Wealth and Asset Ownership,* 1994; *Educational Attainment in the United States,* 1995; *Marital Status and Living Arrangements,* 1995; *Money Income in the United States,* 1995; *Poverty in the United States,* 1995.
Committee on Ways and Means, U.S. House of Representatives, *Green Book,* 1996.
Department of Health and Human Services, *Characteristics and Financial Circumstances of AFDC Recipients,* 1995.

ACKNOWLEDGMENTS AND SOURCES

Internal Revenue Service, *Individual Income Tax Returns,* 1979; *Statistics of Income Bulletin,* 1993–96.
National Center for Health Statistics, *Natality,* 1995.
Office of Personnel Management, *Occupations of Federal White-Collar and Blue-Collar Workers,* 1993.
Social Security Administration, *Annual Statistical Supplement,* 1995.

OTHER DOCUMENTS, REPORTS, AND BOOKS

Altman Weil Pensa, *Law Firm Salary Survey,* 1995.
American Medical Association, *Physician Marketplace Statistics,* 1995.
Association of American Medical Colleges, *Medical School Faculty Salaries,* 1994–95.
Executive Leadership Council, *1996 Membership Roster.*
McGraw-Hill Relative Value Studies, 1996.
Organization for Economic Cooperation and Development, *Income Distribution in OECD Countries,* 1995.
Roper Reports, 1995.
World Bank Atlas, 1996.

Graef Crystal, *In Search of Excess: The Overcompensation of American Executives* (1991)
Robert H. Frank and Philip J. Cook, *The Winner-Take-All Society,* 1995.
John Kenneth Galbraith, *American Capitalism: The Concept of Countervailing Power,* 1952.
Robert Reich, *The Next American Frontier,* 1983.
Lester Thurow, *The Zero-Sum Society,* 1986.

COURT CASES AND STATUTES

American Federation of State, County, and Municipal Employees v. *State of Washington,* 578 F.Supp. 846.
California Federal Savings & Loan v. *Guerra,* 758 F.2d 390.
Educational Amendments of 1972, Public Law 92–381, title 9.
Equal Employment Opportunity Act of 1964, Public Law 88–354.
Equal Employment Opportunity Commission v. *Sears, Roebuck & Co.,* 628 F.Supp. 1286.
Equal Pay Act of 1963, title 29, sec. 206(d).

INDEX

Blacks *(cont.)*
  in middle class, 157
  occupational representation, 151,
    152, 153, *154,* 155–58, *156*
  poverty and, 14–15, *15,* 237
  in public employment, 155–56, 157
  race consciousness in America and,
    145–46
  in top-income tier, 94, 158
  See also Racial money gap
Blank, Arthur, 91
Bloomberg, Michael, 100
Boards of directors, 112–13
Bok, Derek, 69, 208
Bonfire of the Vanities (Wolfe), 207
Bowden, Bobby, 142
Britain, 18
Bronfman, Edgar, 94
Brooks, Garth, 201
Buffett, Warren, 27, 89, 97, 205
Bullock, Sandra, 27, 74
Bulow, Claus von, 101
Bureau of Labor Statistics, 26, 75, 125,
  131, 156, 189
Busch, August, III, 117–18
Business schools, 141–42
BusinessWeek, 27–28, 107

Calculus, 47
Cambodian immigrants, 162
Canada, 18
Capitalism, 43–44
  acquisitiveness and, 42–43
  employment and, 44–46
  technology and, 44
Carnegie, Andrew, 92, 100
Carrey, Jim, 74
Caterpillar company, 45
Census Bureau, 26, 55, 62, 85, 131, 132,
  148–49, 171, 186, 199, 213
Central American immigrants, 166
CEO compensation, 24–25, 53, *108,*
  115, 233
  appearances issue, 114, 116
  controversy surrounding, 107
  golden parachutes, 112
  in higher education, 121, *122*
  leadership issue, 107, 109

  in nonprofit organizations, 121, *122*
  $1 million incomes, 74–77
  in privately held enterprises, 118–19
  of promoted executives, 110
  of recruited executives, 109–10
  retention of valued executives and,
    111
  size of compensation, determination
    of, 109, 112–13
  total company costs, percentage of,
    114
CEOs
  anonymity of, 105
  backgrounds of, 113–14, 167
  dismissals of, 107, 112
  influence on corporate outcomes,
    111–12
  market forces, insulation from, 37
  ownership interests, 116–18, *117*
  public figures, 106
  See also CEO compensation
Charitable contributions, 79–80
Childbearing, 60–61, *170,* 171
Child care, 180
Child-care credits, 79
Children
  in black families, 14–15, *15*
  economic value of, 29
  poverty and, 14–15, *15,* 65, 66, 239,
    240
Child support, 177, 179–80
Chinese immigrants, 23
Chronicle of Higher Education, 28
Clancy, Tom, 82, 201
Classes in American society, 226–30
Clemenceau, Georges, 29
Clinton, Bill and Hillary, 67–68
Coaches in athletics, 28, 142, 220–21
Cochran, Johnnie, 150
College education. *See* Higher
  education
College Retirement Equities Fund,
  119
Collins, Jackie, 201
Comparable worth, 219–21
Computerization of workplace, 45
Condit, Philip, 227
Contingent employment, 120